JOB, BOETHIUS, AND EPIC TRUTH

By the same author

The Song of Songs in the Middle Ages

JOB, BOETHIUS, AND EPIC TRUTH

ANN W. ASTELL

Cornell University Press

Ithaca and London

809,132
As82j

Copyright © 1994 by Cornell University

All rights reserved. Except for brief quotations in a review, this book, or parts thereof, must not be reproduced in any form without permission in writing from the publisher. For information, address Cornell University Press, Sage House, 512 East State Street, Ithaca, New York 14850.

First published 1994 by Cornell University Press.

Library of Congress Cataloging-in-Publication Data
Astell, Ann W.
    Job, Boethius, and epic truth / Ann W. Astell.
       p.   cm.
    Includes bibliographical references (p.   ) and index.
    ISBN 0-8014-2911-0 (alk. paper)
    1. Boethius, d. 524. De consolatione philosophiae. 2. Epic literature—History and criticism—Theory, etc. 3. Bible. O.T. Job—Criticism, interpretation, etc. 4. Literature, Medieval—Classical influences. 5. Influence (Literary, artistic, etc.) 6. Typology (Theology) in literature. 7. Imitation in literature. 8. Bible in literature. 9. Literary form. I. Title.
    PA6231.C83A88   1994
    809.1'32—dc20   93-27265

TO MY FATHER
"Vir Patiens Forti Melior"

CONTENTS

PREFACE

This book rewrites a long chapter in literary history by asserting what is usually denied: the existence of medieval secondary epic and a correspondent medieval theory of heroic poetry. I argue for a continuous epic tradition from antiquity through the Middle Ages into the Renaissance. The late antique and medieval *imitationes* of Homer and Virgil are primarily related to their classical exemplars, however, not through the outward, formal resemblance of literary convention, but by their adherence to "epic truth," as the allegorical exegesis of heroic myth—atomist, Stoic, Neoplatonic, and Christian—had successively defined and redefined it. This "truth," in its most fundamental terms, answers to the Delphic oracle and thus recalls us to self-knowledge by delineating human nature in the mirrored images of heroic (and therefore "true") human beings—suffering, striving, and ultimately divinized.

Boethius' sixth-century *Consolation of Philosophy* echoes Homeric poetry and interprets it in precisely this anthropomorphic and pedagogical fashion, bringing its originally veiled meaning into the foreground of a philosophical quest for a threefold self-knowledge. In so doing, Boethius gained acclaim as an imitator of Virgil and provided the major conduit for the transmission of classical epic into the Christian Middle Ages, as well as the literary model for its generic reformulation.

Saint Gregory the Great's influential *Moralia in Job*, composed shortly after Boethius' *Consolation*, firmly established the Book of Job as a divinely inspired heroic poem, depicting the trials of a "true man" and innocent sufferer. Following both Jerome and Gregory, Isidore of Seville, Bede, and Rabanus Maurus point to Job as a biblical example of heroic poetry comparable to the epics of Homer and Virgil.

The generic designation of Job as a heroic work, initially surprising by modern standards, becomes comprehensible when one
considers the exegetical tradition as a whole, as it affected the reception of classical epic, and the close affinities between the books of Job
and Boethius. Medieval readers tended to interpret Boethius' prosimetric work, not in isolation, but rather paired with the Book of Job
as its authoritative biblical analogue and complementary scriptural
"other-speaking." The similarities between them, explicitly high-
lighted in Saint Thomas Aquinas' thirteenth-century Joban commentary, are obvious enough. Both feature an innocent sufferer who
addresses the problem of evil in the form of complaint and questions within the framework of a philosophical dialogue. Both works
assert the existence and benevolence of providential design. These
overt similarities, corroborated by Boethius' virtual canonization as a
Christian martyr, led medieval readers to consider the books of Job
and Boethius as *translationes* of each other, conveying the same
message and therefore belonging to the same literary genre.

At the same time, however, the differences between the two works
and the interpretation of Job at discontinuous levels gave rise to an
amazing array of literary expressions when medieval writers imitated
either Job or Boethius or both and placed their books allusively in
dialogue with one another. As we shall see, depending on which of
the two—Job or Boethius—is foregrounded and in what context, the
hero assumes a different face; his story, a different pattern. The
shifting relationship between the biblical sufferer and his Boethian
counterpart delineates a typology of medieval heroes and enables, to
some extent, an archeology of heroism. Indeed, the creative tension
between the Book of Job and the *Consolation of Philosopy*, which
characterizes the complexity of their intertextual relationship, accounts for many of the distinctive features of hagiographic, amatory,
and chivalric romance as they developed in the Middle Ages.

This book thus affords a new approach to the well-established
problem of the ascendancy of romance over epic. I argue that the
relative formlessness of medieval romance, which stands as the generic "other" of classical epic, derives historically from epic's "other-
speaking," as the exegetes interpreted it. That is to say, the formal
discontinuity that has led most literary historians to deny the very
existence of secondary (i.e., imitative) epic in the Middle Ages actu-

ally demonstrates the conscious continuation of heroic poetry, not in its false (and therefore rejected) letter, however, but in its underlying, allegorical truth—a truth revealed most clearly in the paired books of Job and Boethius and the writings patterned (albeit diversely) after them.

When I was a little girl I saved my father's life in a swimming accident. Afterward the state of Wisconsin awarded me a certificate for heroism. At the time the honor puzzled me a great deal, and I wondered, "What does it really mean to be a hero?" Perhaps the first origins of this book lie in those childhood musings.

In his Letter to Leander, which prefaces his *Moralia in Job*, Saint Gregory the Great enumerates his administrative burdens, pastoral worries, and physical ailments. In the plan of God, he says, all of these troubles have helped him to understand better the sufferings and heroism of Job. For my part, I will spare my readers any account of personal sorrows. Surely all of us have burdens to bear. I will say, however, that it has been a source of strength and comfort for me to meditate on Divine Providence in the course of writing this book.

The thought of God's Providence awakens deep gratitude, some of which I hope to express. The National Endowment for the Humanities awarded me a fellowship for 1991–92, during which time I wrote this book. The Institute for Research in the Humanities at the University of Wisconsin–Madison graciously welcomed me as an honorary fellow that same year. I enjoyed the use of a studio at Memorial Library on campus, and the Department of English there kindly afforded me access to their computer lab.

These gifts were made possible, in turn, by others. Alger N. Doane, Allen J. Frantzen, Dolores W. Frese, and Christina Von Nolcken all wrote letters of recommendation on my behalf—for which I am very grateful. The English Department at Purdue University allowed me a year's leave and generously supported my work with their good wishes. My students and fellow medievalists made the sacrifice of missing me.

In the various stages of writing this book, I have drawn strength from conversations with friends and colleagues—among whom I wish to name Barbara Fowler, Shaun F. D. Hughes, Douglas Kelly, Christopher Kleinhenz, Fannie J. LeMoine, Peggy McCracken,

Thomas Ohlgren, Lea Olsan, Carol Braun Pasternack, Sherry Reames, Mary Beth Rose, Charles S. Ross, Albert Rossi, Donald Rowe, Margaret Moane Rowe, and Larry Scanlon. I owe special thanks to two dear classicist friends and teachers of mine, Keith Dickson and Martin Winkler. Without their good example, constructive criticism, personal support, and simple affection, I would have lacked the courage to write this book.

The editors and readers at Cornell University Press have been enormously helpful. I thank in particular Bernhard Kendler, for his unfailing support; Lisa Turner and Liz Holmes, for their careful attention to the manuscript; and Sherron Knopp, whose detailed and thoughtful response to my first book guided me in writing this second one.

Sections of Chapters 4, 5, and 7 are revisions of previously published articles, and I thank the journals' editors for permission to use them here. "Apostrophe, Prayer, and the Structure of Satire in 'The Man of Law's Tale'" appeared in *Studies in the Age of Chaucer* 13 (1991): 81–97, copyright © 1991 by The New Chaucer Society, the University of Tennessee, Knoxville. "Orpheus, Eurydice, and the 'Double Sorwe' of Chaucer's *Troilus*" was published in *Chaucer Review* 23.4 (1989): 283–99; copyright 1989 by The Pennsylvania State University; reproduced by permission of The Pennsylvania State University Press. "The Medieval *Consolatio* and the Conclusion of *Paradise Lost*" appeared in *Studies in Philology* (1985): 477–91.

On a more personal note, I thank my parents and brothers and sisters for their love and support. My heartfelt gratitude goes to the Schoenstatt Sisters of Mary with whom I lived and worked during the fellowship year, and to all the sisters whose prayers, sacrifices, and practical faith in Divine Providence have contributed to the completion of this book. I am happy to use this opportunity to thank in particular my provincial and filiation superiors who, over the course of the years, have valued, protected, and nurtured my work as a scholar—Sisters M. Felicia, Helma, Jacoba, Barbara, Elizabeth, Mary, and Carol.

I have dedicated this book to my father. That title refers, first of all, to my beloved "pappa," John M. Astell. It also refers to Alger N. ("Nick") Doane, who directed my dissertation and whose encouragement and good humor have given me life as a medievalist. Finally, it names the priest who has been for me an earthly image of my Father in Heaven, Fr. Joseph Kentenich.

ANN W. ASTELL

West Lafayette, Indiana

ABBREVIATIONS

AJP	*American Journal of Philology*
ASE	*Anglo-Saxon England*
BASOR	*Bulletin of the American Schools of Oriental Research*
CCSL	Corpus Christianorum, Series Latina. 176 vols. Turnhout: Brepols, 1954–.
CJ	*The Classical Journal*
EETS	Early English Text Society
ELH	*English Literary History*
JBL	*Journal of Biblical Literature*
JEGP	*Journal of English and Germanic Philology*
MLN	*Modern Language Notes*
MLQ	*Modern Language Quarterly*
MP	*Modern Philology*
NLH	*New Literary History*
NM	*Neuphilologische Mitteilungen*
PG	Patrologiae Cursus Completus, Series Graeca. Ed. J. P. Migne. 162 vols. Paris, 1857–66.
PL	Patrologiae Cursus Completus, Series Latina. Ed. J. P. Migne. 221 vols. Paris, 1844–64.
PMLA	*Publications of the Modern Language Association*
PQ	*Philological Quarterly*
SAC	*Studies in the Age of Chaucer*
SP	*Studies in Philology*
TSL	*Tennessee Studies in Literature*

INTRODUCTION

The Middle Ages singled out the enig-
matic Book of Job as a biblical counterpart to the epics of antiquity.
Considered literally, the Old Testament story chronicles the multiple
sufferings of Job, the just man, whom Satan afflicts with a series of
terrible trials, beginning with the loss of his property and the sudden
death of his seven sons and three daughters. Stricken with boils,
tormented by the despair of his wife and the cyclic, pious speeches of
would-be consolers, Job responds to his affliction with both silent
submission and bitter complaint, until a powerful divine epiphany
inaugurates the miraculous restoration of his health and household.

A mysterious text, Job raises serious theological problems that the
early Church addressed in commentaries and homilies emphasizing
Job's exemplary patience under trial and his allegorical significance
as a type of the suffering and resurrected Christ. Origen in the third
century, and Saint John Chrysostom in the fourth, described Job as a
heroic model of Christian fortitude, an athlete of God wrestling with
God's Adversary. On the authority of Josephus, Saint Jerome (A.D.
340–420) advanced the mistaken notion that the Joban dialogues
(Job 3:1–42:7) were written in hexameters, the meter appropriate to
epic. In the sixth century, Saint Gregory the Great's voluminous
Moralia in Job confirmed Job's heroic and typological status and
discovered, in addition, an encyclopedic range of orthodox teaching
hidden as "other speaking" beneath the superficially blasphemous
letter of Joban outcry. Isidore of Seville (seventh century) describes
the Book of Job as heroic in both its subject matter and mixed form—
a judgment echoed and elaborated upon by Bede (eighth century)
and Rabanus Maurus (ninth century), both of whom point to Job as a
biblical instance of heroic poetry comparable to Homer's *Iliad* and

Odyssey and Virgil's *Aeneid*.[1] As Barbara K. Lewalski has shown, this exegetical tradition, "according to which Job's encounter with Satan is a heroic combat of cosmic significance," continued through the seventeenth century.[2] Like modern biblical exegesis, recent literary history has, in Lewalski's words, "virtually lost contact with this tradition" and largely overlooked the medieval reading of Job as epic.[3] The omission is in many ways understandable. Job, after all, bears no obvious formal resemblance to either the Homeric poems or the *Aeneid*, the literary exemplars that traditionally define the conventions of the genre. It cannot easily be designated as either primary or secondary epic, the familiar categories normally used by historians of epic poetry.[4] Job is not a heroic poem with the oral features characteristic of primary epics like Homer's. Nor is its text, like Virgil's, an artistically self-conscious, literary imitation of oral epic. Indeed, the Book of Job resists displacement into these categories and thus, as a biblical model for medieval epic, fails to accommodate the notion of a continuous epic tradition, defined in purely formal terms.[5]

1. See Origen, "Selecta in Iob," PG 12, c1033; St. John Chrysostom, "Fragmenta in Beatum Job," PG 64, c506; St. Jerome, "Interpretatio Chronicae Eusebii Pamphili," PL 27, c36, and "Liber Iob," PL 28, c1081–82; Isidore of Seville, *Etymologiae* I.xxxix.9–11, PL 82, c118–19; Bede, *De arte metrica* I.xxv in *Opera Didascalica*, CCSL 123A, ed. C. B. Kendall (1975), pp. 139–41, and PL 90, c174; Rabanus Maurus, *De universo* XV.ii, PL 111, c419–20.

2. Barbara K. Lewalski, *Milton's Brief Epic: The Genre, Meaning, and Art of "Paradise Regained"* (Providence: Brown University Press, 1966), p. 17.

3. Ibid.

4. In a typical handbook entry, Chris Baldick defines "epic" as "a long narrative poem celebrating the great deeds of one or more legendary heroes, in a grand ceremonious style." He goes on to explain: "Virgil and Milton wrote what are called 'secondary' or literary epics in imitation of the earlier 'primary' or traditional epics of Homer, whose *Iliad* and *Odyssey* (c. 8th century B.C.) are derived from an oral tradition of recitation" (*The Concise Oxford Dictionary of Literary Terms* [Oxford: Oxford University Press, 1990], p. 70). Baldick lists no example of biblical epic or medieval secondary epic.

5. Studies that have argued for a continuous formal tradition in epic poetry include Thomas M. Greene, *The Descent from Heaven: A Study in Epic Continuity* (New Haven: Yale University Press, 1964); Rodney Delasanta, *The Epic Voice* (The Hague: Mouton, 1967); Albert Cook, *The Classical Line* (Bloomington: University of Indiana Press, 1966). Such studies, as Stephen G. Nichols, Jr., has observed, displace medieval epic "in the direction of the classical 'model' " in a way that provides at best

Acceding to the dominance of the classical model, historians of epic poetry generally discuss the acknowledged primary epics of the Middle Ages—such as *Beowulf*, the *Nibelungenlied*, and the *Song of Roland*—and mark the category of the secondary epic with a hiatus that ends only with the Renaissance and Tasso's neoclassical *Gerusa-lemme Liberata* (1581). J. B. Hainsworth, for one, notes the loss of Aristotle's *Poetics* during the Middle Ages and characterizes the period as a time "when even an intuitive perception of the literary kinds was lost."[6] In his view, medieval poets, lacking a theoretical concept of epic as a genre, inevitably failed to write epic poems. Dante's *Commedia*, for instance, is completely "innocent of the form of an epic poem in the classical tradition," and, according to Hainsworth, "the more the formal characteristics are dispensed with, the harder it is to call a poem an epic."[7]

The historical witness of Bede, Rabanus Maurus, and others, however, cites Job as an instance of epic comparable to the classical epics. The identification implies both a medieval theory of epic and its derivation from Homeric and Virgilian models. It prompts us to ask not only how the people of the Middle Ages read the Book of Job, but also how they read the *Iliad*, the *Odyssey*, and the *Aeneid*. As we shall see, medieval commentators grouped them together as examples of a single literary kind not because of any perceived formal similarity but because they conveyed the same message, taught the same truth. By the early Middle Ages, the allegory of classical epic

---

"only superficial insights into the poems so treated" ("The Spirit of Truth: Epic Modes in Medieval Literature," *NLH* 1 [Spring 1970]: 366). A more satisfactory approach explores a tradition of classical as well as medieval formal discontinuity on the basis of Callimachean principles. See John Kevin Newman, *The Classical Epic Tradition* (Madison: University of Wisconsin Press, 1986).

6. J. B. Hainsworth, *The Idea of Epic* (Berkeley: University of California Press, 1991), p. 139.

7. Ibid., pp. 140, 144. John Clark (*A History of Epic Poetry* [New York: Haskell House, 1900, 1964]) and Henry Osborn Taylor (*The Classical Heritage of the Middle Ages*, 4th ed. [New York: Frederick Ungar, 1957]) apply similar formal criteria to "epical" medieval works. For specific treatments of the *Commedia*'s relationship to epic tradition, see David Thompson, *Dante's Epic Journeys* (Baltimore: Johns Hopkins University Press, 1974), and John Freccero, "Dante's Ulysses: From Epic to Novel," in *Concepts of the Hero in the Middle Ages and the Renaissance*, ed. Norman T. Burns and Christopher J. Reagan (Albany: State University of New York Press, 1975), pp. 101–19.

had become so identified with epic itself in the reading process—
a practice that systematically joined text with interpretation—that
commentators had no trouble accommodating radical formal dis-
similarities among epic works, both pagan and Christian.

This kind of reading, in turn, prompted medieval imitations of
classical works as the commentaries had contextualized them. Homer and Virgil, after all, could only be rewritten as they were being
read—that is, in the necessarily double, figurative *translatio* of word
and interpretation. In each case, as Robert Lamberton observes, "the
author conceives his relationship to a tradition as one of imitation,
or at least of participation, but his own historicity (given concrete
form . . . by the commentaries that mediate between him and the text)
has transformed that text and imposed on the imitation a radical new
structure of meaning."[8] Bernard Silvestris in the twelfth century, for
instance, treats Martianus Capella's allegorical *De nuptiis Philologiae
et Mercurii* as a literary imitation of Virgil's *Aeneid*, and Boethius' *De
consolatione philosophiae* as an imitation, in turn, of Martianus' *De
nuptiis*, on the grounds that all three works deal figuratively with the
same thing: "Que quidem tres figure fere idem exprimunt. Imitatur
ergo Marcianus Maronem, Boecius Marcianum."[9] Bernard goes on
to draw an analogy between Aeneas, who journeys *per inferos* guided
by the Sybil, and Boethius, who journeys *per falsa bona* guided by
Philosophy.[10]

Bernard's linkage of Virgil with Martianus and Boethius suggests
a paradigm for medieval secondary epic, for a practice of literary
imitation grounded in the *conversio* of allegory rather than the *con-
ventio* of formal resemblance. As we shall see, the classical epic
tradition, continuous in spirit, discontinuous in form, survived and
flourished in the Middle Ages as the "other speaking" of itself, its

8. Robert Lamberton, *Homer the Theologian: Neoplatonist Allegorical Reading
and the Growth of the Epic Tradition* (Berkeley: University of California Press, 1986),
p. 286.

9. Quoted by Winthrop Wetherbee, *Platonism and Poetry in the Twelfth Century*
(Princeton: Princeton University Press, 1972), pp. 124, 267. Brian Stock (*Myth and
Science in the Twentieth Century: A Study of Bernard Silvester* [Princeton: Princeton
University Press, 1972], pp. 36–37) contests the attribution of this commentary to
Bernard Silvestris but agrees that it "illustrates a view of literature and philosophy
currently in fashion at both Chartres and Tours."

10. See Wetherbee's discussion and partial translation of Bernard's commentary
on Martianus in *Platonism and Poetry*, pp. 104–25, 267–72.

allegorical deep structure brought to the surface in new forms. The Middle Ages did not merely, as Domenico Comparetti suggests, disregard "the aesthetic side of antiquity" in favor of a one-sided interest in "the moral and religious side of the classical works."[11] Rather, as Stephen G. Nichols, Jr., has insisted, the epics of the Middle Ages "explicitly reject the form of the earlier phase as falsifying the truth of the epic matter."[12]

Defining Epic Truth

The definition of epic truth began at least as early as the fifth century B.C. "The ancients," Michael Murrin observes, "wished to explain away the scandal of Homer's gods."[13] Plato's *Republic* lists the crimes Homer ascribes to the immortal gods and concludes that his works should by no means be included in the curriculum of the ideal state lest the youth be corrupted by them. It makes no difference, Socrates says, whether they be allegories or not (*Rep.* 2.378d: οὔτ᾽ ἐν ὑπ- ονοίαις . . . οὔτε ἄνευ ὑπονοιῶν), because young people are unable to distinguish on their own between the literal and the allegorical.[14] As Lamberton observes, the passage bears oblique witness to the pedagogical practice of the Sophists under whose leadership "Greek education took the form of commentaries on texts, commentaries

---

11. Domenico Comparetti, *Vergil in the Middle Ages*, 2d ed., trans. E. F. M. Benecke (London: George Allen & Unwin, 1908, 1966), p. 173.

12. Nichols, "The Spirit of Truth," p. 371. Nichols argues that Renaissance secondary epic consciously distances the epic world by emulating the "salient formal features of the primary model" out of "an express desire to point out the differences between the epic world—now seen as a lost, but not irretrievable ideal—and the real world" (p. 384). It has a focused temporal perspective. Medieval secondary epic, on the other hand, typically brings its heroes and heroines into the present, making them contemporary in order to enhance their role as models for imitation. Thus "the second phase carries forth the basic themes and events of the first phase, but *never* the form" (p. 371).

13. Michael Murrin, *The Allegorical Epic: Essays in Its Rise and Decline* (Chicago: University of Chicago Press, 1980), p. 3. For essays emphasizing the positive, not defensive, motive behind allegorical interpretation, see J. Tate, "On the History of Allegorism," *Classical Quarterly* 28 (1934): 105–14; "Plato and Allegorical Interpretation," *Classical Quarterly* 23 (1929): 142–54 and 24 (1930): 1–10.

14. Plato, *The Republic*, vol. 1, trans. Paul Shorey, Loeb Classical Library (London: W. Heinemann; New York: G. P. Putnam's, 1930), pp. 182–83.

oscillating between the poles of allegory and irony, but doubtlessly favoring the former."[15]

The allegorical readings took various forms, ranging from the derivation of moral precepts from *exempla* to etymological glosses to the scientific demythologizing of a nymph's rape by the god Boreas as a maiden's sudden, accidental fall off a cliff in a gust of wind. (For the latter, see *Phaedrus* 229c.) The most powerful and influential interpretations arose out of the conjunction of philosophy and myth and concerned nothing less than the nature of God and humankind and their respective places in the order of the cosmos. When the myths that gained expression in the epics of antiquity were read from the point of view of specific philosophical schools—atomist, Stoic, Neoplatonist—the great poems became transparent coverings of the truths they simultaneously veiled and conveyed. Stoic exegetes, for instance, found adumbrated in Homer their own cosmological scheme, the actions of the gods and goddesses mirroring the inter-action of the four primary elements—fire (Zeus), air (Hera), water (Poseidon), earth (Hades)—and their respective qualities: hot, dry, moist, cold.[16] These macrocosmic readings, in turn, accommodated and encouraged microcosmic interpretations of the epics as mirrors of human nature within an encyclopedic frame.[17] Epic truth thus became the knowledge of a person's own self. Plato documents this tendency when Socrates tells Phaedrus that mythic allegories, no matter how clever and appealing, serve no purpose if they only concern things external to human nature and do not lead to the self-knowledge commanded by the Delphic oracle: "Know thyself."[18]

The ancient philosophers gave three answers to the question "What is a human being?" Each of these found its confirmation in the inspired poetry of Homer. The first answer recalls our mortality, our necessary subjection to death and to fortune as bodily creatures

15. Robert Lamberton, "Introduction" to *Porphyry: On the Cave of the Nymphs*, trans. Robert Lamberton (Barrytown, N.Y.: Station Hill Press, 1983), p. 6.

16. The standard work on Greek allegorical interpretation is Félix Buffière, *Les mythes d'Homère et la pensée grecque* (Paris: Belles Lettres, 1956).

17. Jon Whitman traces the historical shift from macrocosmic to microcosmic allegorical interpretation in *Allegory: The Dynamics of an Ancient and Medieval Technique* (Oxford: Clarendon Press, 1987).

18. Plato, *Phaedrus*, trans. Harold N. Fowler, Loeb Classical Library (Cambridge: Harvard University Press, 1914, 1960), 229e, pp. 420–23.

existing in time, exposed to temporal change, and fated to die. As Seneca writes to Marcia (circa A.D. 37):

Hoc videlicet dicit illa Pythicis oraculis adscripta vox: NOSCE TE. Quid est homo? Quolibet quassu vas et quolibet fragile iactatu. . . . Quid est homo? Imbecillum corpus et fragile, nudum, suapte natura inerme, alienae opis indigens, ad omnis fortunae contumelias proiectum.

[This, clearly, is the meaning of that famous utterance ascribed to the Pythian oracle: Know Thyself. What is man? A vessel that the slightest shaking, the slightest toss will break. . . . What is man? A body weak and fragile, naked, in its natural state defenceless, dependent upon another's help, and exposed to all the affronts of Fortune.][19]

Seen from the perspective of this answer, the tragic action of Troy and the long suffering of Odysseus on his voyages eloquently indicate man's corporeal and mortal nature—a definition basic to the materialism of both the atomists and the Stoics and the beginning of their wisdom. When Lucretius, therefore, seeks to banish the fear of dying by recalling the death of great poets and philosophers, he first mentions Homer as the only king of poets (*De rerum natura* 3.1037–38: "adde Heliconiadum comites, quorum unus Homerus / sceptra potitus") and then the atomist philosophers Democritus and Epicurus, applying to Epicurus the epigram that Leonidas of Tarentum composed in praise of Homer:

ipse Epicurus obit decurso lumine vitae,
qui genus humanum ingenio superavit et omnis
restinxit, stellas exortus ut aetherius sol.
                    (*De rerum natura* 3.1042–44)

[Epicurus himself died when the light of life had run its course, he whose intellect surpassed humanity, who quenched the light of all as the risen sun of heaven quenches the stars.][20]

19. Seneca, "Ad Marciam de consolatione," in *Moral Essays*, vol. 2, trans. John W. Basore, Loeb Classical Library (Cambridge: Harvard University Press, 1932, rev. ed. 1958), XI.3, pp. 32–35.

20. Lucretius, *De rerum natura*, trans. W. H. D. Rouse, rev. Martin Ferguson Smith, 2d ed., Loeb Classical Library (Cambridge: Harvard University Press, 1924, 1982), pp. 270–71. Subsequent citations are parenthetical.

The passage, the only one in *De rerum natura* to name Epicurus, makes Homer a philosopher and Epicurus another Homer, both of them teaching the truth of mortality. In recalling the death of better men (*De rerum natura* 3.1026: "qui melior multis quam tu fuit"), Lucretius himself echoes the wisdom of Homer: "Even Patroclus died, and he was a far better man than you" (*Il.* 21.107: κάτθανε καὶ Πάτροκλος, ὅ περ σέο πολλὸν ἀμείνων).²¹

The second answer to the question "Quid est homo?" recalls human rationality, the power of a person's higher nature over his passions, his body, and his external situation. Whereas the first answer points to the body and the existential necessity of suffering, the second accords to human nature the possibility of mastering the body and its weakness with one's mind and will. The *logos* implanted in human nature, according to the Stoics, enables people to will freely what has been willed for them by the eternal *Logos*, the mind of god; to bring themselves in harmony with the *cursus* of the universe and its concatenated causes. "The wise man," Seneca writes, "is next-door neighbor to the gods and like a god in all save his mortality" (*De constantia sapientis* 8.2: "sapiens autem vicinus proximusque dis constitit, excepta mortalitate similis deo").²² The practice of virtue and the exercise of judgment set him over the changes of fortune, draw him into the divine current, and render him invulnerable. "Relying on reason," such a person "marches through mortal vicissitudes with the spirit of a god, has no vulnerable spot where he can receive an injury" (p. 73) (*De constantia* 8.3: "Qui rationi innixus per humanos casus divino incedit animo, non habet ubi accipiat iniuriam").

From this philosophical perspective, the Stoic moralists found in the person of Homer's Odysseus—impervious to Circe's dehumanizing charms, self-restrained when seduced by Siren-song—a model of wisdom and tested virtue. Seneca affirms and continues this tradition when he numbers Ulysses among the wise-men ("sapientes") who were "unconquered by struggles, despisers of pleasure, and victors over all terrors" (p. 51) (*De constantia* 2.1: "invictos laboribus

21. Quoted from Homer, *Iliad*, ed. Thomas W. Allen, 3 vols. (Oxford: Oxford University Press, 1931).

22. Seneca, "De constantia sapientis," in *Moral Essays*, vol. 1, trans. John W. Basore, Loeb Classical Library (Cambridge: Harvard University Press, 1928, 1958), pp. 72–73. Subsequent citations are parenthetical.

et contemptores voluptatis et victores omnium terrorum"). Fulgentius later allegorizes the story of Ulysses and the Sirens, observing that the crafty Ulysses triumphs over their alluring song "because wisdom is a stranger to all things of this world" (*Mitologiae* II.viii: "Quia sapientia ab omnibus mundi rebus peregrina est").[23]

The third response to the call for self-knowledge requires a person to recall the immortality of his soul, its divine origin and end. The Platonic and Neoplatonic view of human nature, which identifies the self with the disembodied spirit, thus directly counters the materialism of the first answer and its exclusive emphasis on the mortal body. Macrobius (fifth century) gives expression to this tradition when he writes:

"de caelo descendit γνῶϑι σεαυτόν." nam et Delphici vox haec fertur oraculi. consulenti ad beatitatem quo itinere perveniret: si te, inquit, agnoveris. sed et ipsius fronti templi haec inscripta sententia est. homini autem, ut diximus, una est agnitio sui, si originis natalisque principii exordia prima respexerit, nec se quaesiverit extra. Sic enim anima virtutes ipsas conscientia nobilitatis induitur, quibus post corpus evecta eo unde descenderat reportatur. (*In Somnium Scipionis* I.9.2–3)

["From the sky has come to us the saying, 'Know thyself.'" Indeed, this is said to have been the advice of the Delphic oracle. To one desiring to know by what path blessedness is reached the reply is, "Know thyself." The maxim was inscribed on the front of the temple at Delphi. A man has but one way of knowing himself, as we have just remarked: if he will look back to his first beginning and origin and "not search for himself elsewhere." In this manner the soul, in the very cognizance of its high estate, assumes those virtues by which it is raised aloft after leaving the body and returns to the place of its origin.][24]

With the rise of Neoplatonism in the second century A.D., this third aspect of epic truth came to be discovered in Homer, and the figure of

23. Fulgentius, *The Mythologies*, in *Fulgentius the Mythographer*, trans. Leslie George Whitbread (Columbus: Ohio State University Press, 1971), p. 73; Fulgentius, *Mitologiae*, in *Opera*, ed. Rudolph Helm (Leipzig: Teubner, 1898, 1970), p. 48. For a full exposition of Odyssean allegory, see William Bedell Stanford, *The Ulysses Theme: A Study in the Adaptability of a Traditional Hero*, 2d ed. (Oxford: Blackwell, 1963).

24. Macrobius, *Commentarii in Somnium Scipionis*, ed. Jacob Willis (Leipzig: Teubner, 1970), p. 40; Macrobius, *Commentary on the Dream of Scipio*, trans. William Harris Stahl, Records of Civilization, Sources and Studies 48 (New York: Columbia University Press, 1952), pp. 124–25. Subsequent citations are parenthetical.

Odysseus received yet another reading. No longer merely the moral exemplar of the Stoics, he became for Numenius a religious symbol, a type of the soul on its homeward journey. Numenius' lost work, to which Porphyry refers in his essay on the cave of the nymphs in *Odyssey* 13.102–12, contributed to an influential series of Neo-platonic readings of Homer. Plotinus (b. A.D. 205) describes Odysseus as the blessed soul, in love with Eternal Beauty, who flees to the Fatherland away from the material universe which imprisons him, a universe figured in the sensory delights of the isles of Circe and Calypso (*Enneads* I.6.8, 16–21).[25] Porphyry (A.D. 233–301) treats Odysseus at the end of his travels as "the symbol of man passing through the successive stages of γένεσις and so being restored to his place among those beyond all wavecrash"—that is, beyond "the material universe."[26] Proclus (c. A.D. 410–85) interprets the wanderings of Odysseus as the "wanderings and circlings of the soul" in its quest for the "mystical harbor of the soul" (*In Parm.* 1025a.29–37).[27] In the West, Proclus' contemporary Macrobius includes Porphyry's allegory of Odysseus in his commentary on Cicero's *Dream of Scipio* (I.12.2–3) to explicate the soul's origin and final destiny, its descent and ascent. "This," Macrobius explains, "is what Homer with his divine intelligence signifies in his description of the cave at Ithaca" (p. 134) (*In Somnium Scipionis* I.12.3: "Hoc est quod Homeri divina prudentia in antri Ithacensis descriptione significat").

The three interpretations of Homer we have just surveyed—atomist, Stoic, and Neoplatonic—with their respective emphases on the mortal, rational, and spiritual aspects of human nature, inspired a succession of rewritings of Homer in antiquity, all of them based on a figurative reading of Greek myth as a mirror of self-knowledge and a means to know the universal causes of things. As we shall see, whereas Virgil imitates the Homer of cosmological allegory, the authors of Greek and Roman romance continue the epic tradition by imitating a moralized Homer for a popular audience. Both the Virgilian and the romantic imitations of Homer were then given Neoplatonic readings that affected, in turn, the ways that they were imitated by late-antique writers such as Apuleius (second century),

25. Plotinus, *Enneads*, trans. A. H. Armstrong, vol. 1, Loeb Classical Library (Cambridge: Harvard University Press, 1966), pp. 256–57.
26. Porphyry, *On the Cave of the Nymphs*, p. 39.
27. Quoted by Lamberton, *Homer the Theologian*, p. 226.

Martianus Capella (fifth century), and his close contemporary, Fulgentius (A.D. 480–550).

Boethius' *De consolatione philosophiae* (A.D. 525) gives a summary expression to this tradition of Homeric rewritings and stands as the major conduit for the continuation of the classical epic tradition in the Middle Ages. A prosimetric composition, the *Consolation* admits an encyclopedic range of literary forms into its own imitation of epic as a mixed kind, even as its narrative quest for self-knowledge focuses on, and systematically unfolds, the tripartite definition of epic truth derived from figurative readings of Homeric myth. At the outset Lady Philosophy encounters the despairing prisoner with blazing eyes ("oculis ardentibus"), even as Athena meets the wrathful Achilles in *Iliad* 1.200.[28] As we shall see, she quotes Homer repeatedly to Boethius, aligning her philosophy with his inspired poetry. After the prisoner lays bare the wound of his grief (in response to a Homeric command in Greek on Philosophy's lips), she assesses his condition by asking him to define his own human nature: "Quid . . . homo sit" (I.p6,15).[29] The incompleteness of his answer, "rationale animal atque mortale," leads her to conclude that he has forgotten who and what he is, his celestial origin and end.

Lady Philosophy then helps Boethius to regain self-knowledge, using three mythological metra to impress upon him the full, threefold definition of his humanity. The failed romance of Orpheus and Eurydice (III.m12) underscores the lesson of mortality and transience. The tale of Ulysses and Circe (IV.m3) enforces the Stoic teaching that rationality and moral choice elevate human beings over both other animals and their own passions. Finally Boethius joins in a single metrum (IV.m7) the myths of Agamemnon, Odysseus, and Heracles to recall the Neoplatonic doctrine of a celestial homeland and the heroism of the philosopher's laborious journey *ad patriam.*

There are only three mythological metra among the thirty-nine in Boethius' *De consolatione.* They all follow Lady Philosophy's climactic, metrical request for poetic and philosophical inspiration, "O qui perpetua" (III.m9), and insist self-consciously on the correspondence between epic action (however briefly presented) and epic

---

28. See Lamberton, *Homer the Theologian,* p. 276; Whitman, *Allegory,* pp. 114–15.

29. Quotations from Boethius, cited parenthetically, are taken from *De consolatione philosophiae,* ed. Ludovicus Bieler, CCSL 94 (Turnhout: Brepols, 1957).

truth, the self-knowledge commanded by the Delphic oracle. The Boethian rewriting of Homer, mediated through Virgil, Seneca, and the various Neoplatonic texts echoed in the *De consolatione*, thus brings the allegorical tradition we have been tracing to its synthetic climax, embedding the images of epic poetry in a dialogic and philosophical discourse that carefully discloses its own limits in order to transcend them.

Lady Philosophy's development of providential themes, her insistence on human inability to see things from a divine viewpoint, her final exhortation to humble prayer, and the absence of explicit reference to Christ in the *Consolation* as a whole encouraged medieval readers to supply what Boethius, revered as a Christian martyr, had omitted by coupling his *Consolation* with a complementary Old Testament text, the Book of Job. There are some obvious similarities between the works, which were subsequently underscored and elaborated by biblical exegetes. Boethius, like Job, is an innocent sufferer confronted in a deeply personal way with the problem of evil. His complaints and queries in dialogue with Philosophy parallel those of the stricken Old Testament saint in conversation with his consolers and God. Indeed, as we shall see, Boethius' mental journey *per falsa bona* closely resembles the psychological and philosophical progress that prepares Job for a divine epiphany.

Two major biblical commentaries attest to a close assimilation of the texts of Boethius and Job during the medieval period. When Saint Gregory the Great (c. A.D. 540–604), Boethius' near contemporary, wrote his *Moralia in Job*, he discovered in the Old Testament *vir bonus* a philosophical hero and a Christian martyr like Boethius. The *Moralia*, which Lawrence Besserman terms "the best known and most authoritative commentary on the Book of Job in Western Christendom," largely shaped the reading of Job during the Middle Ages and directed its literary imitation.[30] When Saint Thomas Aquinas, another student of Boethius, wrote his thirteenth-century commentary on Job, he explicitly likened the biblical book to *De consolatione*.[31] According to Aquinas, "Job disclosed his sadness by speak-

30. Lawrence L. Besserman, *The Legend of Job in the Middle Ages* (Cambridge: Harvard University Press, 1979), p. 56.
31. See Ralph McInerny, *Boethius and Aquinas* (Washington, D.C.: Catholic University of America Press, 1990). McInerny does not treat Aquinas' commentary on Job.

ing," even as "Boethius in the beginning of *On the Consolation of Philosophy* disclosed his sadness to show how to mitigate it with reason."[32] The purpose of the Book of Job is, moreover, identical with that of *De consolatione*: to show "through plausible arguments that human affairs are ruled by divine providence."[33]

Boethius paraphrases Job 1:21 in *De consolatione* II.p2,8 when a personified Fortune declares her right to exercise change. Awaiting execution in Pavia for a political crime he did not commit, Boethius may well have meditated deeply on the Book of Job and the misfortunes of its righteous hero. Whether or not Boethius did, however, his *Consolation* clearly prepared the way for the medieval reception of Job as heroic poetry on the basis of both content and form.

Boethius' figural reading of Homer as an avenue to epic truth found its complement in the allegorical reading of Job. As we shall see, Gregory the Great's *Moralia* (circa A.D. 595) uses an extended allegory of martial combat, not unlike the Virgilian personification allegory of Prudentius' *Psychomachia* (A.D. 405), to interpret the struggle between Job and Satan. In this reading the truth revealed in the inspired biblical Word corresponds to the truth veiled and obscured by the letter of pagan epic, even as it insists on the literal falsity of the latter. Job appears as a hero who displays heroic, godlike virtue in the face of great adversity and whose particular story reveals from the perspective of moral philosophy the universal truth of human nature.

Asserting the heroism of Job as a "true man" ("homo verus") to rival Virgil's *vir*, Aeneas, required the exegetical redefinition of heroism itself and its constitutive virtues, in particular, wisdom and courage ("sapientia et fortitudo"). In Gregory's *Moralia*, therefore, "fortitudo" ceases to manifest itself in the Aristotelian terms of fearless, freely chosen, public military action and becomes identified closely with the private virtues of patient endurance and long-suffering. Similarly, "wisdom" loses its pragmatic, prudential associations and becomes instead the Pauline foolishness that rejoices in the cross (1 Corinth. 1:18–25) and discovers in it a means of salvation, of

32. Thomas Aquinas, *The Literal Exposition on Job: A Scriptural Commentary Concerning Providence*, trans. Anthony Damico, ed. Martin D. Yaffe, Classics in Religious Studies 7 (Atlanta: Scholars Press, 1989), p. 100.
33. Ibid., p. 68.

providential return from a mutable world to the eternal Fatherland. "Heroic virtue," in general, becomes the special characteristic, not of demigods like Achilles and Hercules, but of saints, the heroes and heroines of the new, Christian social order.

Perceived similarities in content between Job and Boethius thus accomplished a figural continuation of the Homeric tradition in its Odyssean and Iliadic modalities of homeward journey and battle. At the same time, however, their formal resemblance as prosimetric compositions enabled a medieval departure from the literary conventions of classical epic as an outward expression of both Christianity's countercultural stance vis-à-vis paganism and its characteristic emphasis on the spirit of a text over, and even against, its letter, in accord with the oft-quoted Pauline dictum, "The letter killeth, but the spirit giveth life" (2 Corinth. 3:6).[34] To a world fascinated by allegorical interpretation and the Augustinian insight that multiple *signa* point to a single *res*, the literal alternation of prose and verse hinted at a deeper, underlying Word, at the One behind the many, at a single, universal Truth that could be expressed in infinitely many different ways.[35]

In his Preface to Job, Saint Jerome describes the Book as a prosimetric composition. The frame narrative of Job's lost and restored fortune, which makes up the beginning and the end of the Book, is, he says, in high style biblical prose ("prosa oratio"), whereas the middle section from Job 3:3 through 42:6 consists in the original language of "hexameter verses running in dactyl and spondee": "hexametri versus sunt, dactylo spondaeoque currentes."[36] Jerome's division casts the greater part of Job in the meter traditionally used for epic poetry. It also suggestively associates third-person narrative

34. See James J. Murphy, *Rhetoric in the Middle Ages: A Study of Rhetorical Theory from Saint Augustine to the Renaissance* (Berkeley: University of California Press, 1974, 1990), pp. 48–64.

35. Modern critics are apt to disparage the *prosimetrum* as an "unpromising structure" (to borrow a phrase from F. J. E. Raby, *The History of Christian-Latin Poetry* [Oxford: Clarendon Press, 1927], p. 112). It indicates, however, as Ernst Robert Curtius observes, the great "variety of the linguistic art forms in the Middle Ages"— plain prose, artistic prose, rhymed prose, mixed prose, metrical and rhythmic poetry— and the delight medieval writers took in "uniting and crossing these stylistic devices" out of a "childish delight in play and variegated color" and an urge toward the incarnational mingling of "the sacred and burlesque" (*European Literature and the Latin Middle Ages*, trans. Willard R. Trask, Bollingen Series 36 [New York: Harper and Row, 1953, 1963], pp. 150–54).

36. Saint Jerome, "Preface" to *Job*, PL 28, c1081.

(in the frame) with prose and first-person narrative (in the dialogic monologues) with poetry.[37] Jerome's metrical assessment of the book certainly disposed subsequent readers to compare Job to the poems of Homer and Virgil. As we have seen, Isidore of Seville considers it a heroic work, written in heroic meter.[38] Bede cites Job as an example of dactylic hexameter, the "heroic verse" ("heroicum") appropriate to both long and short works ("opusculis tam prolixis quam succinctis") that sing "of the greatest heroes" ("maxime heroum").[39] He goes on to classify it as a work written in a "mixed mode": "The combined or mixed kind is where the poet himself speaks and speaking characters are also introduced, as in Homer's *Iliad* and *Odyssey* and Virgil's *Aeneid* and, among our [Christian] works, the history of holy Job" (*De arte metrica* I.xxv, pp. 140–41: "Coenon est uel micton in quo poeta ipse loquitur et personae loquentes introducuntur, ut sunt scripta Ilias et Odyssia Homeri et Aeneidos Virgilii et apud nos historia beati Iob").

The distinction of three poetic voices (*tres characteres dicendi, tribus modis carmen*), familiar to the Latin Middle Ages through the commentaries of Servius and "Probus" on Virgil's *Eclogues*,[40] is a commonplace of medieval literary criticism.[41] Rabanus Maurus (ninth century), for instance, repeats Bede's listing of classical and biblical examples of each mode almost verbatim, singling out the Book of Job as representative of the mixed kind.[42] In medieval dis-

---

37. Although Jerome's characterization of the Joban verse as hexameter is based on a mistaken notion of Hebrew poetry, his tentative choice of epic meter displays a remarkable sensitivity to the formal quality of the language in the book. As Marvin H. Pope notes, "The Prologue-Epilogue . . . presents a number of literary features and motifs which are characteristic of Semitic epic, as known from Akkadian literature and more recently from the Ugaritic texts. These epic literary features appear as a sort of substratum which may well derive from a very ancient Job epic" ("Introduction," in *Job*, Anchor Bible Series [Garden City, N.Y.: Doubleday, 1965], p. xxxi). Pope cites the following studies: N. M. Sarna, "Epic Substratum in the Prose of Job," *JBL* 76 (1957): 13–25; H. L. Ginsberg, "The Legend of King Keret, a Canaanite Epic of the Bronze Age," *BASOR*, Supp. Studies 2–3 (1946).

38. See Isidore, *Etymologiae* I.xxxix.9–11, PL 82, c118–19.

39. Bede, *De arte metrica*, ed. M. H. King, CCSL 123A (Turnhout: Brepols, 1975), I.x, p. 108. Subsequent citations are parenthetical; translation, mine.

40. See Servius, *Commentatio in Vergilii Bucolica*, ed. G. Thilo and H. Hagen (Leipzig, 1881), III.1, p. 29; *Explicatio in Vergilii Bvcolica* I, p. 2.

41. See *Medieval Literary Theory and Criticism c.1100–1375: The Commentary Tradition*, ed. A. J. Minnis and A. B. Scott, with the assistance of David Wallace (Oxford: Clarendon Press, 1988), pp. 23, 344.

42. Rabanus Maurus, *De universo* XV.ii, PL 111, c420.

cussions of the three modes, the "mixed mode" appropriate to heroic poetry designates a kind of narrative that combines the exegematic or didactic mode, in which the poet speaks in his own voice as a teacher and a teller, and the dramatic mode, appropriate to comedy and tragedy, in which the poet never speaks in his own person but rather impersonates others.[43]

The threefold scheme—didactic, dramatic, mixed—has its classical origin in Plato's *Republic* 3 and Aristotle's *Poetics* 3.48a19–24. As Gerald F. Else has shown, Aristotle converted an essentially bipartite distinction between dramatic and narrative mimetic modes into a tripartite "*scala* of the purity of realization of Μίμησις, reaching from the lowest to the highest": narrative, mixed, dramatic.[44] According to this Aristotelian *scala*, Homeric poetry, which makes a "*dramatic use* of direct speech," anticipates the peak mimetic achievement of Greek tragedy and, from the viewpoint of Aristotle's literary history, actually fathers it.[45]

Unlike Plato and Aristotle, however, who begin their discussions with the mixed kind and end with the dramatic mode as an instance of pure imitation, medieval commentators typically begin with didactic poetry and end with a treatment of the encyclopedic mixed kind, thus elevating heroic poetry as an all-inclusive genre over both drama and exposition. Neither Plato nor Aristotle directly correlate the distinction among the various mimetic modes with the distinction between poetry and prose. Nonetheless, the classical perception of Homer's works as mixed, together with the common pedagogical practice of glossing his poetry with prose, may help to explain the late-antique popularity of prosimetrical epic imitations in the form of Menippean satire: Petronius' *Satyricon*, Martianus Capella's *De nuptiis Mercurii et Philologiae*, and Boethius' *De consolatione philosophiae*.[46]

43. See P. B. Salmon, "The 'Three Voices' of Poetry in Medieval Literary Theory," *Medium Aevum* 30 (1961): 1–18, and my *Song of Songs in the Middle Ages* (Ithaca: Cornell University Press, 1990), pp. 162–67.

44. Gerald F. Else, *Aristotle's Poetics: The Argument* (Cambridge: Harvard University Press, 1963), p. 101.

45. Ibid. Else (pp. 90–101) gives a thorough discussion of the theory of three modes in Plato and Aristotle and surveys the subsequent history of the threefold distinction.

46. For a discussion of prosimetric form, see Joachim Gruber, *Kommentar zu Boethius de consolatione philosophiae* (Berlin and New York: de Gruyter, 1978), pp.

Job, designated as the biblical counterpart to Homer, Virgil, and Boethius, displays precisely this mixture of prose and poetry. "It is written in its own language," Bede says, "in a style that is not totally poetic, but partly rhetorical, partly metrical or rhythmical" (*De arte metrica* I.xxv, pp. 140–41: "in sua lingua non tota poetico, sed partim rhetorico, partim sit metrico uel rithmico scripta sermone"). Bede's vague description reflects the uncertainty of Jerome's when he first terms the Joban frame narrative an oration in prose ("prosa oratio") and then goes on to describe the central dialogue as dactylic hexameter interspersed with rhythmic sections, sweet and ringing, set free from the law of meter: "interdum quoque rhythmus ipse dulcis et tinnulus fertur numeris lege metri solutis."[47]

As a mixed kind, as a summative genre—narrative and dramatic, prosaic and poetic, metrical and rhythmical, Latin and vernacular—epic lost its formal distinctiveness for the Middle Ages. Paradoxically, formal conjunction increasingly admitted the translative possibility of disjunction: long or short, prose or verse, metrical or rhythmical, Latin or vernacular. Indeed, as a literary kind, recognizable by distinctive formal features, "epic" was unknown to the Middle Ages.[48] The typical medieval designation, "heroic poetry," names something else. It points to an epic tradition continuous not in its letter but in its truth: the truth of human nature providentially revealed in the virtuous *homo*, the Joban saint.

The complex, intertextual relationship between Boethius' *Consolation* and the Book of Job, which defined them as exemplars of the same literary kind, generated multifarious imitations in the Middle Ages. As heroic works mixed in their form, combining not only first and third person narration with the direct speech of characters, but also prose with poetry in a variety of meters, the books of Boethius and Job could virtually be imitated in any imaginable outward form or combination of forms. Indeed, the relative formlessness that we associate with medieval romance, and which makes it impossible for

---

16–19. Twelfth-century examples include Bernard Silvestris' *De universitate mundi* and Alain de Lille's *Anti-Claudianus*.

47. Saint Jerome, "Preface," PL 28, c1081–82. For an instructive discussion of Jerome's Preface to Job, see James L. Kugel, *The Idea of Biblical Poetry: Parallelism and Its History* (New Haven: Yale University Press, 1981), pp. 233–36.

48. The *Oxford English Dictionary* notes the first appearance of the word "epic" in 1589.

us to define "romance" at all, except with descriptive qualifiers like "hagiographic," "amatory," and "chivalric," derives in large part from the radical medieval disassociation of epic form from epic truth. Heroic literature in the Middle Ages was simply poetry or prose about heroes and heroines. Depicting true heroism, however, meant discovering the truth that pagan epic had veiled. There is, in short, a close relationship between epic allegory and medieval romance, between the twinned double otherness of epic's hidden message, as defined by Boethius and Job, and its complementary literary kind.

The medieval understanding that the *Consolation of Philosophy* and the Book of Job teach a common message and mirror each other structurally helps to explain the frequent collocation of allusions to them in vernacular works. The historical pairing of the two works as textual analogues was complicated, however, by the exegesis of Job on three different levels—literal, tropological, and allegorical (in the narrow sense of that word, as referring to Christ.) In every case, therefore, the conjoining of Boethian and Joban elements looks different, depending on which of the two is foregrounded and how they interact as allegories of each other. Hagiographic romance typically emphasizes *ironia* in the relationship between the two, whereas amatory romance often posits a typological, even sacramental, relationship between them. In chivalric romance the two texts, Joban and Boethian, tend to meet as moral analogues.

As we shall see, hagiographic romance, exemplified in the popular *legenda* of Eustace, Griselda, and Constance, foregrounds the Joban archetype of the so-called frame story in which the steadfast saint endures without complaint the assaults of the devil in an infinitely expandable series of terrible misfortunes. In these *legenda* Boethian laments on the lips of other characters, or as narratorial intrusions, replace the Joban outcries of the central dialogue (Job 3:3–42:6) as an index of the superhuman intensity of the trials, while the saint remains silent or speaks in prayer. An ironic contrast between Job and Boethius, in short, diverts attention from the biblical split between the pious and the despairing Job, emphasizes the difference between the divine and human view of things, and enables a fairly static characterization of the saint in the midst of a violently mutable world.

The tales of Boethian lovers, on the other hand, as instances of amatory romance, foreground the *Consolation of Philosophy* as a love story, configured according to both the lovers' triangle formed in the opening scene by the meretricious Muses, the male sufferer, and Lady Philosophy and its central representation in the myth of Orpheus and Eurydice (III.m12). In Peter Abelard's *Historia calamitatum*, Dante's *Commedia*, and Chaucer's *Troilus and Criseyde* a single beloved woman plays in succession the disparate roles of strumpet muse, Philosophia, and divine grace as the lover's cruel sufferings and experiences of loss assimilate him gradually to Job and Christ. The story of Job, in short, as a foreshadowing of the passion and resurrection of Christ, serves to extend the Boethian account of spiritual growth, remembering, and self-knowledge into a heroic tale of personal redemption through divine and human love.

In the case of chivalric romance, the different faces of Job and Boethius enable a complete archeology of medieval knighthood. As we shall see, in the early Christian period, Job, as a spiritual warrior and the patron of saints like Martin of Tours, stands radically apart from the world of physical combat. At the beginning of the Crusades, Job becomes the Galahad-like patron of the Knights Templar and the laity in general, whose literal warfaring has sacramental significance as the pure, outward expression of *psychomachia*. In the late Middle Ages the moral scandal of the Crusades and the evident disparity between chivalric ideals and practice focus attention not on the Job of Christological allegory, but on the tropological Job, who models for penitent knights like Malory's Lancelot the path from lost to regained virtue, from earthly to heavenly knighthood. This face of Job especially recalls the image of Boethius as a patient and a learner and emphasizes the distance in his spiritual progress between "before" and "after," time and eternity. The rhetorical thrust of this late-medieval tropological reading tended to give increased importance to the *pathos* of the Book of Job, until finally, in the sixteenth century, Job as a literally despairing sinner and sufferer serves as a model for Spenser's mutable Redcrosse Knight, and indeed for every Protestant Christian engaged in the spiritual quest for holiness in the midst of an ever inconstant world.

At the end of the English Renaissance, Milton's "argument / Not less but more Heroic than the wrath / of stern *Achilles*" (9.13–15) rediscovers and renews the medieval idea of epic, consciously departing from antique epic form in search of an "answerable style" (9.20) appropriate to the "better fortitude / of Patience and Heroic

Martyrdom / Unsung" (9.31–33), the heroism of Job.[49] Through the figure of Satan, Milton rejects a literal reading of classical epic, even as he uses Boethian allusions to enforce a figurative interpretation of Homer and Virgil, thus leading back from the classics to the Bible, to the epic truth revealed in the Book of Job.

Indeed, taken all together, Milton's three great works constitute an exegetical trilogy inspired by Protestant theology and poetics, each work imitating Job at a different level of interpretation. *Paradise Regained* imitates the static, Christlike Job of allegory; *Samson Agonistes*, the Job of literal despair; *Paradise Lost*, the tropological Job of moral growth and Boethian instruction. While the three Miltonic faces of Job as sinless saint (Christ), despairing sinner (Samson), and virtuous penitent (Adam) distantly reflect the ancient threefold definition of human nature as divine, mortal, and rational, Milton's mirror affords a self-knowledge that separates, rather than combines, these human qualities in a nearly schizophrenic array of possibilities. Formally diverse, Milton's heroic works thus find their common subtext in the Book of Job, a book whose single epic truth has, however, become disturbingly several. Indeed, Milton's last work, *Samson Agonistes*, which represents the Book of Job as tragedy, reflects contemporary Protestant exegesis in a way that anticipates the modern view of Job as drama, not epic.[50] It asks, more than it answers, the question: "God of our Fathers, what is man!"[51]

49. John Milton, *Paradise Lost*, in *Complete Poems and Major Prose*, ed. Merritt Y. Hughes (New York: Odyssey Press, 1957). Subsequent citations are parenthetical.

50. For a discussion of the modern and Reformation view of Job as drama, see Lewalski, *Milton's Brief Epic*, pp. 17–20. As Lewalski observes, whereas the Middle Ages emphasized the so-called frame-story (Chapters 1, 2, and the last portion of Chapter 42), which recounts Job's affliction, patient acceptance, and ultimate reward, contemporary exegetes focus on the dramatic dialogues that constitute the problematic center of the book. Whereas Gregorian commentary seeks to reconcile (via allegorical interpretation) the central speeches with the narrative that introduces them, present-day scholars deny Job's textual integrity, treating the outer narrative as an inherited folktale that occasions, at the heart of the work, a sophisticated philosophical discussion of the problem of evil. Indeed, from the point of view of recent scholarship, "the interpretations of Job in the premodern period advance our understanding of the book very little"; instead, as Nahum N. Glatzer insists (*The Dimensions of Job: A Study and Selected Readings* [New York: Schocken Books, 1969], p. 11), "they add to our appreciation of the period, the writers, and their concerns" as records of reader response. See also Morris Jastrow, Jr., *The Book of Job: Its Origin, Growth, and Interpretation* (Philadelphia: J. B. Lippincott, 1920), and Marvin H. Pope, ed., *Job*.

51. John Milton, *Samson Agonistes*, in *Complete Poems*, line 667. The Chorus echoes Job 7:17.

1   Allegories of *Logos* and *Eros*

Before we take up the central concern of this book—the Boethian and Joban mediation of the classical epic tradition in the Middle Ages and Renaissance—we need to recall some of the literary contexts in which Boethius wrote his sixth-century *De consolatione philosophiae.* As we have seen, Bernard Silvestris considered Boethius' work to be an imitation of both Virgil's *Aeneid* and Martianus Capella's *De nuptiis Philologiae et Mercurii,* and thus the expression of a continuous Homeric tradition. All three works, he says, deal figuratively with the same thing.[1] This chapter examines the historical basis for that critical judgment.

The bizarre combination in *De nuptiis* of weighty textbook material on the seven liberal arts with a fanciful, allegorical love story seems, to be sure, far removed from both Virgil's *Aeneid* and Boethius' *Consolation.* It does, however, call attention to two clearly marked lines of allegorical development in antiquity. As we shall see, both Boethius and Martianus, albeit in strikingly different ways, join these two lines. The first, emphasizing *logos* and the intellectual discovery of the causes of things, proceeds from Homer through Virgil, Macrobius, and Fulgentius. The second, emphasizing *eros* and the moral application of truth, also finds its origins in Homer, but proceeds through popular romance, both Greek and Roman.

1. Quoted by Winthrop Wetherbee, *Platonism and Poetry in the Twelfth Century* (Princeton: Princeton University Press, 1972), p. 124.

Virgil and the Allegory of *Logos*

The *Vitae Vergilianae* and Virgil's own remarks in *Georgics* 2.475–82
indicate that Virgil wanted to imitate Lucretius in writing a philosophical poem, a poem unveiling the causes of things.[2] Despite
Lucretius' opening invocation of Venus as "Aeneadum genetrix," the
Aeneid is seldom read as Virgil's response to *De rerum natura*.[3]
Although there are clear differences in form and content between the
two, Lucretius' poem offers a suggestive model for Virgil's own philosophical rewriting of Homer. As we have already seen, Lucretius
draws a strong parallel between Homer and Epicurus (*De rerum
natura* 3.1037–44). Elsewhere Lucretius summarizes the action of
the *Iliad* to show that historical events result accidentally from body
and void ("eventa . . . corporis atque loci") as first causes:

> denique materies si rerum nulla fuisset
> nec locus ac spatium, res in quo quaeque geruntur,
> numquam Tyndaridis forma *conflatus* amore
> *ignis*, Alexandri Phrygio sub pectore *gliscens*,
> clara *accendisset* saevi certamina belli,
> nec clam durateus Troianis Pergama partu
> *inflammasset* equos nocturno Graiugenarum.
>
> (*De rerum natura* 1.471–77, emphasis added)

> [Again, if there had been no material for things, and no place and space in
> which each thing is done, no *fire fanned to flame* by love through the
> beauty of Tyndareus' daughter, and *glowing* beneath the breast of Phry-
> gian Alexander, would ever have *set alight blazing* battles of savage war;
> no wooden horse, unmarked by the sons of Troy, would ever have set
> Pergama in *flames* by its night-born brood of Grecians.] (pp. 40–41,
> emphasis added)

2. See Michael Murrin, *The Allegorical Epic: Essays in Its Rise and Decline* (Chicago: University of Chicago Press, 1980), pp. 11–13.
3. I quote from Lucretius, *De rerum natura*, trans. W. H. D. Rouse, rev. Martin F.
Smith, 2nd ed., Loeb Classical Library (Cambridge: Harvard University Press, 1975,
repr. 1982). Philip R. Hardie advances the "perhaps disconcerting" thesis that *De
rerum natura* is "a central model" for the *Aeneid* in *Virgil's "Aeneid": Cosmos and
Imperium* (Oxford: Clarendon, 1986), p. 157. Murrin suggestively anticipates this
approach in *The Allegorical Epic*.

The imagery of the passage, which links in a causal chain the fire of love with the flames of war and the eventual burning of Troy, offers a prologue to the long philosophical discussion that follows, in which Lucretius refutes Heraclitus, Empedocles, and the Stoics, all of whom consider fire, not solid matter, to be the original substance of things: "primordia rerum / mollia" (1.753–54).[4] Lucretius, in short, first envisions a Stoic reading of Homer, a reading that posits fire as the elemental beginning and end of the Trojan war, and then argues on behalf of the atomists for solid matter as antecedent to fire.

Lucretius' imagined Stoic reading derives from Stoic allegoresis of the *Iliad.* As Cicero's Balbus bears witness, Stoic theory deified the air lying between the sea and the sky, naming it Hera (later, Juno) because of its close connection with aether, the cosmic fire associated with Zeus (later, Jove), Hera's brother and husband.[5] The Stoics thus discovered behind Homer's imagistic pantheon a true natural philosophy according to which, for instance, Hera's cloud-covered copulation with Zeus on Mt. Ida (*Il.* 14.153–355; 15.1–84) encoded an elemental description of a springtime thunderstorm—air (Hera) coupling with fire (Zeus).[6] Lucretius, however, goes beyond such sporadic exegesis, which served to explain problematic passages individually, in isolation from the *Iliad* as a whole, and gives to fire (and thus to Jove) ultimate causality for the whole action of Homer's epic, unifying it from beginning to end.

The Stoic reading of Homer that Lucretius first posits and then rejects bears striking resemblance to Virgil's own reading and rewriting of Homer. It is virtually a critical commonplace to recognize Stoic elements informing the *Aeneid.* The epic's proem, which makes a wrathful Juno responsible for Aeneas' sufferings, introduces a specifically Stoic concern ("secundum Stoicos dicit") for, as Servius notes, the Epicureans pictured the gods as disinterested in human affairs: "nam Epicurei dicunt deos humana penitus non curare" (*In*

---

4. Hardie treats this passage briefly as a Lucretian precedent for the Virgilian literary device whereby "initially figurative" events become narrative actualities. See *Cosmos and Imperium*, pp. 232–33.

5. Cicero, *De natura deorum*, trans. H. Rackham, Loeb Classical Library (Cambridge: Harvard University Press, 1933, 1979), II.xxvi.66, pp. 186–87. See also Macrobius, *Commentary on the Dream of Scipio*, trans. William Harris Stahl (New York: Columbia University Press, 1952), I.xvii.12–15, pp. 157–58.

6. See Murrin, *Allegorical Epic*, pp. 4–7, 15.

Vergilii Aeneidos I.11).[7] Aeneas' piety ("pius Aeneas") marks him as a Stoic hero, rendering his filial duty to his father and the gods; his paternal due to those entrusted to his care.[8] Aeneas' heroic action and suffering result from his free acceptance of his appointed destiny, and the combination of human virtue and divine affliction in his *labores* make the epic as a whole a Stoic exploration of the problem of evil in a providentially ordered universe. As Servius phrases the question: "If Aeneas is just, why does he suffer under the hatred of the gods?" (*In Aen.* I.10: "si iustus est Aeneas, cur odio deorum laborat?").

Whereas Virgil's Juno is the agent of disorder, personified opposition to destiny, and the source of storms and madness, Virgil's Jupiter is, as Hainsworth phrases it, "an allegory of his historical determinism" who speaks "as if he were the mouthpiece of Fate."[9] "Jupiter's will," Servius writes, "is Fate" (*In Aen.* IV.614: " 'fata' dicta, id est Iovis voluntas"). When Jupiter, in answer to Venus' fears, declares Fate immovable (*Aen.* 1.257–58: "manent immota tuorum / fata"), he expresses the Stoic teaching ("dogma Stoicorum ostendit") that Fate cannot be altered (*In Aen.* I.257: "nulla ratione posse fata mutari").[10] Elsewhere Servius treats the word "fata" as a past participle indicating what the gods have decreed: " 'fata' modo participium est, hoc est, 'quae dii loquuntur' " (*In Aen.* II.54)—words that the gods themselves must obey once they have been spoken. As Jupiter tells Venus: "necque me sententia vertit" (*Aen.* 1.260).[11]

Virgil couples this explicit treatment of Jupiter's will as the fixed, necessary cause of things with imagery appropriate to Stoic cosmology. Jupiter makes his first appearance "aethere summo" (*Aen.*

7. Quotations from Servius are all taken from *Servii Grammatici qui feruntur in Virgilii Carmina commentarii*, ed. Georg Thilo and Hermann Hagen (Leipzig, 1881– 87), 3 vols. Translations of Servius are mine.

8. For an excellent study of Stoic ethics, see Brad Inwood, *Ethics and Human Action in Early Stoicism* (Oxford: Clarendon Press, 1985).

9. J. B. Hainsworth, *The Idea of Epic* (Berkeley: University of California Press, 1991), p. 106.

10. All quotations from Virgil are taken from *The Aeneid of Virgil*, 2 vols., ed. R. D. Williams (Basingstoke and London: Macmillan, 1972).

11. For studies of the antique understanding of fate, see Vincent Cioffari, *Fortune and Fate from Democritus to St. Thomas Aquinas* (New York: Columbia University Press, 1935); Jerold C. Frakes, *The Fate of Fortune in the Early Middle Ages: The Boethian Tradition* (Leiden and New York: E. J. Brill, 1988).

1.223), in the upper, fiery air. The passage recalls the Stoic deification of aether as Jove, the primal, creative Fire that is the material
origin of everything. According to this view, aether is both the world
and its god ("mundus deus"), the animate force governing the muta-
tion of its elements (air, water, earth).[12] Virgil's Anchises enunciates
this Stoic dogma when he associates fiery energy and a heavenly
origin with the seeds of things: "igneus est ollis vigor et caelestis
origo / seminibus" (*Aen.* 6.730–31). Twice Virgil calls Jupiter "hominum sator atque deorum" (*Aen.* 1.254, 11.725), the sower ("sator") of
gods and men, thus linking his paternity to the seeds of fire ("seminibus"), the warmth from the sky ("caldor e caelo") that is, according
to Zeno, the seed of animate creatures: "animalium semen ignis is
qui anima ac mens."[13]

Virgil's strong association of Jupiter with both fate and fire allows
him to rewrite Homer from the unified Stoic perspective Lucretius
first suggested when he posited divine fire as the first and last cause
of the Trojan war (*De rerum natura* 1.471–77). When Aeneas tells of
his escape from burning Troy, he dwells upon his solitary encounter
with Helen (*Aen.* 2.567–87).[14] Filled with vengeful fire (2.575: "exar-
sere ignes animo"), he almost kills her as the cause of Troy's destruction (2.581: "Troia arserit igni"), but Venus herself intervenes to
exculpate both Helen and Paris and blame instead the cruelty of the
gods: "divum inclementia, divum" (2.602). Aeneas will learn this
lesson over and over again as his own divine and fiery destiny casts
him repeatedly, in relation to both Dido and Lavinia, in the role of
another Paris.

When Aeneas speaks of the fall of Troy, Venus has already con-
spired with Cupid to girdle Dido with the flame of love (1.673:
"cingere flamma") and kindle fire in her very bones: "incendat regi-
nam atque ossibus implicet ignem" (1.660). Ignorant of fate (1.299:
"fati nescia"), Dido receives as a gift from Aeneas the dress and veil of

12. See Cicero, *De natura deorum* II.xlvi.118, pp. 234–35; III.xvi.40, pp. 322–23.
13. See Varro, *De lingua latina*, vol. 1, trans. Roland G. Kent, Loeb Classical
Library (Cambridge: Harvard University Press, 1938, 1977), V.59, pp. 54–57.
14. This passage (lines 567–88), supposedly suppressed and deleted by Varius and
Tucca, early editors of the *Aeneid*, survives only in Servius' commentary. The general
scholarly consensus is that the much disputed passage is authentic and provides a
startling insight into Virgil's concept of the character of Aeneas. (See the commentary
of R. G. Austin, *Aeneidos liber secundus* [Oxford: Clarendon Press, 1964], pp. 217–29.)

Helen (1.650). When she finds herself responding to Aeneas as she had to her husband Sychaeus—"agnosco veteris vestigia flammae" (4.23)—she begs Jupiter to prevent her dishonor by using lightning to send her to the underworld: "pater omnipotens adigat me fulmine ad umbras" (4.25). That prayer gains an ironic answer when Jupiter's own lightning flash during the storm occasions her pseudo-marriage to Aeneas in the cave: "fulsere ignes et conscius aether / conubiis" (4.167–68). Servius calls attention to lightning as Jupiter's characteristic sign (*In Aen.* I.42, I.230) and, citing Varro, interprets the celestial fire ("fulsere ignes") coupled with rain as a divine nuptial observance.[15]

Iarbas, however, protests that Jupiter's avenging thunderbolts (4.209: "in nubibus ignes") should not overlook Dido's scandalous affair with Aeneas. Dido's vow never to remarry, to remain faithful to her dead husband, makes her, in relation to Aeneas, another Helen; Aeneas, another Paris (4.215: "ille Paris cum semivio comitatu"). As once in Troy, the flames of love lead to battle and funeral fires as Dido, abandoned by Aeneas at Jupiter's command, kills herself upon a pyre, after cursing the Dardanians and prophesying that one of her race will pursue them with firebrand and sword: "face . . . ferroque" (4.626). The departing Trojans see the walls of Carthage, like the walls of Troy, aflame: "moenia respiciens, quae iam infelicis Elissae / conlucent flammas" (5.3–4).[16]

Virgil's language makes his protagonists the followers of the gods, drawn irresistibly into a preordained course. All their actions are fated, sequenced in a causal chain. Aeneas does not freely strive to gain Italy: "Italiam non sponte *sequor*" (4.361, emphasis added). The dead Dido follows Aeneas and haunts him with blackened firebrands: "*Sequar* atris ignibus absens" (4.384). The Carthaginian Hannibal will pursue with fire the descendants of Troy: "qui face Dardanios ferroque *sequare* colonos" (4.626).

15. See Varro, *De lingua latina* V.61–62, pp. 58–59. See also J. W. Jones, Jr., "Allegorical Interpretation in Servius," *Classical Journal* 56 (1960–61): 217–26, and Hardie's comments on storms and *fulmen* in Lucretius and Virgil, pp. 176–93. Seneca discusses lightning from a Stoic perspective as a sign of Jupiter and fate in *Naturales quaestiones* II.33–50, vol. 1, trans. Thomas H. Corcoran, Loeb Classical Library (Cambridge: Harvard University Press, 1971), pp. 154–81.

16. Hardie lists various studies of the linked imagery of amatory and actual wounds and fire in Book 4 (*Cosmos and Imperium*, n. 183, p. 232).

Even when Juno or Venus seem to initiate an action, Virgil's fiery imagery makes them agents of Jupiter and the larger, providential plan. In Book 5, for instance, the Trojan women, weary of their journey and infuriated by Juno, set the ships ablaze. Just before that turbulent scene takes place, however, Jupiter intervenes in the funeral games with a strange omen when the arrow shaft of Acestes catches fire in flight: "volans liquidis in nubibus arsit harundo / signavitque viam flammas" (5.525–26). That Jovian fire, which singles Acestes out for glory, anticipates the women's furious assault on the ships and the founding of a new Trojan city under Acestes' rule. In the end, Jupiter's own thunderbolts initiate a rainstorm to save the remnant of the fleet.

Another fiery omen underscores Jupiter's determination of the course of events in Book 7 when the sacrificial fire seems to catch in Lavinia's long hair (7.73: "visa (nefas) longis comprendere crinibus ignem") and set aflame her jewelled crown. A portent of war (7.80: "magnum portendere bellum"), it signals yet another repetition of Iliadic action. The Sibyl foretold that a foreign bride would again bring destruction to the Trojans (6.93–94) and that they would find another Achilles in Latium (6.89). Turnus' wrathful strength in battle makes him another Achilles (9.742), but his prior engagement to Lavinia likens him to Menelaus, his wife stolen, as Helen had been, by an Aeneas playing the part of another Paris (7.321: "Paris alter"). Amorous fire turns imagistically once more into the fire of war when the blush on Lavinia's burning cheek (12.65–69) awakens Turnus' love and increases his ardor for battle: "ardet in arma magis" (12.71). The capital city in flames—like the Stoic conflagration of an old world—moves Turnus at last to accept the will of the gods and embrace his own death at the hands of a wrathful Aeneas. The burning city thus recalls the burning of Troy and the epic ends as it began, with the tears of things (1.462: "lacrimae rerum") answering to primal fire.

Whereas Virgil, answering Lucretius, reads and rewrites Homer from a Stoic perspective, Virgil's readers come to interpret him, in turn, from a Neoplatonist point of view. As Michael Murrin observes, Virgil's polyvalent mode of divine representation, which associates Jupiter with both fate and fire, Juno with both rebellion and rain, "encouraged an allegorical reading of the *whole* epic" as a continuous allegory.[17] Virgil's depiction of Stoic *logos* in the will of Jupiter thus extended itself into interpretations of Virgil's words as instances of deliberate verbal allegory concealing natural secrets of all kinds. We find in Servius' fourth-century commentary and in Macrobius' *Saturnalia* (c. A.D. 400) the early flowerings of that impulse, but Fulgentius' *De continentia Vergiliana* (sixth century) stands as the first reading of the *Aeneid* as a systematic exposition of the life of Everyman.

The work of Fulgentius bears comic witness to what must have been common pedagogical practice at the time: the use of Virgil's writings as a pretext for discussing "the innermost profundities [*interna viscera*] of almost every art," veiled references to which grammarians found in the line-by-line analysis of his poems.[18] Fulgentius casts himself in the role of a pupil instructed by Virgil himself, who appears before him as a frowning, notebook-carrying, preoccupied schoolmaster. Virgil begins by explaining, "In all my writings I have introduced themes of natural order, whereby in the twelve books of the *Aeneid* I have shown the full range of human life" (p. 122) (pp. 86–87: "In omnibus nostris opusculis fisici ordinis argumenta induximus, quo per duodena librorum uolumina pleniorem humanae uitae monstrassem statum"). In the dialogue that follows, Virgil interprets his own epic allegorically, using etymologies to discover a coherent (albeit digressive) account of "the complete state of man" (p. 124)—his natural development from infancy to old age, his gradual acquisition of wisdom through practical experience and disciplined study, his acceptance of toil, his moral struggle against evil and passion, and his heroic encounter (in the image of Juturna's chariot) with Fortune's ever-turning wheel.[19]

In the twelfth century Bernard Silvestris and John of Salisbury,

17. Murrin, *Allegorical Epic*, p. 23.
18. Fulgentius, "The Exposition of the Content of Virgil according to Moral Philosophy," in *Fulgentius the Mythographer*, trans. Leslie George Whitbread (Columbus: Ohio State University Press, 1971), p. 119. I quote the Latin text from *Opera*, ed. Rudolph Helm (Stuttgart: G. B. Teubner, 1970).
19. Jon Whitman astutely observes that "about the time that Fulgentius was closing his interpretive allegory with the concept of Fortune's wheel, Boethius was turning that wheel into the starting point for his own compositional design" (*Allegory: The Dynamics of an Ancient and Medieval Technique* [Oxford: Clarendon Press, 1987], p. 112).

following Fulgentius, unfolded more sophisticated allegorical readings of Virgil, employing a similar anthropocentric scheme. To read
the *Aeneid* in this way, Bernard says, is to take seriously the Delphic
oracle's exhortation to self-knowledge. It is, moreover, a very useful
thing for a person to know himself: "homini enim magna est uti-
lias . . . se ipsum cognoscere."[20] The commentators thus discovered
in Virgil a moral philosopher; in Aeneas, a type of the soul imprisoned in the body.[21] In his actions they perceived *sub integumento* "all
that the human soul does or suffers during its temporary abode in the
body" ("quid agat vel quid patiatur humanus spiritus in humano
corpore temporaliter positus").[22] Thus Aeneas' literal warfare and
wanderings, parallel to those of Odysseus, came to be read as his had
been: as the homeward journey of the soul to the Fatherland.

The Romancers and the Allegory of *Eros*

Whereas the allegory of *logos* aims at the intellectual discovery of
truth, at naming the cosmological and microcosmic causes of things,
the allegory of *eros* aims at the personal application of truth; at
feeling, willing, and doing, rather than knowing. Romance, as the
"other speaking" of epic, thus aligns itself especially with the otherness of moral allegory, the reading which defines epic action as
exemplary. Sir Philip Sidney bears witness to this connection when
he names Heliodorus as an epic poet comparable to Homer and
Virgil on the grounds that "it is not rhyming and versing that maketh
a poet," but moral exemplification, the "feigning notable images of
virtues" as "delightful teaching."[23]

Unlike Virgil, who subordinated the *Odyssey* to the *Iliad* in his
refiguration of Homer, the authors of the ancient romances—among

20. Bernard Silvestris, *The Commentary on the First Six Books of the "Aeneid" of
Virgil Commonly Attributed to Bernard Silvestris*, ed. Julian Ward Jones and Elizabeth
Frances Jones (Lincoln: University of Nebraska Press, 1977), p. 3.

21. John of Salisbury, following Fulgentius, describes the *Aeneid* as a book in
which Virgil explores the secrets of all philosophy: "libro in quo totius philosophiae
rimatur arcana" (*Polycraticus* ii, PL 199, c430).

22. Bernard Silvestris, *The Commentary*, p. 3.

23. Sir Philip Sidney, *An Apology for Poetry; or, The Defence of Poesie*, ed. Geoffrey
Shepherd (London: Thomas Nelson, 1965), p. 103.

them, Chariton, Xenophon of Ephesus, Heliodorus, Achilles Tatius, and Apuleius—gave prominence to the *Odyssey*, thematizing its epic truth (as a Platonizing Stoicism had defined it) in popular forms accessible to general audiences. The Stoic moralists, as we have seen, discovered in Odysseus the figure of the virtuous man, bravely bearing the assaults of Fortune, whereas the Neoplatonists saw in him the image of the perfected soul, empowered by heavenly love to detach itself from earthly goods. These two interpretations, as we shall see, conjoin in the romances where literary imitation is self-consciously rhetorical and aimed at the imaginative participation of its audience.

Reading Homer's Odysseus as a moral exemplar (a reading that was common pedagogical practice) encouraged the audience's identification with him; that identification, in turn, promoted a rewriting of Homer in which his larger-than-life heroes became ordinary people, middle-class heroes and heroines. The moralization of Homer thus established a parallel between the Homeric stories and their retelling in analogous tales that invited similar personal application by the reader. To use Ben E. Perry's phrase, the romance as "latter-day epic for Everyman" translated the exemplariness of Homer's heroes and the moral message of their struggles into forms readily accessible to, and imitable by, general audiences.[24] Thus it became, as Tomas Hägg says, "the epic of the Hellenistic period, fulfilling the functions of epic in a new age."[25] In this sense Perry's words hold true: "Romance and epic are basically the same genre."[26] Radically different in form, they convey the same epic truth.

Although the romances are seldom treated in discussions of an-

24. Ben Edwin Perry, *The Ancient Romances: A Literary-Historical Account of Their Origins*, Sather Classical Lectures 1951 (Berkeley: University of California Press, 1967), p. 48. According to Perry, the audience of the romances was a "morally and realistically minded, middle class citizenry" (p. 63).

25. Tomas Hägg, *The Novel in Antiquity* (Berkeley: University of California Press, 1983), p. 111.

26. *Ancient Romances*, p. 45. Perry attributes the formal differences between epic and romance to the social conditions surrounding their production, epic arising in "closed," centripetal societies; the novelistic romance in "open," centrifugal ones. His treatment of epic and romance in many ways parallels that of M. Bakhtin, *The Dialogic Imagination*, ed. Michael Holquist, trans. Caryl Emerson and Michael Holquist, University of Texas Press Slavic Series, No. 1 (Austin: University of Texas Press, 1981).

cient epic, they themselves lay an explicit internal claim to a continuous epic—that is, Homeric—tradition through multiple verbal
echoes, allusions, and plot parallels. As Robert Lamberton has suggested, the author's intent in each case is imitation.[27] Chariton's
Chaereas and Callirhoe (first or second century A.D.), for example,
begins with a wedding "like the wedding of Thetis on Pelion as poets
describe it" (p. 24)—the strife-troubled marriage feast that sets the
stage for the Trojan war: Τοιοῦτον ὑμνοῦσι ποιηταὶ τὸν Θέτιδος
γάμον ἐν Πηλίῳ γεγονέναι (I.I, p. 416).[28] This Iliadic opening is
matched by an Odyssean conclusion when husband and wife, faithful
to one another through a long separation and multiple trials, are reunited, a euphoric moment Chariton narrates using Homer's words
(*Od.* 23.296): "they fell into each other's arms and 'gladly turned to
the pact of their bed as of old' " (p. 112) (VIII.I, p. 493: περιπλακέντες
ἀλλήλοις 'Ασπάσιοι λέκτροιο παλαιοῦ θεσμὸν ἵκοντο). Callirhoe,
the heroine, worships Aphrodite, whose beauty she embodies. That
Helen-like beauty causes her the misfortune to be the wife of two
husbands (Chaereas and Dionysius), to awaken desire in a series of
would-be lovers, and to occasion discord. At the same time, her
chastity and her dilemma in the face of ardent suitors liken her to
Penelope—a parallel Chariton underscores by weaving quotations
from the *Odyssey* into his prose narrative. Callirhoe's husband Chaereas similarly combines in his person the qualities of several Homeric
figures. He grieves like Achilles at the death of Patroclus (*Il.* 18.22–
24) over his separation from Callirhoe: " 'with both hands he took
dark dust and poured it over his head, defiling his lovely countenance' " (p. 77) (V.II, p. 463: 'Αμφοτέραις χερσὶ περιελὼν κόνιν
αἰθαλόεσσαν Χεύατο κακκεφαλῆς, χάριεν δ' ἤσχυνε πρόσωπον).
He goes into battle with Hector's words (*Il.* 22.304–05) on his lips

27. Robert Lamberton, *Homer the Theologian: Neoplatonist Allegorical Reading
and the Growth of the Epic Tradition* (Berkeley: University of California Press, 1986),
p. 286.
    28. The English translations of the cited romances—Chariton's *Chaereas and
Callirhoe* by B. P. Reardon, Xenophon of Ephesus' *An Ephesian Tale* by Graham
Anderson, Achilles Tatius' *Leucippe and Clitophon* by John J. Winkler, Heliodorus' *An
Ethiopian Story* by J. R. Morgan—are all taken from *Collected Ancient Greek Novels*,
ed. B. P. Reardon (Berkeley: University of California Press, 1989). The Greek texts of
Heliodorus and Chariton are taken from *Erotici Scriptores Graeci*, ed. G. A. Hirschig
(Paris: Didot, 1875). Page references are parenthetical.

(p. 102) and proves himself as brave as Diomedes (*Il.* 9.48–49) in a contest resembling that at Troy (*Il.* 13.131, 16.215): " 'Shield pressed against shield, helmet against helmet, man against man" (p. 105) (VII.IV, p. 487: 'Ασπὶς ἄρ' ἀσπίδ' ἔρειδε, κόρυς κόρυν, ἀνέρα δ' ἀνήρ). Throughout the romance, direct quotation assimilates the domestic trials of the young couple, their friends, and their parents to the suffering undergone by Homer's legendary heroes. Public interest, we are told, focuses on the case of Callirhoe when it is brought to trial, even as the gods " 'sitting at Zeus's side' " (p. 80) held debate over Troy (*Il.* 4.1): Οἱ δὲ θεοὶ πὰρ Ζηνὶ καθήμενοι ἠγορόωντο (V.IV, p. 466).

Heliodorus' *Ethiopica* (third or fourth century A.D.), like Chariton's early romance, combines an Iliadic opening with a conclusion that celebrates an Odyssean homecoming. When the heroine Charikleia makes her first appearance in the garb of a Delphic priestess, her Artemisian description (p. 354) recalls that of Apollo, descending with his deadly arrows from Olympos at the start of the *Iliad* (1.46–47). Charikleia's chaste young lover, Theagenes, is a swift-footed descendant of Achilles, whose handsome appearance attests his ancestry (p. 407). Theagenes' character, however, lacks Achilles' "arrogance" (IV.v, p. 284: "οὐχ ὑπέρφρων"), having "a gentle side to temper his pride" (p. 428). Charikleia in her lovesickness first identifies Theagenes as the one she loves by repeating aloud the verse of Homer (*Il.* 16.21): " 'Son of Peleus, far greatest of the Achaians, Achilles' " (p. 430) (IV.vii, p. 286: Ὦ Ἀχιλεῦ Πηλέως υἱέ, μέγα φέρτατ' Ἀχαιῶν). Once wounded in a boar hunt, Theagenes has a scar on his knee like that of Odysseus, which serves him also as a token of recognition (p. 449). In a vision one night Odysseus himself appears to the travelers and extends to Charikleia on her dangerous sea voyage Penelope's special blessing "since she esteems chastity above all things" (p. 462) (V.xxii, p. 311: διότι πάντων ἐπίπροσθεν ἄγει τὴν σωφροσύνην). Those who try to force Charikleia into marriage find the wedding "bitter" (p. 469) (V.xxx, p. 316: πικρόγαμος), even as Penelope's suitors did (*Od.* 1.266, 4.346, 17.137). As beautiful and faithful as Penelope, Charikleia experiences in the end the reward of her tested virtue in a dramatic scene of recognition and reunion.

The character Kalasiris, however, provides the strongest indication that the *Ethiopica* represents Heliodorus' conscious attempt to write a kind of Homeric epic.²⁹ Kalasiris, the wise old man who serves as mentor to the young lovers and whose voice narrates a considerable portion of the romance, begins his tale (p. 394) with the same words Odysseus uses (*Od.* 9.39) to recount his: Ἰλιόθεν με φέρεις (II.xxi, p. 258). An Egyptian priest, Kalasiris figures as a type of Homer himself who, we are told, was an "Egyptian poet" (p. 407) (II.xxxiv, p. 269: ἡ γὰρ Ὁμήρου τοῦ Αἰγυπτίου ποίησις) and "well versed" in the "holy lore" (p. 420) of the Egyptians: Αἰγύπτιος καὶ τὴν ἱερὰν παίδευσιν ἐκδιδαχθεὶς (III.xiii, p. 278). The son of Hermes, Homer "the wise poet" (p. 419) (III.xii, p. 276: ὁ σοφὸς Ὅμηρος) grew up in the precincts of an Egyptian temple where he, trained in the exegetical method usually associated with Alexandria, mastered in his poetry "the typically Egyptian combination of concealed meanings and sheer enjoyment" (p. 421) (III.xv, p. 278: τὸ ἀνειμένον τε καὶ ἡδονῇ πάσῃ σύγκρατον ὡς Αἰγύπτιον). In his own study of Homer's works, Kalasiris understood at first "the superficial import of the lines" (III.xii, p. 277: τὴν μὲν ἐπιπολῆς διάνοιαν) and only afterward became aware of the "religious teaching embedded in them" (p. 419) (III.xii, p. 277: τὴν δὲ συγκατεσπαρμένην αὐτοῖς θεολογίαν ἠγνόηκα). Kalasiris' reading of Homer thus provides a key for understanding his own retrospective narrative, and Heliodorus' romance as a whole, as a latter-day epic, different from the Homeric poems in its external form but conveying the same "true wisdom" (p. 421) (III.xvi, p. 279: ἀληθῶς σοφία).

The epic truth of the romances is twofold, reflecting in a popular way both the Stoic teachings of necessary subjection to, and possibly victory over, Fortune and the Neoplatonist doctrines of *eros* and immortality. As we have seen, Seneca responds to the Pythian oracle "Know thyself" by pointing with Stoic realism to the naked weakness and fragility of human beings who are, by nature, "dependent upon another's help, and exposed to all the affronts of Fortune."³⁰

This mortalist view strikingly informs the romances where the blows of Fortune serve to expose the helplessness and vulnerability of

29. Cf. Lamberton's discussion of Heliodorus in *Homer the Theologian*, pp. 149–57.

30. Seneca, "Ad Marciam de consolatione," in *Moral Essays*, vol. 2, trans. John W. Basore, Loeb Classical Library (Cambridge: Harvard University Press, 1932, rev. ed. 1958), XI.3, p. 35.

the protagonists, all of whom endure serial sufferings. The unfolding plotline of Chariton's *Chaereas and Callirhoe* is punctuated with the heroine's apostrophes to the goddess Fortune (Τύχη) as trial after trial besets the young lovers. Xenophon's *Ephesian Tale*, strongly influenced by Chariton's romance, recounts the adventures of another young married couple, Anthia and Habrocomes, who are separated from one another and finally reunited after a similar series of imprisonments, tortures, travels, and temptations. Like Chariton, Xenophon intersperses pauses in the course of the fast-paced narrative for lamentation, each lament providing an occasion for the preceding misfortunes to be rehearsed. When Heliodorus' heroine, Charikleia, breaks down in a similar fashion under the weight of misfortune, her mentor Kalasiris rebukes her for her "extravagant and unseemly anguish," her "senseless submission to adversity" (p. 481) and exhorts her: "Kindly remember that you are a human being, a creature of change, subject to rapid fluctuations of fortune for good or for ill" (p. 481) (VI.ix, p. 326: οὐκ ἐννοήσεις, ἄνθρωπος οὖσα, πρᾶγμα ἀστάθμητον καὶ ὀξείας ῥοπὰς ἐφ' ἑκάτερα λαμ-βάνον). Taken together, the romances all enforce upon their readers that remembering of human frailty which is, in Seneca's view, essential to self-knowledge and wisdom.

In the romances, however, the recollection of mortality is coupled with the assurance of divine assistance.[31] Constantly in motion, Fortune serves unchanging destiny, the larger, providential plan which is divinely set (*fatum*) and which gains expression in the romances in oracles and prophetic dreams. As Chariton observes, "without [Fortune] nothing ever comes to completion" (p. 54) (III.iii, p. 443: Ἡ τύχη δ' ἐφώτισε τὴν ἀλήθειαν, ἧς χωρὶς ἔργον οὐδὲν τέλειον). When Anthia and Habrocomes and Charikleia and Theagenes set off on their journeys in response to oracles, they enact the part the Stoics assign to the good man who, in Seneca's words, "offer[s] himself to Fate," consoled by the knowledge that we are all swept along (*rapi*) with the universe along the same unchangeable course (*cursus*) and by the same necessity that binds the gods: "eadem

31. As Cicero's Stoic Balbus insists, in opposition to the Epicureans, the care of the gods extends to individuals (*De natura deorum* II.lxv.164), and oracles, prophecies, dreams, and portents offer the strongest proof of that providential concern (II.lxv.162–63).

necessitate et deos alligat."[32] We are all, as Heliodorus' theatrical metaphors emphasize, players in the often spectacular drama of destiny.

Educated and purified by the blows of Fortune, strengthened in virtue, the lovers of the romances gradually achieve a steadfastness that likens them to the fixity of Fate itself.[33] Godlike in the faithfulness of their love, raised above the material sphere where Fortune exerts her influence, the long-suffering couples merit the assistance they receive on their homeward journey. Against terrible odds, Habrocomes and Anthia fulfill their oaths of mutual fidelity and find each other at last in the temple of Helius, the sun god. Callirhoe's loyalty to Chaereas assimilates her to the heavenly Aphrodite, whom she worships, and who presides over the lovers' first meeting and their reunion. Theagenes and Charikleia maintain mutual fidelity and virginal chastity, virtues that ultimately secure their marriage and their consecration as priest and priestess of the Sun and Moon.

The overt religiosity of the romances, coupled with the dominant theme of faithful love and the plot of a homeward journey ("ad patriam"), easily assimilates them to the Platonic scheme of a spiritual ascent inspired by *eros*. Achilles Tatius' *Leucippe and Clitophon* "abounds," as John J. Winkler observes, in "covert references" to Plato's *Phaedrus* and *Symposium*, where Socrates uses Homer to discover the doctrine of love.[34] Heliodorus' *Ethiopica* interprets the opening description of Charikleia gazing at the wounded Theagenes in words reminiscent of *Phaedrus* 252a: "Genuine affection and wholehearted love disregard all external pains and pleasures and compel the mind to concentrate thought and vision on one object: the beloved" (p. 355) (I.II, p. 227: Οὕτως ἄρα πόθος ἀκριβὴς καὶ ἔρως ἀκραιφνὴς τῶν μὲν ἔξωθεν προσπιπτόντων ἀλγεινῶν τε καὶ ἡδέων πάντων ὑπερφρονεῖ, πρὸς ἓν δὲ τὸ φιλούμενον καὶ ὁρᾶν καὶ συννεύειν τὸ φρόνημα καταναγκάζει.). A romance that frequently "hints at mystical allegory,"[35] the *Ethiopica* clearly encouraged its early read-

32. Seneca, "De providentia," in *Moral Essays*, vol. 1, trans. John W. Basore, Loeb Classical Library (Cambridge: Harvard University Press, 1958), V.8, pp. 38–39.

33. Seneca emphasizes the divine pedagogy that allows good people to struggle with misfortune in "De providentia," IV.11–16, pp. 30–35.

34. John J. Winkler, *Leucippe and Clitophon*, in *Collected Ancient Greek Novels*, n. 6, p. 177. For an ironic treatment of the Platonic echoes, see Graham Anderson, *Eros Sophistes: Ancient Novelists at Play* (Chico, Calif.: Scholars Press, 1982).

35. Lamberton, *Homer the Theologian*, p. 157.

ers to discover one. Philip the Philosopher's fragmentary exposition of the *Ethiopica* (late fifth century?) elaborates on Heliodorus' own Platonizing narrative with an allegorical reading that is, as Lamberton has shown, "quite close" to the Neoplatonic allegories of Homer.[36] According to Philip, the lovers are not only models of the "four general virtues"; Charikleia is also the symbol of the soul and of the mind.[37] In her whole-hearted love for Theagenes, she resembles the soul that "transcends the material dyad" and contemplates her "true family." Filled with "the love of highest wisdom," she "scorns her former habits, utterly unmindful of her body, and her thought tends only toward her beloved." Advancing "toward her own country," the soul endures "trial by fire," until, "radiant," she returns to the place of her origin.[38]

The two Odyssean allegories—Stoic and Neoplatonic—we have found refigured in the romances clearly define the outer and inner structure of Apuleius' second-century Latin romance, the *Metamorphoses*. Apuleius' satiric frame tale extends Stoic moral commentary on Homer's Calypso and Circe episodes (*Od.* 5 and 10) into the story of Lucius, a young man whose ungoverned curiosity and lust indirectly cause his magical transformation into an ass. Lacking in wisdom and self-control, Lucius subjects himself to the Fortune over which the wise Ulysses triumphed. The romance begins with a traveler's cautionary exemplum, the story of Socrates. Seduced by Meroe, a Circe-like witch who turns her neighbors into beavers, frogs, and rams, Socrates flees from her clutches only to be murdered in an inn by the self-proclaimed "Calypso," who revenges herself cruelly upon this would-be "Ulysses in his craftiness" (p. 39): "At ego scilicet Ulixi astu deserta vice Calypsonis" (*Met.* I.12).[39] Lucius, however, fails to apply the lesson to himself and in his curiosity about magic falls victim to the concoctions of Pamphile, a sorceress. Near the end of his serial misfortunes in the form of an ass, Lucius

36. Ibid., p. 148.

37. Ibid., p. 308. Lamberton provides a complete translation of Philip's fragmentary commentary, pp. 306–11.

38. Ibid., pp. 310–11.

39. English translations, cited parenthetically, are from Apuleius, *The Golden Ass*, trans. Jack Lindsay (Bloomington: Indiana University Press, 1932, 1962). For the Latin text I use Apuleius, *Metamorphoses*, 2 vols., ed. and trans. J. Arthur Hanson, Loeb Classical Library (Cambridge: Harvard University Press, 1989).

compares himself ironically to Ulysses. Whereas "the Divine Author of the ancient poetry of the Greeks, desiring to depict a man supremely wise and humanly perfected, sang of him who had visited many cities and known many people" (p. 192) (IX.13: "Nec immerito priscae poeticae divinus auctor apud Graios summae prudentiae virum monstrare cupiens, multarum civitatium obitu et variorum populorum cognitu summas adeptum virtutes cecinit"), Lucius can only say of himself and his travels: "hidden under the ass's skin, I perceived all life's variety and acquired much knowledge, if little wisdom" (p. 192) (IX.13: "me suo celatum tegmine variisque fortunis exercitatum, etsi minus prudentem, multiscium reddidit").

As a Neoplatonic counterpart and corrective to the Tale of Lucius, the story of Cupid and Psyche occupies the structural center of the *Metamorphoses*. Like the romances of Chariton and Xenophon of Ephesus, the plot concerns the initial bliss, subsequent trials, and final reunion of a young married couple. The protagonists, however, virtually personify the Platonic doctrine of love and reenact Homer's allegorized *Odyssey*. Psyche refigures and feminizes Odysseus, read as a type of the soul, whereas Cupid, according to Apuleius' own explanation, represents a daemon or genius of the soul, by virtue of which one is perfected through ardent desire of the Good: "bona cupido animi bonus deus est."[40] This *eros* moves the soul, even as Athena, personifying divine wisdom, directed Odysseus.[41] The soul descends when its own desire takes visible form, as when Psyche gazes on Cupid, but the soul in love with Eternal Love (*Met.* V.23: "magis magisque cupidine flagrans Cupidinis") valiantly endures the suffering of purification until, as James Tatum phrases it, "a bond is established between Soul and god through the agency of Love."[42] The soul thus attains knowledge of the divine, a blissful sapience imaged in the Olympian wedding feast.

A Platonic allegory, the Psyche-romance is also an allegory of Lucius' history. The sacrilegious inquisitiveness of Psyche into her husband's identity, like Lucius' curiosity about magic, leads her to

40. Apuleius, *De deo Socratis*, in *De philosophia libri*, ed. Paul Thomas (Stuttgart: B. G. Teubner, 1970), XV, p. 23.
41. See *De deo Socratis* XXIV, p. 35.
42. James Tatum, *Apuleius and the Golden Ass* (Ithaca: Cornell University Press, 1979), p. 61.

lose her happy state as Cupid's bride, and her wanderings and labors in search of Cupid distantly parallel those of the unhappy ass in search of a cure. At one point a jealous Juno afflicts Psyche, even as Virgil's Juno torments Aeneas, and thus becomes the analogue of the blind Fortune ("Fortuna caeca") that abuses Lucius while, at the same time, directing him unknowingly to his goal: "istam beatitudinem improvida produxit malitia" (*Met.* XI.15).[43] In the end Psyche is saved, as Lucius is, by a divine intervention, her restoration and deification prefiguring his physical transformation by Isis and his spiritual conversion to her priestly service. As a counterpart to the Heavenly Venus, symbolized by the harmony of the Olympian marriage between Psyche and Cupid, Isis brings order into Lucius' chaotic quest.

Apuleius' artistry, which establishes the Psyche-romance as the inner allegory of Lucius' ironic *Odyssey*, thus provides an apt contemporary illustration for the reading of ancient romance. As the "other speaking" of epic, romance exemplifies its moral and spiritual meaning. The difficulty, both for an ass-auditor like Lucius and for all of us as unconverted beings, still enslaved by the body and not our true, spiritual selves, is to perceive the analogy and, at the same time, endure the existential difference. Charite, the captive maiden who shares Lucius' lot among the bandits and who, like Psyche, is rescued by the man she loves, experiences no happy ending to her earthly romance. She, like Lucius, draws comfort from the tale of Psyche—a story Apuleius presents as wise foolishness, the (possibly inspired) babbling of a drunken, old woman (*Met.* VI.25)—only to have her own life story depart dramatically from Psyche's when her beloved husband is murdered, and she herself turns into a cruel avenger and suicide.

The allegorical juxtaposition of romance and realism in Apuleius suggests that the romantic figuration of epic truth needs to be grounded constantly in its own "other speaking," in the recall of tragic possibilities.[44] The lover, after all, occupies a precarious position in the Platonic scheme. Possessing a fresh memory of Eternal

43. See Tatum, *Apuleius*, pp. 49–50.
44. Tatum observes that the same "jarring contrasts" that figure in Book VI are characteristic of the "popular philosophy" (p. 64) of the time, as evidenced in the Stoicism of Marcus Aurelius, an emperor contemporary with Apuleius.

Beauty, he is strongly attracted to its embodiment in visible, corporeal beauty and in the beauty of noble souls. That fervent attraction, based on affinity, enables the lover's spiritual ascent, but only at the cost of painful detachment, of recognizing the vast difference between the eternal and the temporal. As Boethius' Orpheus shows, the lover who fails to rise, falls.

The two lines of allegorical interpretation we have been tracing—cosmological and moral, universal and personal—with their respective appeals to *logos* and *eros*, converge in the works of both Martianus Capella (fl. A.D. 410–29) and Boethius (A.D. 480?–526). Martianus' *De nuptiis* combines, albeit in a discordant and mechanical manner, the late-antique pedantry of the first with the amatory interest of the latter, using the episode of Psyche and Cupid from Apuleius' *Metamorphoses* as his principal model for his allegorical frame-story of courtship and marriage.[45] Philologia's union with Mercury, like Psyche's with Cupid, is approved by an assembly of gods and goddesses; she ascends to heaven after suitable labors prove her worthy of immortality; and finally she weds her divine husband, with the consent and assistance of Venus, amid general celestial rejoicing.

Before the marriage is finally consummated, however, the assembled wedding guests must listen to the book-long speeches of each of the personified liberal arts. While the song of Harmony at the conclusion of *De nuptiis* (Book IX) finally unites the erudite discourses of the *artes* with the plot of courtship and actually seals the marriage between Mercury and Philology, readers are likely to join Martianus' Venus in complaint about the long delay and question the effectiveness of Martianus' solution to what Emerson Brown, Jr., has called the "conflict between the classroom and the bedroom."[46]

Boethius' *De consolatione*, in contrast, combines the themes of

45. See William Harris Stahl and Richard Johnson with E. L. Burge, *Martianus Capella and the Seven Liberal Arts*, vol. 1, Records of Civilization Series 84 (New York: Columbia University Press, 1971), pp. 32, 42, 84.

46. See Martianus Capella, *De Nuptiis Philologiae et Mercurii*, ed. James Willis (Leipzig: Teubner, 1983), IX.890, pp. 338–39; Emerson Brown, Jr., "Epicurus and Voluptas in Late Antiquity: The Curious Testimony of Martianus Capella," *Traditio* 38 (1982): 75–106, p. 98. For an interpretation stressing Martianus' attempt to harmonize the universe he imitates, see Fannie J. LeMoine, *Martianus Capella: A Literary Reevaluation* (Munich: Salzer, 1972).

knowledge and love, using not the final speech of a personified Harmony, but rather Philosophia's song of the musician, Orpheus (III.m12).[47] In the myth of Orpheus and Eurydice, central to the *Consolation* as a whole, Boethius brings seamlessly together the two traditions of *eros* and *logos* that Martianus sets side by side. Indeed, as Jon Whitman puts it, Boethius' work begins where that of Martianus and Fulgentius ends and thus "completes the cycle of allegorical transition from late antiquity to the Middle Ages."[48]

In its literal terms, the tale of Orpheus and Eurydice realizes the tragic potential of popular romance and inverts the myth of Psyche. In it a virtuous, newly married couple is separated; the partners undertake a long, difficult journey (in this case, to and from the underworld) in the hope of being reunited; their mutual faithfulness wins the favor of the gods; their quest, however, governed by the laws of love and fate, results not in a happy reunion, but in a second, final separation.

The *Consolation* tells the tale, moreover, in a way that dramatizes the rhetorical impact of romance as a genre. Boethius, listening to Philosophia's song, identifies with Orpheus and, sharing in his sorrow, experiences anew the pain of his own attachment to earthly things (*eros*). With the force of moral allegory, the Orphic romance reveals to Boethius both what he has been and what he must become if he wishes his own life story to have a happy ending.

When Philosophia echoes Virgil's *Georgics* 2 and 4 in her rendition of the myth and then invites Boethius to take flight on her pinions, to succeed in the ascent where Orpheus has failed, she joins *logos* to *eros*. The cosmological vision and the rational insight into the causes of things that she offers Boethius depend on, and are inseparable from, his affective self-knowledge and directed power of love. The *logos* of Boethius' universe is *amor*; his knowing, loving. Philosophia's gown is decorated with emblems of the seven liberal arts, practical and theoretical, but unlike Martianus, who separates them, she decries their partition and insists upon their submission to a single pursuit: the knowledge of one's self. That Boethian pursuit, as we shall see, assumes epic proportions.

---

47. Martianus' Harmony (IX.907, pp. 345–46) tells the story of Orpheus briefly.
48. Whitman, *Allegory*, p. 112.

2 Boethius and Epic Truth

The opening lines of Boethius' prosimetric *Consolation* place it firmly in the epic tradition as a rich series of Stoic and Neoplatonic writings had contextualized it. Echoing at once both the epilogue to Virgil's *Georgics* (4.564–565) and the pseudo-Virgilian prologue to the *Aeneid*,[1] the weeping prisoner recalls the tranquil writings of his youth, even as he sounds the initial theme of a more serious work: "sad songs must I begin" (I.m1,2: "maestos cogor inire modos").[2] Identifying himself with a composite epic hero defined as Everyman, Boethius assumes the posture of an Aeneas (Cf. *Aen.* 6.699) who, in the underworld of afflictive earthly struggle, weeps as he speaks: "ueris elegi fletibus ora rigant" (I.m1,4). At the same time he plays the part of an Odysseus assailed by the pathetic, self-pitying strains and seductive blanishments of the poetical Muses, who accompany him, weeping, on his journey, and whom Lady Philosophy denounces and dismisses as sweetly destructive

1. For Boethius' sources I am indebted to the references in Joachim Gruber, *Kommentar zu Boethius De Consolatione Philosophiae* (Berlin: De Gruyter, 1978), and Helga Scheible, *Die Gedichte in der Consolatio Philosophiae des Boethius* (Heidelberg: Carl Winter, 1972). For a treatment of the pseudo-Virgilian prologue, see P. A. Hansen, "ILLE EGO QUI QUONDAM . . . Once Again," *Classical Quarterly* n.s. 22 (1972): 139–49.
2. For the Latin text of Boethius I use L. Bieler, ed., *De consolatione philosophiae*, CCSL 94 (Turnhout: Brepols, 1957). The literal English translations given for passages indented in my text are from *The Consolation of Philosophy*, trans. S. J. Tester, Loeb Classical Library (Cambridge: Harvard University Press, 1918, 1978).

Sirens: "Sirenes usque in exitium dulces" (I.p1,11). Finally, in his offended sense of justice and passionate despair, the prisoner accosted by a Philosophia with blazing eyes (I.p1,1: "oculis ardentibus") resembles the wrathful Achilles at *Iliad* 1.200 confronted by a towering Athena.[3] Even as Athena, goddess of wisdom, directs Achilles and protects Odysseus, Philosophia fulfills the tutelary function of a Sibyl as she reminds Boethius of his final goal and reiterates the Delphic oracle that recalls Boethius to self-knowledge.

Although these parallels at the outset readily liken the prisoner in our eyes to an epic hero, he is initially blind to any analogy between himself and Homer's and Virgil's protagonists. He sees himself as a victim, not a victor. He can liken his situation only to that of other persecuted philosophers. Philosophia herself begins with that analogy, comparing Boethius' fate to that of Socrates, Zeno, Canius, Seneca, and Soranus, all of them philosophers put to death for opposing wickedness with wisdom (I.p3,9). The prisoner confirms the comparison in his autobiographical complaint when he calls himself one of Philosophia's ill-rewarded, obedient servants (I.p4,4). Later references to Nero and Seneca (III.p5,10–11; III.m4) underscore the close historical comparison between Boethius' fate in the court of Theodoric the Ostrogoth and that of Seneca in Nero's.[4]

Boethius only begins to see himself as an epic hero and thus become one when his understanding of his own situation changes from a literal to a figurative one. At the same time, as we shall see, his philosophical quest advances from a consideration of external causes (material and efficient) in Books I and II to the internal causes of idea and intention in Books III and IV. In both cases Boethius learns to prove into the deeper meaning of things. By the end of Book III the prisoner is able to read the story of his own life allegorically as a heroic descent to the underworld comparable to that of Orpheus (III.m12); as a mental victory over the body and its passions, similar

---

3. See Robert Lamberton, *Homer the Theologian: Neoplatonist Allegorical Reading and the Growth of the Epic Tradition* (Berkeley: University of California Press, 1986), p. 276.

4. For a discussion of Boethius and Seneca see Seth Lerer, *Boethius and Dialogue: Literary Method in "The Consolation of Philosophy"* (Princeton: Princeton University Press, 1985), pp. 245–47. For an excellent introduction to Boethius' life and times, see Henry Chadwick, *Boethius: The Consolations of Music, Logic, Theology, and Philosophy* (Oxford: Clarendon Press, 1981, repr. 1983), pp. 1–68.

to Ulysses' (IV.m3); and even as a victorious ascent to the stars like Hercules' (IV.m7). As Seth Lerer phrases it, "he learns to see himself through the texts he has read."[5]

When Boethius discovers that his own struggle with misfortune is mirrored in the paradigmatic agon of epic heroes like Ulysses and Hercules, he reads the myths much as Seneca and Lucretius did. In *De rerum natura* 5.22–54, for instance, Lucretius exalts the Epicurean philosopher, who conquers the monstrous fear of death, over Hercules, who triumphed in his labors over terrible beasts. The ostensible contrast, however, turns into a metaphor, and Hercules becomes for Lucretius an image of the heroic philosopher. Seneca, like Lucretius, assigns the myths of monster-killers to a primitive past ("excussa iam antique credulitate") while at the same time using them to represent the greatness of a man like Cato, who struggled against ambition and the greed for power and stood alone against the hydra-like vices of a degenerate state.[6] For Seneca, as Villy Sørenson observes, "Cato is the Hercules of his day."[7] For Boethius, as we shall see, everyman is called to be a Hercules.

In the prose section immediately preceding the Hercules-metrum, Philosophia makes the epic comparison explicit. Not only does a true hero combine in himself the classical, martial virtues of prudence and courage; his wisdom actually *is* his strength. The *vir sapiens*, she reminds Boethius, enters into his battle with fortune as fearlessly as a strong man (*vir fortis*) aroused by battle-cry. As she explains it, the word *virtus* derives from *vis*, meaning force or strength, because the virtuous man, relying on his own powers (IV.p7,19: "suis viribus nitens"), is not overcome by adversities.

Boethius' thrice-repeated glance into the mythic mirror which represents the self archetypally in the form of an epic hero brings to a climax the educational process Lady Philosophy begins when she asks Boethius whether he remembers who he is: "hominemne te esse

5. Lerer, *Boethius and Dialogue*, p. 168. Lerer's pioneering work, to which I am indebted, focuses particularly on Boethius' pedagogical use of dialogue as a literary form and his revision of selected Senecan sources.

6. Seneca, "De constantia sapientis," in *Moral Essays*, vol. 1, trans. John W. Basore, Loeb Classical Library (Cambridge: Harvard University Press), II.i–iii, pp. 50–53.

7. Villy Sørensen, *Seneca: The Humanist at the Court of Nero*, trans. W. Glyn Jones (Edinburgh: Canongate; Chicago: University of Chicago Press, 1984), p. 203.

meministi?" (I.p6,14). As we have noted, there are only three mythological metra among the thirty-nine in Boethius' *Consolation*. Although few in number, these poems, as Gerard O'Daly insists, have a
"significance" that "must not be underestimated."[8] Not merely "in-
terludes in the argument or decorative embellishments of it,"[9] the
metra featuring Orpheus (III.m12), Ulysses and Circe (IV.m3), and
Agamemnon, Ulysses, and Hercules (IV.m7) are placed "at important
junctures in the work"[10] to summarize and advance its themes by
relating them to the allegorical exegesis of heroic myth practised in
the Hellenistic and Neoplatonic philosophical schools. While Lerer,
O'Daly, and others have related the mythological metra in general
terms to the pedagogical progression of the *Consolation*, no one has
drawn a direct correlation between the three metra and the threefold
definition of human nature that Philosophia helps her pupil, Boethius, to recall. Even as the allegorical reading of ancient myth,
deeply grounded in moral philosophy, had defined a threefold self-
knowledge as epic truth, Lady Philosophy assesses Boethius' condition and effects his cure according to a tripartite definition of human
nature.

When Philosophia cross-examines the prisoner to determine his
mental state, she asks him, first of all, about his belief in divine
providence. When he avers that the course of the world is directed
not by mere chance but by God, she applauds his answer but presses
him more closely to discover the cause of his obvious despair. Further
questioning reveals that although he remembers the origin of everything, he has forgotten the final cause of the universe, the end at
which the whole of creation aims and moves. He has similarly lost
sight of his own telos as a human being. He confesses himself to be
a man ("homo"), defined in Aristotelian terms as a rational and mortal animal (I.p6,15: "rationale animal atque mortale") and nothing
more (I.p6,16: "nihil"). He has, in short, forgotten the third part of
the hominal definition, according to which a human being possesses
an immortal soul and a divine destiny. As Philosophia pointedly tells
him, he no longer knows what he is: "quid ipse sis, nosse desisti"
(I.p6,17).

8. Gerard O'Daly, *The Poetry of Boethius* (Chapel Hill: University of North Carolina Press, 1991), p. 178.
9. Ibid., p. vii.
10. Ibid., p. 178.

As we shall see, the three mythological metra, as fables teaching truth, constitute a step-by-step unfolding of the three essential features of human nature. The Orpheus metrum (III.m12) represents the linked truths of mortality and love. The Circe-Ulysses metrum (IV.m3) offers an imagistic reflection on human rationality. Lastly, the metrum that narrates the homeward voyages of Agamemnon, Ulysses, and Hercules (IV.m7) recalls the forgotten truth of telos. Boethius' meditation on the mythic past becomes a means for, and an expression of, his remembrance of himself. At the same time, as Richard A. Dwyer has suggested, the simultaneous vision of past and present that Boethius achieves marks his transcendence of propositional logic, his approach to a figural and providential "intelligence of divine order."[11] Each of the mythological metra marks itself as type and figure, ending with a pointed comment on the metrum's moral message that works to fuse moral philosophy with epic poetry.

The Platonic matching of word and thing, *verbum* and *res*, achieved in the metra enables Lady Philosophy's final victory over the Siren-like "poeticae Musae," whom she drives from Boethius' bedside. From the beginning she sets her poetry and her own wholesome Muses in opposition to their sweet poisons (I.p1,8). Music, Philosophia says, is a little servant in her household, and the suasions of sweet rhetoric have their proper use in philosophical instruction (II.p1,8).

The prisoner complains at first that Philosophia's lovely songs and honey-sweet music offer him only a temporary relief from his misery, a comfort that vanishes with the sound of her voice (II.p3,2). He, in short, responds to the metra superficially. The early poems, moreover, as Lerer has observed, versify "the palpable experience of history and nature" and require only a literal understanding.[12] The lasting consolation the prisoner seeks, one which Lady Philosophy gradually offers him, necessitates a meeting between the "altior sensus" (II.p3,2), the deeper sense of his sorrow, and the hidden meaning, the allegorical "sensus" of poetry.

Together, the three mythological metra occasion that kind of consolation and reveal to Boethius the truth of himself. Lady Philosophy

---

11. Richard A. Dwyer, *Boethian Fictions: Narratives in the Medieval French Versions of the Consolatio Philosophiae* (Cambridge, Mass.: Medieval Academy of America, 1976), p. 22.

12. Lerer, *Boethius and Dialogue*, p. 166.

sets them apart from earlier verses, placing them all after the great Timaean hymn, "O qui perpetua" (III.m9), which, at the structural center of the *Consolation*, invokes the Father of All Things with a request for divine aid.[13] As a self-conscious "exordium" (III.p9,33), the hymn adopts Virgilian language (Cf. *Georgics* 4.228; *Aeneid* 10.62; 11.789) to beg for philosophical and poetic inspiration in addressing the topic of the highest Good and the beatitude it confers:

> Da, pater, augustam menti condescendere sedem,
> da fontem lustrare boni, da luce reperta
> in te conspicuos animi defigere uisus.
>
> (III.m9,22–24)

[Grant, Father, to my mind to rise to your majestic seat, / Grant me to wander by the source of good, grant light to see, / To fix the clear sight of my mind on you.]

The Orpheus metrum, which closes the third book, echoes this invocation in its opening lines: "boni / fontem uisere lucidum" (III.m12,1–2). The lesson of its "fabula" (III.m12,52) thus becomes identified with revealed truth. The prose section immediately preceding the Orpheus metrum also prepares the way for an identification of its poetry with the affective truth that offers lasting consolation. First of all, Lady Philosophy quotes Wisdom 8:1, a biblical quotation to which Boethius calls special attention by praising Philosophia's delightful words (III.p12,23).[14] Lady Philosophy then introduces this, the first of the three mythological metra, with a Platonic reminder that words, also the words of poetry, properly resemble the things about which they speak (III.p12,38) and affect us accordingly.

In her role as a poet of truth, Lady Philosophy identifies herself closely with Homer. As Robert Lamberton has observed, "it is always Philosophia and not Boethius who quotes or alludes to Homer."[15]

---

13. Gruber has shown that the poems in the *Consolation* are grouped according to their respective metres in a symmetrical arrangement around "O qui perpetua." See *Kommentar*, p. 22. See also Chadwick, *Consolations of Music*, p. 234.

14. As Chadwick notes, while there are several possible biblical allusions in the *Consolation*, this is the only one to which Boethius calls specific attention. Wisdom 8:1 inspired the Advent antiphon "O Sapientia" as early as the ninth century and probably earlier. See *Consolations of Music*, pp. 237–38.

15. Lamberton, *Homer the Theologian*, p. 276.

Not only does she celebrate Homeric myth in the metra depicting the underworld to which Orpheus descends, Circe's island, and the voyages of Agamemnon and Ulysses; she also refers explicitly to Homer four times in the prose passages and once in verse. When Philosophia urges Boethius to lay bare his wound (I.p4,1: "uulnus detegas"), she assumes the motherly role of a Thetis consoling Achilles and quotes Homer (*Il.* 1.363) in Greek: "'Εξαύδα, μὴ κεῦθε νόῳ" (I.p4,1). She counters the prisoner's mistaken notion that Fortune rules the world with a reminder in Homeric Greek (*Il.* 2.204) that a provident God is the only king in Boethius' true Fatherland: "εἷς κοίρανός ἐστιν, εἷς βασιλεύς"(I.p5,4). Later, when Lady Philosophy impersonates Fortune, she quotes in Greek the familiar proverb of the two jars, found in Homer (*Il.* 24.527–28), to remind Boethius that one must take the bitter things in life as well as the sweet, the bad along with the good (II.p2,13). In Book IV, when Philosophia has virtually exhausted herself in her approach to Theology, she quotes Homer again in Greek (*Il.* 12.176) to confess her inability to speak like a god about divine things: "'Αργαλέον δέ με ταῦτα θεὸν ὣς πάντ' ἀγορεύειν" (IV.p6,53). Finally Lady Philosophy dares to make Homer's poetry not only part of her prose, but also part of her verse. In Book V the second metrum begins with a line in Greek from *Iliad* 3.277 and *Odyssey* 11.109; 12.323:

Πάντ' ἐφορᾶν καὶ πάντ' ἐπακούειν
puro clarum lumine Phoebum
melliflui canit oris Homerus.
(V.m2,1–3)

[That Phoebus shining with pure light "sees all and all things hears," So Homer sings, he of the honeyed voice.]

The metrum goes on to show that since the sun cannot literally see all things, cannot penetrate the depths of the earth and sea, Homer's verse actually refers allegorically to the Creator, the true Sun, who with his provident eyes beholds the past, present, and future (V.m2,11).

Philosophy's use of Homer as a pedagogical touchstone bears witness to the exegetical context in which he was commonly read. She clearly affirms the tradition that found the truths of moral philosophy adumbrated in Homeric verse. As Lamberton phrases it, "For Boethius Homeric language and myth, properly understood, yield truths about the nature of man and the universe compatible with Platonism."[16] Philosophia does not, however, typically begin with Homer and then comment expansively on him, as earlier exegetes did. Instead she begins with the philosophic truths that an earlier tradition had found veiled in Homer and introduces Homeric myth into that context as a symbol with the power to render truth not only rationally but also emotionally compelling. The parallels she systematically establishes between philosophical dialogue and epic narrative ultimately lead beyond analysis to synthesis, beyond reason to intuition, beyond philosophy to theology. Neoplatonic exegesis had discovered in the *Odyssey* the pattern of spiritual descent, purification, and enlightenment. Philosophia reverses that process, making the mental and spiritual quest of her pupil into an epic journey.

The imagistic language of the *Consolation* embeds the prisoner's gradual reorientation toward final causality within an unfolding epic narrative of return to the Fatherland. The process of Platonic remembrance, which constitutes the discursive plot of the dialogue, thus becomes a heroic action as the prisoner's mental journey in conversation with Lady Philosophy parallels the arduous journeys of Odysseus to Ithaca and of Aeneas to Italy. Indeed, Lady Philosophy constantly uses the word *patria* ("fatherland") to designate the goal of her philosophical hero.[17] When she first encounters the prisoner, she finds him far from his spiritual homeland (I,p5,3: "quam procul a *patria*")—not as an outcast, but as a wanderer who has lost his way. Confused by the blows of Fortune, he needs to remember the country of his origin (I.p5,4: "si enim cuius oriundus sis *patriae* reminiscare") and the divine king who governs its affairs. Spiritually uprooted, he necessarily finds himself in exile, whereas others, enduring the same situation with grateful, inner calm, consider themselves at home: "Hic ipse locus, quem tu exilium uocas, incolentibus *patria* est" (II.p4,17). In the end, however, the prisoner's increasingly firm belief that the harmony in the universe does result from God's governance

16. Ibid., p. 279.
17. Cf. Lerer, *Boethius and Dialogue*, n. 19, pp. 130–31; p. 184. I have used Lane Cooper, *A Concordance of Boethius* (Cambridge, Mass.: Medieval Academy of America, 1928) to trace, in particular, Boethius' employ of *patria* and *causa*.

offers hope for his happiness and safe return: "ut felicitatis compos *patriam* sospes reuisas" (III.p12,9). By Book IV, Lady Philosophy readily promises Boethius that he will indeed return to his Fatherland through her direction, by her path, and with her wings: "sospes in *patriam* meo ductu, mea semita, meis etiam uehiculis reuertaris" (IV.p1,9). When his ascendant soul has taken flight, she says, he will clearly recognize the place of his origin: " 'Haec,' dices, 'memini, *patria* est mihi' " (IV.m1,25). The fifth and last book opens with a renewal of Philosophia's promise to disclose the route of sure return: "uiamque tibi qua *patriam* reueharis aperire" (V.p1,4).

Boethius's epic journey *ad patriam*—a progress expressed throughout the *Consolation* in contrasting images of darkness and light, clouds and stars, night and day, descent and ascent—represents analogously the direction of his mental quest for the causes of things—a search that begins with an examination of external causes, material and efficient; turns to internal, formal causes; and ends with the final causes of human and divine intention. For Boethius, arrival in the Fatherland means the heroic recognition and acceptance of one's own final cause.

As we have seen, atomist, Stoic, and Neoplatonic allegoresis had discovered universal principles of causation beneath the veil of Homeric verse, and Lucretius and Virgil, influenced by such readings, had sought to probe the causes of things in the philosophical poetry of *De rerum natura*, the *Georgics*, and the *Aeneid*: "Musa mihi causas memora" (*Aen.* 1.8). Boethius not only rewrites Virgil's *Georgics* 2.490 ("Felix, qui potuit rerum cognoscere causas") in the famous opening line of the Orpheus metrum (III.m12); his language also echoes Virgil, Homer, Plato, and Seneca throughout the *Consolation* as the dialogue between the prisoner and Lady Philosophy focuses systematically on the various issues of causality. It is, after all, the proper task of Philosophia to unfold the causes of hidden things (IV.p6,1: "latentium rerum causas euoluere"), and she enables Boethius, in turn, to continue in an epic mode the philosophical enquiry that characterized his youthful, bucolic writings: "naturae uarias reddere causas" (I.m2,23).

When Lady Philosophy first questions the cause of the prisoner's distress, he answers solely in terms of external, material, and efficient causes, all of them symbolized in the cruelty of a personified Fortune, who has proven two-faced and capricious in her dealings with him (I.m1,19). Asked to lay bare his wound, Boethius speaks at length about his own innocence and the wickedness of his enemies. His virtue in public office, he says, has earned him the hatred of Theodoric's courtiers. Because he dared to defend Albinus and the senate as a whole against the charge of conspiracy, he exposed himself to false accusations of treason and sorcery. Condemned while absent from the court and unable to defend himself, he must endure a general loss of public esteem, because people tend to associate misfortune with guilt. His imprisonment and fast-approaching execution encourage the wicked, discourage and dishonor the good. Heavily burdened, he cannot easily reconcile the existence of God with manifold injustice (I.p4,30) and concludes that God's providence attends everything in creation except the acts of humankind: "hominum solos . . . actus" (I.m5,26).

Lady Philosophy listens patiently to Boethius' outburst, then counters it by exposing the inward cause of his unhappiness, his forgetfulness of a universal and personal telos: "Iam scio, inquit, morbi tui . . . causam" (I.p6,17). Because the prisoner still erroneously attributes his misery to Fortune and the loss of Fortune's goods— freedom, honor, power, riches—Lady Philosophy impersonates Fortune and allows her to speak in self-defense. Fortune reminds Boethius that nothing external to human beings can directly cause or destroy their happiness which, as Philosophia demonstrates, is an internal, spiritual possession, a resting in the good of true love and lasting friendship. Indeed, the loss of external goods often assists one in discovering what really endures, the faithfulness of true friends: "amicorum tibi fidelium mentes" (II.p8,6).

Proceeding one step further in her examination of causes, Lady Philosophy distinguishes in Book III between the true and false forms and causes of happiness (III.p9,24). Because temporal things yield a happiness that is incomplete and therefore fails to satisfy, they point beyond themselves to the perfect, eternal Good, the possession of which yields lasting happiness (III.p10,6). The outward forms of happiness—riches, honors, power, fame, sensory pleasures (III.p2,12)— that motivate human desire and action are but partial expressions of a single, higher Good, which Philosophia identifies with God, the origin and end of human nature. The greed for earthly things is, therefore, a compelling, misdirected hunger for the one Good that satisfies, and which is the chief and cardinal cause of everything that people seek (III.p10,38). God alone, according to Lady Philosophy's Timaean hymn, acts creatively in total freedom as the first cause, independent of external, secondary causes (III.m9,4). People, however, resemble God and approach His freedom to the extent that they emancipate themselves from control by external causes and act out of inner principles.

The opening of Book IV echoes the beginning of the second book (II.p1,12: "tanti causa maeroris"), but at a higher level of abstraction. The greatest cause of Boethius' sorrow (IV.p1,3: "maxima nostri causa maeroris") is, he says, the existence of evil in a universe governed by a good God. Unless one understands the reason behind God's action, his governance looks like mere chance, if not cruelty (IV.p5,6). Lady Philosophy responds by reasoning that the divine *intentio*, the final cause for God's action, must be love, since He himself is the supreme Good. If the desire for the Good defines the telos of human being and acting, so much so that nothing is done for the sake of evil, even by evil men (IV.p6,22), then all the more so is God's intention good.

Indeed, the divine telos is revealed by the love ("alternus amor," "concordia") that moves the universe at its origin and end. Because all things necessarily flow back to the cause that gave them being (IV.m6,48) and that sustains them in existence, a beneficent intention stands behind everything that occurs. That *intentio* makes every fortune that befalls us good: "omnem . . . bonam prorsus esse fortunam" (IV.p7,2). Everything has its purpose in the pedagogy of love. Viewed correctly, every occurrence that seems harsh, actually strengthens us by trial, corrects, or punishes us (IV.p7,22). Even if we do not know God's immediate purpose, we should remain firm in our belief that a good God directs the world: "bonus mundum rector temperat . . . ne dubites" (IV.p5,7).

Whereas Book IV examines final causality from a perspective based on affirmative, analogical reasoning—the correspondence between human and divine intent—Book V takes a negative approach that underscores the limits of philosophy and human reasoning in addressing questions relating to God. Having demonstrated that no fortune is bad and that nothing occurs by chance, Lady Philosophy has emphasized the First and Last Cause almost to the exclusion of secondary causes. Boethius then asks about the place of human freedom in the series of linked causes that begins with God (V.p2,2). Does not the chain of fate ("fatalis catena") constrain the very minds of people and thus compel their acts? As the dialogue continues, the question of human freedom becomes an issue of divine freedom. Are human actions the cause of God's foreknowledge? Or does God's foreknowledge cause human acts?

Philosophia explains that the darkness which shrouds these issues results from the inability of human reason to approach the simplicity of divine foreknowledge. Our vision is necessarily partial. Human beings cannot know as God does, because his faculties exceed ours. Indeed, we cannot know God objectively—that is, as He is in him-self—but only subjectively, according to our own nature. Failing to recognize our limits, and the essential dissimilarity between divine and human modes of apprehension, is a continuous source of error (V.p4,24). Human reason must be drawn beyond itself by grace into the simplicity of the *mens divina*. Only there will it see what it cannot see by itself: "illic enim ratio uidebit quod in se non potest intueri" (V.p5,12). Lady Philosophy concludes that, given the greatness of God, a person's best recourse is humble prayer, steadfast hope, and the willing practice of virtue before the face of a judge who sees all that we see, and more: "ante oculos agitis iudicis cuncta cernentis" (V.p6,48).

When Philosophia insists repeatedly in the last book of the *Conso-lation* that everything known is known not according to its own nature but according to the nature of its knower (V.p6,1), she underscores the moral and epistemological importance of human self-knowledge, the guiding theme of her instruction from beginning to end. Human beings can only know God to the extent that they know themselves, both the creaturely limits that make them dissimilar to God and the higher powers that liken them to him. Reason alone, however, with its definition of *homo* as a rational biped (V.p4,35: "animal bipes ra-tionale"), does not afford a complete self-understanding: As we shall see, the final metrum of the *Consolation* (V.m5) positions humankind within the cosmos in a threefold way that echoes and corrects Bo-ethius' first, incomplete hominal definition. At the same time, it recalls the language and synthesizes the key images found in the three mythological metra, which, as fables of truth, have recalled him step by step to a full self-knowledge. Before considering that final metrum as a poetic and philosophical *summa*, however, we should consider in greater detail Boethius' rendering of the stories of Orpheus and Eurydice (III.m12), Circe and Ulysses (IV.m3), and Agamemnon, Ulysses, and Hercules (IV.m7) and their respective emphases on human mortality, rationality, and divinity.

Orpheus and Eurydice

In the concluding metrum of Book III, Lady Philosophy recounts the myth of Orpheus, the divinely gifted Thracian musician, who, moved by love for his dead wife, Eurydice, descends into Hades in an attempt to regain her. The language of Philosophia's song echoes three other texts—Virgil's *Georgics*, Seneca's Herculean tragedies, and the earlier descriptions of Boethius in the *Consolation* itself—and thus, through a complex matrix of intertextual reference, builds upon various previous interpretations of the myth and the reasons they offer for Orpheus' failure. As I hope to show, Virgil, Seneca, and Boethius all discover in the Orphic tale the universal truth of human mortality. Boethius' Philosophia, however, supplementing Stoic materialism with Neoplatonic precepts, teaches mortality in a transcendent context that simultaneously confirms and denies its necessity.[18] Indeed, Philosophia's own musical descent into Boethius' prison cell to rescue him offers a paradigm for a successful return *ad patriam* that incorporates the story of Orpheus as a literary model while supplying a different ending that redirects its narrative telos from tragedy to comedy. Boethius thus shapes the allegory of epic, the admonitory lesson derived from the original Orphic *fabula*, into a new form that displays the generic features of romance.

Boethius' strategy in embedding the Orphic tragedy within a larger, comic narrative parallels Virgil's strategy in *Georgics* 4. There Virgil tells the story of Orpheus as a tale within the tale of Aristaeus, the bee-keeper. Aristaeus' lamentation over his dead bees parallels

18. Cf. Chadwick's perception of a general movement in the Consolation "from a Stoic moralism to a Platonic metaphysical vision" (*Consolations of Music*, p. 228).

Orpheus' grief over Eurydice, and Aristaeus' descent to his mother Cyrene in the world under the sea resembles the Orphic descent to the underworld. Like Orpheus, who contends with the gods of the dead, Aristaeus wrestles with Proteus, seeking an answer to his predicament. Proteus then relates the story of Orpheus to explain why Aristaeus has been cursed. Whereas the tale of Orpheus ends in Eurydice's second death and Orpheus' savage dismemberment, Aristaeus' story ends happily in the discovery of the agricultural art that produces bees out of the bodies of dead steers.

As Friedrich Klingner has observed, the juxtaposition of the two tales establishes a typically Virgilian tension between the survival of the species and the death of individuals.[19] For the bee species as part of the divine mind, there is no place for death: "nec morti esse locum" (*Georg.* 4.226).[20] Not so for individuals like Orpheus and Eurydice who die, and die cruelly. At the same time the constrasting tales of Orpheus and Aristaeus establish a polarity between the mortal human subjects of art and the immortal art that objectifies them. As Adam Parry puts it, "For Virgil, work, *labor*, is important—because it in turn necessitates *art.*"[21] In this sense the honey of bees provides an analogue for the honey of poetry, and the relationship between agricultural *labor* and *ars* prefigures the dependence of epic poetry as art on the struggles, *labores*, of not only a suffering Orpheus, but also a weeping Aeneas.[22]

Virgil's linked tales of Aristaeus and Orpheus play a key part in the classical epic tradition. As Parry and others have observed, Virgil places the Aristaeus episode as a miniature epic at the conclusion of the *Georgics.*[23] It begins at 4.315 with a six-line invocation of the Muses and an inquiry about divine causation. Homer's wrathful

19. Friedrich Klingner, *Virgil: Bucolica, Georgica, Aeneis* (Zurich and Stuttgart: Artemis, 1967), p. 360.

20. I use Virgil, *Georgics*, trans. H. Rushton Fairclough, rev. ed. Loeb Classical Library (Cambridge: Harvard University Press, 1935, repr. 1986).

21. Adam Parry, "The Idea of Art in Virgil's *Georgics*," in *Virgil: Modern Critical Views*, ed. Harold Bloom (New York: Chelsea House, 1986), p. 98; reprinted from *Arethusa* 5.1 (1972): 35–52.

22. See J. H. Waszink, "Biene und Honig als Symbol des Dichters und der Dichtung in der griechischrömischen Antike," *Rheinisch-Westfälische Akademie der Wissenschaften* (1973), nr. G-196, pp. 26–28.

23. See Parry, "The Idea of Art," p. 97; Charles P. Segal, "Orpheus and the Fourth Georgic," *AJP* 87 (1966): 307–25; Brooks Otis, *Virgil: A Study in Civilized Poetry* (Oxford: Clarendon Press, 1964), pp. 190–214.

Achilles reappears in the form of Aristaeus, who complains to his nymph-mother that he has been denied due honor. Aristaeus then refigures Odysseus (*Od.* 4) in his capture of Proteus. Orpheus, too, recalls both Achilles (in his interview with the ghost of Patroclus in *Il.* 23.62–107) and Odysseus (in his encounter with his dead mother in *Od.* 11.152–224) when he grasps vainly at Eurydice's phantom and hears her reproachful lament.

As an epic episode, the Aristaeus-Orpheus sequence at the end of the *Georgics* clearly anticipates the *Aeneid.* As many have observed, Virgil replays the scene of Orpheus' encounter with Eurydice several times in the *Aeneid,* most notably in Aeneas' loss of Creusa (*Aen.* 2.559–795) and in his meeting with Dido in the underworld (*Aen.* 6.450–76).[24] The story, in short, has an archetypal force in Virgil's art as a recurrent, poignant symbol of death and personal loss, especially of death caused by the madness of love (cf. *Georg.* 4.495: "tantus furor"). Again and again, Virgil counters individual finitude stoically with the promise of collective *aeternitas* and continues in his own epic poetry the broken song of Orpheus.

Boethius clearly wants his readers to recall Virgil's *Georgics* and his version of the Orpheus story. The opening lines of the metrum, "Felix, qui potuit boni / Fontem uisere lucidum, / Felix, qui potuit gravis / Terrae soluere uincula" (III.m12,1–4: Happy was he who could look upon / The clear fount of the good; / Happy who could loose the bonds / Of heavy earth) echo with the force of anaphora *Georgics* 2.490–92:

> Felix, qui potuit rerum cognoscere causas,
> atque metus omnis et inexorabile fatum
> subiecit pedibus strepitumque Acherontis avari.

> [Blessed is he who has been able to win knowledge of the causes of things, and has cast beneath his feet all fear and unyielding Fate, and the howls of hungry Acheron!]

As Joachim Gruber rightly observes, however, Boethius substitutes a single ultimate cause, the "clear fount of the good," for Virgil's

---

24. See especially Ward W. Briggs, *Narrative and Simile from the Georgics in the Aeneid*, *Mnemosyne*, Supplement 58 (Leiden: E. J. Brill, 1980), pp. 99–103; C. P. Segal, "'Like Winds and Winged Dream': A Note on Virgil's Development," *CJ* 69 (1973–74): 97–101. In earlier versions of the Troy legend, Aeneas' wife was named Eurydica, not Creusa. See Austin's commentary on *Aeneid* 2, pp. 287–89.

multiple causes.[25] The change in wording signals an altered philosophical perspective on the myth as a whole. Indeed, Boethius' understanding of the reason for Orpheus' failure and the means he
recommends for conquering the fear of death depart significantly
from Virgil's. As we shall see, he recalls the Virgilian text in order to
set it in dialogue with his own, which, as a conscious "other speaking" of the Orpheus myth, exposes in a new form the deeper Neoplatonic meaning the Virgilian letter had veiled.

In a similar fashion, Boethius uses verbal echoes to incorporate
Seneca's interpretive renditions of the story of Orpheus into metrum
12 and subordinates them to a Neoplatonic scheme. Seneca tells the
story of Orpheus in three different tragedies—*Hercules furens, Hercules Oetaeus,* and *Medea.* (Discussion of the last mentioned follows
below.) *Hercules furens* emphasizes the literal parallel between the
stories of Orpheus and Hercules. As the chorus indicates, the underworld conquered by Orpheus' song will also submit to Hercules'
strength: "Quae vinci potuit regia carmine, / haec vinci poterit regia
viribus" (lines 590–91).[26] The tragic implications of Orpheus' hasti-
ness in looking upon his prize are then played out in the murderous
madness that overwhelms Hercules at the very moment when he, at
the end of his labors, expects to be immortalized.

Hercules Oetaeus, on the other hand, stresses the contrast between
Orpheus and Hercules and attaches a moral lesson to both stories
similar to that found in Boethius' metra. In this play, which Norman
Pratt has called "the culmination of Senecan drama," Seneca embeds the tragic story of Orpheus and Eurydice within the comic story
of the dying, but ultimately rising, Hercules.[27] The chorus spells out
three times the truth of mortality that is taught by Orpheus' autobiographical song. Seneca prefaces the myth of Eurydice with the
choric comment:

Verum est quod cecinit sacer
Thressae sub Rhodopes iugis

25. Gruber, *Kommentar,* p. 315. Gruber cites M. Galdi, *Saggi boeziani* (Pisa, 1938), p. 241.

26. I use Seneca, *Hercules furens,* in *Tragedies,* vol. 1, trans. Frank Justus Miller, Loeb Classical Library (Cambridge: Harvard University Press, 1960).

27. Norman Pratt, *Seneca's Drama* (Chapel Hill: University of North Carolina Press, 1983), p. 128. Pratt argues for the *Oetaeus* as an authentically Senecan work against those who consider it the work of a Senecan imitator.

aptans Pieriam chelyn
Orpheus Calliopae genus,
aeternum fieri nihil.
    (*Herc.O.* 1031–35)

[True sang the bard beneath the heights of Thracian Rhodope, fitting the word to his Pierian lyre, e'en Orpheus, Calliope's blest son, that naught for endless life is made.][28]

At the end of the tale, the chorus repeats the lesson "that all which has been and shall be born shall die" (*Herc.O.* 1099: "quod natum est, quod erit, mori"). Seeing Hercules in his death throes, the chorus attributes to Orpheus prophetic powers: "The overthrow of Hercules bids us to believe the Thracian bard [that all must die]" (*Herc.O.* 1100–01: "Vati credere Thracio / devictus iubet Hercules").

Hercules' final fate, however, offers a partial exception to the Orphic rule. A demigod, the son of Alcmene and Zeus, Hercules is immortalized. Only his maternal part, his mortal body, experiences death; his paternal part ascends victoriously to the stars. In keeping with Stoic cosmology, Seneca contrasts the destructive, temporal flames of the pyre with the creative, primal fire that is eternal and god.[29] Nevertheless, as Pratt observes, the dramatic "distinction between the survival of Hercules' soul and the death of his body" tends "to differentiate sharply between body and soul and to stretch the traditional Stoic tenet that the soul also is material."[30] That imagistic body/soul division, which anticipates a Neoplatonic stance, finds its moral analogue in *Hercules Oetaeus* when Hercules himself contrasts the fear that leads into death with the fortitude that draws one to superhuman heights: "virtus in astra tendit" (*Herc.O.* 1971).

Seneca's Herculean dramas, like Virgil's *Georgics* and Boethius' *Consolation*, contextualize the myth of Orpheus as a tale-within-

---

28. I use Seneca, *Hercules Oetaeus*, in *Tragedies*, vol. 2, trans. Frank Justus Miller, Loeb Classical Library (London: Heinemann and New York: Putnam, 1917). Although Gruber cites the parallel passages, Lerer omits any treatment of this Senecan play, presumably because of its questionable authorship. O'Daly (*Poetry of Boethius*, pp. 194–95) discusses the *Oetaeus* in a tentative but suggestive way.

29. See Seneca, "De beneficiis," in *Moral Essays*, vol. 3, trans. John W. Basore, Loeb Classical Library (Cambridge: Harvard University Press, 1958), IV.8.1, pp. 218–19. See also Thomas G. Rosenmeyer, *Senecan Drama and Stoic Cosmology* (Berkeley: University of California Press, 1989), p. 128.

30. Pratt, *Seneca's Drama*, p. 127.

a-tale that serves to raise vital issues, which are then answered by the framing narrative. Virgil attributes the responsibility for Eurydice's second death not to Orpheus, but to an undefined, cruel outside force, the sudden madness that seizes him unexpectedly at the threshold of the underworld: "subita incautum dementia cepit amantem" (*Georg.* 4.488). Because Virgil's *causa* is outside Orpheus, Virgil's answer to the problem of death is also external to the individual and takes the form of artistic and national continuance. After the final loss of Eurydice, Orpheus sings like the mournful nightingale (*Georg.* 4.511: "qualis ... maerens philomela"), his archetypal status as a poet achieved in part by personal suffering. The music of Orpheus, which tames the tigers and makes the oaks attend, is described at length *after* his failure to retrieve Eurydice, a Virgilian strategy that makes art the fruit of afflictive *labor.* Virgil's Orpheus, a tragic figure, thus anticipates in his art the practical invention of his comic double, Aristaeus the beekeeper.

Even more clearly than Virgil, Seneca exonerates Orpheus, indicating that the gods are also under the law of material necessity (*Herc.O.* 1093: "leges in superos datas") and cannot dispense anyone from death. In *Hercules Oetaeus* the constant theme of Orpheus' song, whether he sings to the trees, the animals, or the denizens of Hades, is the universality of death. His song thus articulates his spiritual penetration of the order of things—the mortalist order to which Hercules heroically submits. Seneca's solution to the Orphic problem of death has a distinctly moral character. One triumphs over death by accepting its inescapability, by stepping fearlessly like a Hercules into the flames, by conforming inwardly to the law of the universe.

Boethius goes beyond Seneca when he contrasts the positive law given by Pluto to the lovers (III.m12.47: "Quis legem det amantibus?") with the greater natural law of love itself: "Maior lex amor est sibi" (III.m12.48). Orpheus' obedience to that higher law establishes a powerful, mysterious parallel between Orpheus' love, which occasions Eurydice's second death, and the love of God that first drew her into the underworld. The parallel, once established, serves to mitigate the tragedy of necessary death by placing it within a larger scheme in which divine love is the final cause.

The Orphic metrum at the end of Book III recalls the great hymn to love with which Book II of the *Consolation* closes. In that hymn the same love that governs the universe, reconciling its opposite elements and harmonizing its seasonal changes, expresses itself in human love, especially marital fidelity, ruling hearts as its rules the heavens and bringing them happiness: "O felix hominum genus, / si uestros animos amor / quo caelum regitur regat!" (II.m8,28–30). The song of Orpheus makes it clear that faithful human love also brings sadness, the pain of physical separation, the endurance of vicissitude. Boethius thus takes up the Stoic idea that the same creative cosmic love which, as a force of cohesion or elemental attraction, brings about harmony, also spreads contagion and causes cyclic disintegration.[31] Boethius, however, uses the image in a distinctly Neoplatonic manner that emphasizes the immortality of the individual soul, which is providentially freed by death from its physical limitations.

Because Boethius, unlike Virgil and Seneca, represents the cause of death as love, his solution to the problem of death is distinctly individual, inward, and centered on love. One must in the midst of darkness seek the light; in the face of loss, one must recall the love that is lasting and thus unite one's human affections with the divine *amor* that perdures and vivifies. The Boethian problem posed by death is not, in short, a matter of *why*, but rather, *wherefore*. Death in his view is not an end, but a means to an end, the telos Lady Philosophy represents in the light-filled fountain of the good into which the blessed gaze.

Boethius' Orpheus cannot, however, perceive an eternal end behind the temporal end of death. He calms the woods and rivers, the hounds and lions, but he cannot soothe himself. That self-defeat anticipates the second. In the underworld Orpheus moves the gods to release Eurydice, but he himself loses her through a forbidden backward glance. In both cases Orpheus fails to lead his own mind (III.m12,54: "mentem ducere") into the light, into a consideration of final causality. The Boethian Orpheus thus combines in his person the archetypal lover and musician, who, according to Plotinus, are attracted to the Supreme Good through the beauties of nature that foreshadow it, but are unable to reach their final goal without the aid of philosophical instruction. As lover and musician, Orpheus stands

---

31. According to Rosenmeyer, "Some Stoic sources, falling back upon the ready mechanism of a divine nomenclature signalling cohesion, refer to *sumpatheia* as Aphrodite, or Love" (*Senecan Drama*, p. 109).

in contrast to the Plotinian philosopher, whose mind is winged and able to ascend.[32]

That contrast, and the threefold Plotinian (ultimately Platonic) typology from which it originates, helps to explain the direction of Lady Philosophy's instruction. Boethius has been, like Orpheus, a lover and a musician.[33] Orpheus expresses his grief in weeping measures (III.m12,7: "flebilibus modis"), even as Boethius composes tearful complaints at the dictation of the strumpet Muses: "fletibusque meis uerba dictantes" (I.p1,7). Like Orpheus, who cannot conquer himself, Boethius lacks the kingly freedom to leave his own misery behind: "miserasque fugare querelas / non posse potentia non est" (III.m5,9–10). Orpheus looks back into the Tartarean cave, turning the light of his eyes away from the supernal light: "lumina flexerit" (III.m12,56). Similarly, Boethius' eyes are beclouded by the mist of earthly affairs (I.p2,6: "lumina eius mortalium rerum nube"), and his mind tends to go into the shadows of his grief (I.m2,2–3: "mens . . . / tendit in externas ire tenebras") rather than into the light.

With a shock of recognition, Boethius sees himself mirrored in Orpheus. Philosophia's tale, he says, has reminded him of his own deep sorrow, and he submits with new eagerness to her instruction. Lady Philosophy responds by inviting Boethius, who has been like Orpheus, to succeed where he failed by taking flight on her pinions homeward to the Fatherland. Philosophia, moreover, offers in her own person a model for the successful Orpheus. Not only has she descended into Boethius' cavelike prison cell to lead him out from his spiritual bondage into the light; she has taken Orpheus' very own death-song upon her lips, singing it gently and sweetly (IV.p1,1), and incorporated it into a romantic epic of return to the Fatherland in which she and her philosophical hero are the chief protagonists.

Circe and Ulysses

Whereas the Orpheus metrum enables Boethius to recall the truth of human mortality within a Neoplatonic frame, the second mythologi-

---

32. See Plotinus, *Enneads* I.3, in *Works*, vol. 1, trans. A. H. Armstrong, Loeb Classical Library (London: Heinemann; Cambridge: Harvard University Press, 1966), esp. pp. 152–57.

33. For a general comment on the parallels between Orpheus and Boethius, see Gruber, pp. 314–15.

cal metrum recalls the truth of rationality. Boethius selects a Homeric scene, Ulysses' encounter with Circe, which the Stoics had interpreted allegorically to celebrate Ulysses' triumph as personified Reason over animal passions and sensual allurement. This interpretation originally derived from the close analogy between a bestial body and a vicious soul and the Stoic identification of both as material. Boethius accepts the inherited moral, begins with it, and retells the tale of Circe and Ulysses from a Neoplatonic perspective that stresses the difference between the material body and the immaterial soul. In so doing, Boethius shifts the focus away from Ulysses to Circe and her attempt to dehumanize Ulysses and his men. In the process Circe becomes the anti-type of both Orpheus and Hercules in their superhuman strivings toward the depths and the heights.

Boethius' Circe, like Orpheus in III.m12, is a singer. She mixes for her guests enchanted drinks—literally, cups touched by song (IV.m3,7: "tacta carmine pocula"). Orpheus tamed the animals with his music:

Iunxitque intrepidum latus
Saeuis cerua leonibus,
Nec uisum timuit lepus,
Iam cantu placidum canem.
        (III.m12,10–13)

[And the hind's fearless flank / Lay beside savage lions, / Nor was the hare afraid to look upon / the hound, made peaceful by his song.]

Circe exercises a similar control over the men she changes into the form of beasts:

Hunc apri facies tegit,
Ille Marmaricus leo
Dente crescit et unguibus.
Hic lupis nuper additus,
Flere dum parat, ululat.
Ille tigris ut Indica
Tecta mitis obambulat.
        (IV.m3,10–16)

[This one the shape of boar conceals, / That one, a lion of Africa, / Grows fangs and claws; / Another just becoming one with wolves, / While he essays to weep, but howls; / Another like an Indian tiger / Prowls tame around the house.]

Finally, Circe's victims are lost in voice and body (IV.m3,26: "uoce, corpore perditis"), even as Eurydice is lost to Orpheus: "Orpheus Eurydicen suam / uidit, perdidit, occidit" (III.m12,50–51).

In constructing Circe as an Orphean anti-type, Boethius follows Seneca's treatment of Medea. Verbal echoes of Seneca's *Medea* in the three mythological metra prove Boethius' close familiarity with that drama and suggest a close intertextual connection between and among them. The heroine of Seneca's tragedy traces her descent from the Sun (*Med.* 210: "avoque clarum Sole deduxi genus"), as does Boethius' Circe (IV.m3,5: "Solis edita semine").[34] Both Circe and Medea are witches. Circe is "herbipotens" (IV.m3,9), skilled in herbal magic, and Seneca's Medea gathers a similar store of deadly herbs: "mortifera carpit gramina" (*Med.* 731). Even as Circe's insular spells assume global dimensions in the form of African lions and Indian tigers, Medea spreads her poisonous influence from the Libyan sands to the arctic snow (*Med.* 682–83).

Even more importantly, Seneca's Medea directly compares her incantations to Orpheus' song.[35] She herself claims to have the gift of Orpheus (*Med.* 228: "munus est Orpheum meum") and to surpass him in power. Drawn by her singing (*Med.* 684: "tracta magicis cantibus"), serpents leave their lairs to come to her, even as the savage beasts flocked to hear Orpheus. The whole world trembles at her singing (*Med.* 739: "mundus vocibus primis tremit"), and her invocation momentarily causes the torments to end in hell (*Med.* 734–49), even as Orpheus holds the trees, rocks, and rivers spellbound and captivates the underworld.

In Seneca's *Medea*, the references to Orpheus associate both him and Hercules with the voyage of the Argo, a voyage parallel in many ways to Ulysses' adventurous homeward journey. Orpheus like Ulysses, for instance, triumphs over the Sirens (*Med.* 355–60). Medea's

34. I quote from Seneca, *Medea*, in *Tragedies*, vol. 1. Lerer does not treat this play.
35. For a discussion of Medea as an Orphean anti-type, see Charles Segal, "Dissonant Sympathy: Song, Orpheus, and the Golden Age in Seneca's Tragedies," in *Seneca Tragicus: Ramus Essays on Senecan Drama*, ed. A. J. Boyle (Berwick, Victoria: Aureal, 1983), pp. 229–56.

spiritual rivalry with Orpheus, then, suggestively prefigures Circe's trial of Ulysses, even as Medea's frenzied undoing of the Argonauts provides an analogue for Circe's destruction of Ulysses' crew.

Medea uses the song of the dead Orpheus, even as she uses the ashes soaked with the blood of Hercules (*Med.* 777–78), to revenge herself on Jason. Indeed, she seeks to undo and reverse all the heroic labors of the Argonauts by the downfall of their leader. She calls for the return of the Hydra and every serpent killed by the hand of Hercules (*Med.* 701–2); she stirs hell with Orpheus' appropriated song, not to restore a dead bride (Eurydice), but to kill a living one (Creusa). In her total microcosmic submission of reason to passion, Medea threatens to overturn the macrocosmic order, drawing the physical elements of the universe into her madness: "With me let all things pass away" (*Med.* 428: "mecum omnia abeant").

Part of the horror and energy of Medea as a protagonist derives from Seneca's Stoic sense of the material continuity of body and soul and their intimate interrelation. Boethius' Circe reflects an opposed, Neoplatonic perspective on things. She exerts power over the bodies of men, but the mind of each remains firm and unchanged: "sola mens stabilis" (IV.m3,27). Her drugs are powerless to change human hearts: "corda uertere non ualent" (IV.m3,32). The bestial bodies she intends as prisons only serve to disclose the hidden citadel of unconquered spiritual strength.

The closing lines of the metrum invert the image of a healthy soul trapped in a deformed body to consider the possibility of a poisoned, vicious soul in an unharmed body. The spiritual poisons that drag a man down, away from himself (IV.m3,35–36: "uenena . . . / Detrahunt hominem sibi") into the abyss are much more potent than the herbs of a Circe. The person who practices vice, Lady Philosophy insists, ceases to be human (IV.p3,21: "homo esse desierit") and turns himself into a beast. One can, in short, be one's own Circe, both host and guest, self-victimized—a paradox Boethius suggests earlier in the metrum by the wordplay on "hospitibus" (line 6) and "hospitis" (line 20). To do so is to repeat at a moral level Orpheus' loss of Eurydice, to experience the death, not of the body, but of the soul. Choosing the downward path precludes the possibility of ascent, even as becoming bestial in one's attitude prevents the opposite human possibility, apotheosis: "cum in diuinam condicionem tran-

sire non possit" (IV.p3,21). In this sense, to stay on Circe's island is
never to return home.

Hearing Lady Philosophy's song of Circe enables Boethius to
recognize himself at a deeper level. Physically imprisoned by Theodoric, Boethius can defend and maintain his freedom of mind and
heart. In doing so he stands superior to his tormentors, who have the
savage and wicked mind (IV.p4,1: "atrox scelerataque mens") of a
beast. Boethius thus recalls his own dignity as a moral being possessing reason and free will. Reason alone does not give him back his full
humanitas, however. He is still incapable of pitying his tormentors,
perceiving their suffering, forgiving them. Reason, as the final mythological metrum shows, often distorts justice into revenge, whereas a
higher intelligence counsels the mercy that enables one to receive
mercy, the Herculean gift of the stars.

Agamemnon, Ulysses, and Hercules

The last of the three mythological metra takes up the theme of
revenge and retribution within a larger narrative of mythic return as
Lady Philosophy relates in succession the homeward journeys of
Agamemnon, Ulysses, and Hercules. The repeated prefix *re* assumes
metaphysical force as Lady Philosophy exposes revenge as a false
means to regain lost happiness, to return home. Hercules alone
escapes the cyclic pattern of revenge and finds the true path *ad
patriam.*

Lady Philosophy tells the stories of the three heroes briefly, allusively. Discovering their significance depends therefore on one's
memory, the recollection of words one has heard before and the
contexts in which they appeared. The exercise of memory enables
Boethius to remember what he has forgotten, his own immortal telos
as a child of God. Like Hercules, the son of Zeus, Boethius traces his
origin to a divine source, the one Father of all (III.m6,2: "Vnus enim
rerum pater est"). That heavenly origin is also his proper end, the
finis symbolized by Hercules' ascent to the stars.

Agamemnon, unlike Hercules, has forgotten his true Father and
Fatherland—a lapse signaled by his own paternal guilt. He has put
off the father (IV.m7,6: "Exuit patrem") and played instead the cruel

part of priest, sacrificing his daughter Iphigenia as a bridal purchase-price for favorable winds. The opening words of the metrum, "Bella bis quinis," echo Seneca's *Agamemnon* 624, and that revenge tragedy contextualizes the whole of Philosophia's song. In Seneca's play, Agamemnon's impious crime against Iphigenia is prefigured in Thyestes' incest with his daughter. Fortune has defiled the father (*Ag.* 28: "Fortuna maculat patrem"), Thyestes announces, in order to beget Aegisthus as the avenger of his House against the House of Atreus.[36] When Agamemnon slaughters Iphigenia in her wedding dress as a holocaust, he commits a symbolic incest that arouses Clytaemnestra's fury. The blood that Agamemnon will repay to Clytaemnestra (*Ag.* 235: "sanguinem reddet tibi") atones for the blood with which he purchased winds: "cruore ventos emimus" (*Ag.* 170). That domestic and dynastic tragedy, moreover, plays itself out against the background of the Trojan War in which a vengeful Agamemnon destroys Troy in revenge for his brother's violated marriage. Crime thus answers crime (*Ag.* 151: "scelus scelere obruit") and, as Jo-Ann Shelton notes, "the desire to redress a wrong" repeatedly "produces a chain of sordid violence."[37] As a consequence, Agamemnon, murdered on his arrival home by Clytaemnestra and Aegisthus, never reaches the true home he seeks.

Even as the Agamemnon section of Lady Philosophy's song echoes Seneca's tragedy, the Ulysses section (lines 8–12) echoes the opening lines of the metrum.[38] Ulysses' comrades, swallowed by Polyphemus, are lost to him (IV.m7,8: "amissos . . . sodales"), even as Helen is lost to Menelaus: "fratris amissos thalamos" (IV.m7,3). Joy compensates ("rependit") for Ulysses' tears, when he succeeds in putting out Polyphemus' eye, even as rising winds answer to the sad purchase-price of Iphigenia's blood: "ventos redimit cruore" (IV.m7,5). Philosophia relates the end of neither Agamemnon's tale nor Ulysses', but a strong pattern of verbal repetition establishes the narrative telos. Agamemnon's distorted reason of revenge leads to the madness of murder, while Ulysses' vengeful escape from the darkness of Polyphemus' cave ultimately exposes him in turn to the

36. I quote from Seneca, *Agamemnon*, in *Tragedies*, vol. II.
37. Jo-Ann Shelton, "Revenge or Resignation: Seneca's *Agamemnon*," in *Seneca Tragicvs*, p. 160.
38. Cf. Lerer, *Boethius and Dialogue*, p. 192.

revenge of both Neptune at sea and Apollo on the Island of the Sun and thus sets at serious risk his return to Ithaca.

In likening Ulysses to Agamemnon as avengers and contrasting them both to Hercules, Boethius reverses traditional interpretations that treated Ulysses and Agamemnon as antitypes and grouped Ulysses and Hercules together as sages.[39] Indeed, Boethius purposefully places Ulysses in the cave of Polyphemus, rather than the Ithacan cave of the nymphs, in order to show the moral limits of mere cunning and the worldly wisdom that dictates an eye-for-eye repayment of wrongs. In Boethius' metrum, Hercules alone proves successful in his homeward journey.[40]

In order to make Hercules a positive exemplum, however, Boethius must remove him from the ironic context in which he appears in Seneca's *Agamemnon*. In that play the chorus of Argive women first praise Hercules and recount his twelve labors, ending with the remembrance that Hercules long ago conquered Troy, and his arrows in the hands of Philoctetes have helped to destroy Priam's Dardanians (lines 808–66). Then Cassandra appears on stage to announce that Troy has been avenged by Agamemnon's murder. Hercules thus figures prominently in the ancient chain of revenge that underlies the Trojan War, determining its epic action and tragic aftermath.

When Lady Philosophy recounts Hercules' labors in IV.m7,13–35, she uses language that echoes Seneca's *Agamemnon* and *Medea*, but she changes the ending of Hercules' story, redirecting its narrative telos from tragedy to comedy. The last labor (IV.m7,29: "ultimus labor") of Philosophia's Hercules is not the punitive destruction of Troy, but the heroic support of the sky, the lifting up of the heavens: "caelum . . . / Sustulit collo" (IV.m7,29–30).

When Lady Philosophy attributes this last labor to Hercules, she imitates Seneca's strategy in his Herculean dramas. In *Hercules furens*

---

39. My close association of Boethius' Ulysses with Agamemnon finds support in Lerer, *Boethius and Dialogue*, p. 192. For a counterargument, see O'Daly, *Poetry of Boethius*, pp. 223–27. It should be remembered that Ulysses had a mixed reputation, even in antiquity—sometimes celebrated as a wise man, sometimes denounced as a cruel, unprincipled sophist and calculating trickster.

40. For a general study of the literary uses of the Hercules legend, see G. Karl Galinsky, *The Herakles Theme: The Adaptations of the Hero in Literature from Homer to the Twentieth Century* (Oxford: Blackwell, 1972).

Hercules explicitly rejects the choice of revenge, choosing not to kill himself after he, momentarily insane, has slain his wife and children. To go on living, to be merciful to himself and his adoptive father, is for Hercules the last and greatest labor, greater than the previous twelve: "ingens opus, labore bis seno amplius" (*Herc.f.* 1282). As Anna Lydia Motto and John Clark put it, "his greatest labor proves to be his self-mastery, his self-control."[41] *Hercules Oetaeus* also focuses on the last labor of Hercules. That play includes Hercules' battle with fire as the last of his labors: "inter labores ignis Herculeos abit" (*Herc.O.* 1616). As he fearlessly mounts his own funeral pyre, Hercules' gaze seeks the stars, not the flames (*Herc.O.* 1645: "vultus petentis astra, non ignes erat") and anticipates his apotheosis.

The unbowed neck (IV.m7,29–30: "inreflexo / . . . collo") of Philosophia's Hercules symbolically opposes the repeated *re* of vengeful retribution (exemplified in Agamemnon ["redimit"] and Ulysses ["rependit"]) and triumphs over the wavering, backward glance of a despairing Orpheus. Indeed, the Herculean neck that nobly bears up the heavens recalls a series of earlier images in the *Consolation* of the prisoner himself: his neck weighed down with heavy chains (I.m2,25: "pressus grauibus colla catenis"); his neck submitted to Fortune's yoke (II.p1,16: "iugo eius colla summiseris"). For Boethius to see Hercules is thus to envision a new positioning of himself in the cosmos.

The stars that the vanquished earth grants to Hercules represent and enable Boethius' return to himself and give new meaning to his sufferings. Properly endured, they are a means for him to merit heaven at the end of his labors and a way of certain return *ad patriam*. When Lady Philosophy points to Hercules as an example for the brave to follow (IV.m7,32: "Ite nunc fortes"), she directly opposes the vengeful, frenzied exhortation of Medea (*Med.* 650) with the closing lesson of the *Hercules Oetaeus*: "The brave live on" (*Herc.O.* 1984: "vivunt fortes") and find their way heavenwards: "iter ad superos" (*Herc.O.* 1988).

The metrum of Agamemnon, Ulysses, and Hercules brings the educational process to a close. In remembering the heroes of the past and

41. Anna Lydia Motto and John R. Clark, *Senecan Tragedy* (Amsterdam: Hakkert, 1988), p. 290.

identifying with them, Boethius has recalled his own mortality and passions, his human reason, and his immortal soul. Gruber rightly observes that the exhortation with which metrum 7 ends joins the conclusion of Book IV to the conclusion of the *Consolation.*[42] Even more importantly, perhaps, the exemplum of Hercules anticipates Philosophia's final metrum (V.m5), which, as an imagistic *summa*, underscores the truths about human nature that the various mythological figures teach us. At the same time the metrum comments self-reflexively on figural representation as an avenue to truth.

The metrum begins with the exclamatory observation that animals abide on earth in various forms and species: "Quam uariis terras animalia permeant figuris!" (V.m5,1). The next six lines distinguish three kinds of animals: those that burrow in the ground, those that fly aloft in the air, and those that move lightly across the surface of the earth as hunters and grazers. Although these visible differences exist, all the animals have a prone posture, and their *sensus*, their capacity for perception, is thus weighed down and gravitates toward the earth. Humankind alone stands erect, lifts its head aloft, and looks down upon the earth. This posture, Lady Philosophy insists, admonishes us that we are to seek heaven and direct our mind to the contemplation of sublime things, lest a base mind (V.m5,14–15: "grauata . . . mens") inhabit an upright body: "corpore celsius leuato."

The initial *distinctio* of three kinds of animals (burrowers, runners, flyers) recalls the geographical *loci* of the three mythological metra. Orpheus descends into hell and Eurydice is buried in the earth. Ulysses travels across the sea to Circe's island. Hercules supports the sky and ascends to the stars. The second *distinctio*, which separates humankind from the other animals, recalls the various moral interpretations that Philosophia attaches to the fables. Orpheus' fate teaches us to free ourselves from earthly chains and direct our mind upward, into the light: "in superum diem / mentem ducere" (III.m12,53–54). The fate of Ulysses' men reminds us that the human mind elevates us above the beasts: "Sola mens stabilis super / monstra" (IV.m3,27–28). The apotheosis of Hercules teaches us that the earth can be overcome by those who follow the high path (IV.m7, 32–33: "celsa . . . via") to heaven.

42. Gruber, *Kommentar*, p. 376.

As Philosophia insists, the ability to apprehend truth through *figurae*—whether the physical forms of animals or poetic images—depends on preexistent forms in the human mind. She explicitly rejects the teaching of the Stoics ("Porticus") that external, material emanations, absorbed through the senses, imprint themselves as images on a passively receptive mind, as one writes on a blank page (V.m4,1–9). Instead, she says, the mind has innate ideas, forgotten memories. Stimulated by sensory experience, one's own active mental power acts to join together external images with internal forms similar to them: "formis miscet imagines" (V.m4,40). True perception, then, depends on the recall and the matching of the proper form—a form belonging to the knower, not the object of one's knowing.

This kind of figural perception makes poetry, especially epic poetry, evocative of truth. Its deeper *sensus* corresponds to the forms of one's own mind which match its images, revealing one's self to oneself as a mortal, rational, and immortal creature. Unlike the verse that brings mere enjoyment, allegory must be remembered in order to be understood and thus brings with it lasting consolation. In Philosophia's school, Boethius' allegorical reading of epic finally enables him to rewrite his own life history as a heroic journey, matching image with form, word with truth, and directing its narrative telos *ad patriam.*

3 Job and
Heroic Virtue

Like Boethius, who made the classical
epic narratives both a means and an expression of human self-
knowledge, the late antique readers of the Book of Job discovered in
it a philosophical mirror of the truth of human nature. According to
this reading, the book's subject is its hero, Job, a man (*vir*) living in
the land of Hus, who was a true man (Job 1:1: "et erat ille homo
verus") by virtue of his likeness to God.[1] As we have seen, Boethius,
under the tutelage of Lady Philosophy, begins his mental journey by
defining himself incorrectly as a mortal and rational animal (I.p6,15:
"rationale animal atque mortale") and nothing more.[2] Saint John
Chrysostom begins his fourth-century Greek commentary on Job
with the same definition of human nature (Ἄνθρωπός ἐστι ζῷον
λογικὸν θνητόν), only to set the opinion of pagan philosophers (Οἱ
μὲν ἔξωθεν σοφοί) in opposition to the scriptural definition of a
human being as someone who preserves his essential similitude to
God through the practice of virtue.[3] The Joban expression "true
man" (*homo verus*) is, according to Chrysostom, a biblical hom-
onym.[4] Job is "true" not only because he is honest in his temporal
dealings, but also because he has safeguarded the timeless divine
image in which he was created.

Chrysostom's philosophical focus on the *vir* and *homo* named in

1. Unlike the Old Latin translation "homo verus," the Vulgate reads "vir simplex."
2. Boethius, *De consolatione philosophiae*, ed. Ludovicus Bieler, CCSL 94 (Turnhout: Brepols, 1957).
3. Saint John Chrysostom, "Fragmenta in beatum Job," PG 64, c509.
4. Ibid., c511.

the opening lines of the Book of Job parallels exegetical treatments of the *vir* mentioned at the opening of Virgil's *Aeneid*: "Arma virumque cano" (*Aen.* 1.1). As we have seen, by the early sixth century the historical tendency to read epic as a moral and metaphysical allegory of the self was so entrenched in the schools that when the mythographer Fulgentius asks a personified Virgil to explicate in his own work the "things that schoolmasters expound, for monthly fees, to boyish ears" ("quae mensualibus stipendiis grammatici distrahunt puerilibus auscultatibus"), Virgil responds by presenting "the full range of human life" (p. 122) as the allegorical content of the *Aeneid*.[5]

According to Fulgentius' Virgil, the opening line of the *Aeneid* announces its hominal subject matter by referring obliquely to the qualities that constitute human perfection: strength of body ("uirtute corporis") and wisdom of mind ("sapientia ingenii"). The phrase "arms and the man," Virgil explains, recalls the power and the wisdom of the perfected human being: "in armis uirtutem, in uiro sapientiam" (p. 87). Although wisdom governs strength, Virgil nevertheless mentions strength first, because, he says, the soul's wisdom unfolds and displays itself in virtuous action: "in uirtute animae sapientia floret" (p. 88). In doing so, Virgil consciously follows the example of Homer who names the wrath of Achilles before Achilles himself and then shows Minerva as personified self-control, grasping Achilles' hair.

In his fictional dialogue, Fulgentius approves Virgil's explanation by citing two scriptural texts: Psalm 1:1, which indicates that the blessed man does not walk in the counsel of the wicked, and 1 Cor. 1:24, which celebrates Christ as the power and wisdom of God ("Christum uirtutem et sapientiam cecinit"), on the grounds that his divinity assumed the perfect human condition: "quod perfectum hominis divinitas adsumpsisse uideretur statum" (p. 87).

Saint Gregory the Great (b. 550) cites the same passage from 1 Corinthians in his explanation of the opening line of the Book of Job: "Vir erat in terra Hus nomine Iob" (I.xi.15, p. 31).[6] Gregory,

---

5. *Fulgentius the Mythographer*, trans. Leslie George Whitbread (Columbus: Ohio State University Press, 1971), p. 121; Fulgentius, *Expositio Virgilianae continentiae secundum philosophos moralis*, in *Opera*, ed. Rudolph Helm (Stuttgart: Teubner, 1898, 1970), p. 86. Subsequent citations are parenthetical.

6. I quote throughout from the standard edition of the *Moralia in Job*, ed. M. Adriaen, CCSL 143, 143A, 143B (Turnhout: Brepols, 1979–85). For an English transla-

moreover, interprets the Joban line in a two-part manner that parallels the "arms and the man" allegory spelled out by Fulgentius' pedantic Virgil. The name "Job," he says, means *dolens* (one who sorrows), whereas "Hus" means *consiliator* (counselor) (I.xi.15, p. 31). As a type of Christ, Job valiantly endures the bodily afflictions that foreshadow Christ's passion. At the same time Job inhabits the land of Hus, his heart ruled by wisdom and right judgment. Interpreted thus, both "Job" and "Hus" characterize the elect, because whoever, sorrowing, hastens from present to eternal things, continually abides in a wise state of mind (I.xxv.34, p. 43).

Isidore of Seville (b. 560) clearly recognized the Virgilian parallel in Gregory's treatment of Job as a strong and wise man. The younger brother of Bishop Leander of Seville, to whom Gregory affectionately dedicated his copious *Moralia in Iob* (A.D. 595), Isidore classifies the Book of Job as a heroic poem ("heroicum carmen") antedating the Homeric epics. Heroic poems, according to Isidore, recount in the heroic hexameter the affairs and deeds of brave men: "uirorum fortium res et facta narrentur."[7] Although Isidore mentions the metrical and mixed form of heroic poems, he clearly understands the genre to be defined by its subject matter: the strong and wise hero (*vir*) whose particular story represents the coming-to-perfection, the true nature of a generalized humankind (*homo*).

According to Isidore, the heroes who are the subjects of such works are literally airy men and worthy of heaven ("viri quasi aerei et coelo digni") on account of their wisdom and fortitude: "propter sapientiam et fortitudinem." Isidore elsewhere defines a hero as a strong and wise man: "vir fortis et sapiens" (*Etym.* X.A.2, c367). The word, he explains, derives from the name of the Greek goddess Hera who represents the heavenly realm (*aer*) where heroes ("viros aerios") desire to dwell: "ubi volunt Heroas habitare" (*Etym.* VIII.xi.98, c325). The hero is strong because he endures adversity (*Etym.* X.F.99, c377: "fert adversa"); wise, because he discerns the truth of things and their causes through a refined spiritual sense analogous to taste: "dictus a sapore" (*Etym.* X.S.240, c392).

---

tion I use St. Gregory the Great, *Morals on the Book of Job*, 3 vols., trans. anonymous (Oxford: John Henry Parker, 1844–50). Subsequent citations are parenthetical.

7. Isidore of Seville, *Etymologiae* I.xxxix.9–11, PL 82, c118–19.

When Isidore emphasizes power and wisdom as heroic virtues, he articulates a critical commonplace. As Ernst Robert Curtius has shown, Homer's *Iliad* represents the two *Heldentugenden* in both isolation (old Nestor's wisdom, Achilles' fearless battle lust) and combination (Odysseus' craftiness and courage) to demonstrate "that strength and intelligence in equipoise (VII,288; II,202; IX,53) represent the optimum in warrior virtue."[8] Virgil's *Aeneid* similarly represents the isolated virtues in his Iliadic characters—Latinus ("all *sapientia*") and Turnus ("all *fortitudo*")—in order to highlight their combination in the *pietas* of Aeneas.[9] After Virgil, as Curtius observes, the polarity between wisdom and fortitude is firmly established as a rhetorical topic and evident as a controlling principle in the works of Statius (*Thebaid*), Dictys (fourth century, *Ephemeris belli Troiani*), and Dares (sixth century, *De excidio Troiae*), as well as the Anglo-Saxon poems *Beowulf* and *Judith*.[10]

Both Curtius and Robert E. Kaske note in passing biblical passages that similarly pair the qualities of wisdom and power. The Book of Job, in particular, abounds in passages associating the two virtues. Job himself has "taught many" and "strengthened weary hands" (4.3: "docuisti multos et manus lassas roborasti").[11] Job praises God as one so "wise in heart and mighty in strength" (9:4: "sapiens corde est et fortis robore") that no one can resist him. With the Lord, Job says, is "wisdom and strength" (12:13: "sapientia et fortitudo"), "strength and wisdom" (12:16: "fortitudo et sapientia"); "By his power the seas are suddenly gathered together, and his wisdom has struck the proud one" (26:12: "in fortitudine illius repente maria congregata sunt et prudentia eius percussit superbum"). Elihu, insisting that no man,

---

8. Ernst Robert Curtius, *European Literature and the Latin Middle Ages*, trans. Willard R. Trask, Bollingen Series 36 (London: Routledge and Kegan Paul, 1953), p. 171.

9. Ibid., p. 173.

10. Ibid., p. 174. For treatments of the Anglo-Saxon poems, see Robert E. Kaske, "*Sapientia et Fortitudo* as the Controlling Theme of Beowulf," *SP* 55.3 (1958): 423–56; repr. in *An Anthology of Beowulf Criticism*, ed. Lewis E. Nicolson (Notre Dame: University of Notre Dame Press, 1963), pp. 269–311, and Jane Mushabac, "Judith and the Theme of *Sapientia et Fortitudo*," *Massachusetts Studies in English* 4 (Spring 1973): 3–12.

11. When I quote the Bible independently, not as an intertext in a particular commentary, I use *Biblia sacra iuxta Latinam vulgatam versionem* (Rome: Vatican, 1951) and the Douay-Challoner translation of the Vulgate.

including Job, can compare with God or contend with him, declares: "God is high in his strength, and none is like him among the lawgivers" (36:22: "Ecce Deus excelsus in fortitudine sua et nullus ei similis in legislatoribus"); "He is great in strength and in judgment" (37:23: "magnus fortitudine et iudicio"). Job responds to Yahweh's majestic speech out of the whirlwind with a similar praise of divine wisdom and power: "I know that thou canst do all things, and no thought is hid from thee" (42:2: "scio quia omnia potes et nulla te latet cogitatio").

Neither Curtius nor Kaske, however, elaborate on the significance of the scriptural parallels for medieval readers. Indeed, Kaske remarks that the biblical combination of *sapientia et fortitudo*, particularly frequent in the Sapiential Books and the Book of Job, is "hardly to be thought of as a heroic ideal."[12] Fulgentius, Gregory, and Isidore, however, explicitly associate biblical wisdom and sapience with heroism and use the scriptural parallels, especially those found in Job, to gloss the truth and falsity of pagan epic. Later, building upon Gregorian exegesis, Saint Thomas Aquinas finds in the Book of Job a biblical analogue of Boethius' *Consolation*, a threefold mirror of human nature, and an elaboration of heroic virtue as the Stoic, Peripatetic, and Neoplatonic exegesis of myth had defined it. As we shall see, this kind of comparative reading of sacred and profane texts led in the Middle Ages to a gradual redefinition of the heroic ideal through a reconceptualization of its essential components: the hero himself, his fortitude, and his sapience.

The Hero: *Vir* and *Virtus*

In classical and medieval understanding, the heroic man (*vir*) excells in power (*virtus*). Cicero derives "virtus" from "vir" and notes that the quality most characteristic of man is strength: "viri autem propria maxime est fortitudo."[13] Isidore, following Cicero, links *vir* with *virtus*, observing that strength (*vis*) is greater in a man than in a

12. Kaske, *"Sapientia et Fortitudo,"* p. 424.
13. Cicero, *Tusculan Disputations*, trans. J. E. King, Loeb Classical Library (Cambridge: Harvard University Press, 1927, 1971), II.xviii.43, pp. 194–97.

woman.[14] This basic etymological association, as we shall see, underlies and enables a gradual reconceptualization of the hero (*vir*) and
his semidivine status as moral philosophers from Aristotle to Saint
Thomas Aquinas unfolded the meaning of *virtus* and shifted its
primary denotation from physical to spiritual power.

Aristotle lays the foundation in the *Nicomachean Ethics* when he
contrasts vice with virtue, unrestraint with self-restraint, and bes-
tiality with its opposite, "Superhuman Virtue, or goodness on a
heroic or divine scale."[15] Aristotle finds the "surpassing virtue" that
"changes men into gods" exemplified in the "surpassing valour" of
Homer's Hector, who seemed even to his father Priam to be not "the
son of mortal man, but of a god" (*Il.* 24.258). Although this particular
Homeric citation associates heroic virtue primarily with fortitude
and martial prowess, Aristotle goes on to argue that intellectual
virtue, more than any other, divinizes a person. Beginning with the
crucial distinction between a person's rational and volitional faculties, he distinguishes correspondent intellectual and moral virtues as
habitual dispositions tending toward good actions. The intellectual
virtues, wisdom (σοφία) and prudence (φρόνησις), are the product of
instruction concerning ends and the choice of means to attain ends,
whereas the moral virtues, directed by prudence, develop through
the practical mastery of pleasure and pain and thus enable the actual
achievement of chosen ends. According to Aristotle, the highest
virtue, σοφία, corresponds to the highest human faculty, the specula-
tive intellect, which as the "ruling and better part" constitutes what is
divine in humankind.[16]

Even more than Aristotle, the Stoics associate the divinization of a
person with intellectual virtue. Indeed, in their view only the Sage
deserves to be called virtuous. As Cicero's Balbus explains it, a special providence shows itself in the gifts of body and soul bequeathed
to humankind. Nature raised human beings up from the earth,
giving them erect bodies, in order that, beholding the sky, they might
gain knowledge of the gods: "ut deorum cognitionem caelum intu-

14. Isidore of Seville, *Etym.* XI.ii.17, PL 82, c417.
15. Aristotle, *The Nicomachean Ethics*, trans. H. Rackham, Loeb Classical Library (London: Heinemann; New York: Putnam, 1926), VII.I, p. 375.
16. Ibid., X.vii.9, p. 619.

entes capere possent."[17] Thus, he says, the reason of wise men has penetrated into heaven and become identical with the divine *ratio* governing the fated course of the material universe.

Unlike Aristotle, however, who clearly distinguishes the moral from the intellectual virtues, the Stoics tend to moralize intellectual virtue as a courageous assent to fate—a tendency that mirrors their essentially materialistic identification of the body with the soul, the mind with volition, the world with god, and god with destiny. The Neoplatonists, on the other hand, intellectualize the moral virtues as exemplars. Whereas both the Aristotelian and Stoic approaches to human divinization are essentially anthropocentric—Aristotle defining virtue as a strictly human excellence, the Stoics actually identifying the human with the divine *ratio*—the Neoplatonist position, as articulated by Plotinus and Macrobius, emphasizes the existence of the cardinal virtues as ideas in the mind of God: "multo magis virtutum ideas esse in mente credendum est."[18] As Macrobius defines them, prudence is the divine mind itself ("mens ipsa divina"); temperance, the unchanging divine intention directed toward God himself; fortitude, divine immutability; justice, the divine governance of works according to eternal law.

According to the Neoplatonists, the civic virtues of prudence, temperance, fortitude, and justice, together with the virtues associated with them, distantly mirror in the social context of human affairs the exemplar virtues that exist in the mind of God: "quae in divina mente consistunt."[19] Practiced in a spirit of detachment from the body and earthly things, the cardinal virtues become purifying virtues that enable the soul's ascent. When the soul is totally directed toward God, the virtues, as practiced by those already purified, take on a perfect, divine quality. As Macrobius notes, as long as the soul inhabits the body, perfect wisdom consists in recognizing the soul's place of origin (and its end): "haec est perfecta sapientia ut, unde orta sit, de quo fonte venerit, recognoscat."[20]

17. Cicero, *De natura deorum*, trans. H. Rackham, Loeb Classical Library (Cambridge: Harvard University Press, 1933, 1979), II.lvi, p. 256.

18. Macrobius, *Commentarii in somnivm Scipionis*, ed. Jacob Willis (Leipzig: B. G. Teubner, 1970), I.8. 10, p. 39. See also Plotinus, "On Virtues," *Enneads* I.2.6–7, trans. A. H. Armstrong, vol. 1, Loeb Classical Library (Cambridge: Harvard University Press, 1966, 1978).

19. Macrobius, *Commentarii*, I.8.10, p. 39.

20. Ibid., I.9.1–2, p. 40.

Unlike the Neoplatonist view, the Christian doctrine of deification makes the soul's ascent radically dependent on the divine descent accomplished in Christ's Incarnation and Atoning Sacrifice and sealed by the outpouring of the Holy Spirit. As the scriptures say, the gift of grace makes human beings "children of God" (see John 1:13; 1 John 3:1, 4:7, 5:1) and actual "partakers of the divine nature" (2 Peter 1:4).[21] Through the indwelling of the Holy Spirit and the infusion of the theological virtues, faith, hope, and charity, the soul acquires a supernatural likeness to God that extends and perfects the natural, formal likeness evident in the intellectual and volitional faculties. Faith, as a superadded *habitus*, perfects the intellect by affording it access to revealed truth and intuitive understanding. Supernatural hope supplies what is lacking in the natural will by directing it toward God and divine goods. Charity accomplishes the lasting union between God and human beings, a union that divinizes them.

Christian saints respond to the infused gift of grace with an equally total gift of themselves, directing all their mental and volitional faculties and the acts of all the virtues, intellectual, moral, and theological, toward the love of God. Having received divine life, the saint heroically conforms himself to the pattern of Christ's earthly life, so that, as Saint Paul says, "It is now no longer I that live, but Christ lives in me" (Galatians 2:20).

When, therefore, Saint Thomas Aquinas accepts Aristotle's idea of superhuman or heroic virtue and aligns it with the Plotinian ideal of the perfect virtue of the purified (*purgati animi*), he does so within a scripturally-informed notion of human personhood and perfection. Citing Christ's command, "You therefore are to be perfect even as your Heavenly Father is perfect" (Matt. 5:48), Aquinas accepts Aristotle's opinion that "it belongs to man to strive as much as possible to attain what is divine" (Q.lxi.Art.5) and applies Plotinus' notion of perfect virtues to Christian saints: "These are the virtues we attribute to the blessed or to those who are most perfect in this life."[22] Aquinas

---

21. Three main schools of Christian thought interpret these passages on human divinization to mean: (1) the substantial identification of man with God, as posited by Meister Eckhart, Molinos, and the pantheists; (2) the moral union of man with God, as postulated by Luther and Calvin; (3) the ontological transformation of the human person, as understood by Catholic theologians. See the articles on "Divine Nature, Partaker of," "Divine Indwelling," and "Grace" in the *New Catholic Encyclopedia*.

22. Saint Thomas Aquinas, "Treatise on the Virtues," trans. John A. Oesterle (Englewood Cliffs, N.J.: Prentice Hall, 1966), p. 116.

then proceeds to discuss the infused theological virtues upon which depends the human attainment of "a happiness surpassing man's nature, which man can arrive at only by the power of God, by a certain participation in divinity (Q.lxii.1).[23] Thus Aquinas makes the Christian saint answer to the Homeric demigod and prepares the way for the Church's formal acceptance of heroic virtue as an official criterion for canonization.[24] The saints, like Isidore's "viri quasi aerei" are "worthy of heaven": "coelo digni."

The Hero's Fortitude

In the *Nicomachean Ethics* Aristotle distinguishes five kinds of courage: the courage of the citizen-soldier, of experience, of passion, of a sanguinic temperament, of ignorance.[25] The truest of these, he says, is the citizen's courage, which is publicly displayed on the battlefield and motivated by both the fear of disgrace and the desire for honor. Aristotle pointedly associates courage with personal initiative, a deliberate choice of fearless action, and public occasion. To be fearless of death by drowning or disease does not, in his view, exemplify fortitude.[26] Rather, fortitude is best illustrated by Homer's heroes in a setting of martial combat.

The Stoics, on the other hand, define fortitude as the subjective *constantia* of the wise man who steels himself to endure the blows of fortune without fear or pain (*apatheia*). As Seneca understands it, the difficult circumstances that beset the *vir bonus* allow him to know himself and display the strength of his mind: "vim animi sui ostenderet."[27] Bad fortune is the adversary that tests men and discovers

23. Ibid., p. 118.
24. The 1492 canonization of Saint Bonaventure included a formal inquiry into his heroic practice of the three theological and four cardinal virtues. By the time of the Renaissance "heroic virtue" was a technical term for the degree of holiness requisite for beatification or canonization. Prospero Lambertini (later Pope Benedict XIV) composed the standard work on the criteria for canonization: *De beatificatione Servorum Dei et de Beatorum canonizatione* (Bologna, 1734–38).
25. Aristotle, *Nicomachean Ethics*, III.viii, pp. 162–71.
26. See *Nicomachean Ethics* III.vi.7–9, pp. 156–57.
27. Seneca, "De Providentia," in *Moral Essays*, vol. 1, trans. John W. Basore, Loeb Classical Library (Cambridge: Harvard University Press, 1958), IV.3, p. 24. Subsequent citations are parenthetical.

among them a great exemplar (*De Prov.* III.4, p.16). The assaults of adversity do not weaken the brave man's spirit ("viri fortis animum"), but rather strengthen it (*De Prov.* II.1, p. 6).

In this Stoic scenario the true hero is best exemplified not by Homer's combatants but by political prisoners and martyred philosophers like Cato and Socrates (*De Prov.* III.4, pp. 16–17). Seneca, however, simultaneously exposes the literal falsity of the archaic understanding of courage and underscores its allegorical truth by using epic images to describe the wise man's fortitude. Even as wrestlers ("athletae") willingly struggle with the strongest opponents, knowing that physical strength diminishes without an adversary to test it, so should good men act in their spiritual confrontation with fate (*De Prov.* II.3–4, p. 8). Fortune, for her part, resembles a gladiator who scorns a victory over an inferior opponent and seeks out instead the bravest men ("fortissimos") in order to try them with all her powers (*De Prov.* III.4, p. 17). A fearless young man may meet a lion's charge, but that contest of man against beast bears no comparison to the wrestling match between a strong man and ill fortune ("vir fortis cum fortuna mala"), which, Seneca insists, is a cosmic spectacle worthy of God's gaze (*De Prov.* II.7–9, p. 10).

Like Seneca, Christian commentators on the Book of Job use the image of the wrestler to describe the hero engaged in spiritual struggle.[28] As Barbara K. Lewalski has observed, both Origen (third century) and Saint John Chrysostom (fourth century) depict Job as an athlete in a theatrical wrestling match, championing the cause of God against Satan.[29] Fulgentius calls Job an athlete in a mighty contest ("ille praecelsi atleta certaminis") and the overcomer of satanic force: "sataelica superator virtutis."[30] Saint Gregory the Great's influential *Moralia in Job* extends the image of the mighty wrestler and gladiator and uses it repeatedly both to unify his encyclopedic exposition of the text and to qualify the Book of Job as a heroic biblical poem.

At first Gregory emphasizes the image of the wrestler. Comment-

28. A persistent tradition numbered Seneca among the Christians in Nero's household and attributed to him correspondence with Saint Paul. See St. Jerome, "De viris illustribus," xii, PL 23, c629; C. Aubertin, *Sénèque et Saint Paul* (Paris: Didier, 1872).

29. Barbara K. Lewalski, *Milton's Brief Epic: The Genre, Meaning, and Art of 'Paradise Regained'* (Providence: Brown University Press, 1966), p. 22.

30. Fulgentius, *De aetatibus mundi et hominis*, in *Opera*, p. 142.

ing on the opening lines of the book, which describe Job as a virtuous man, Gregory likens the listing of virtues to the common practice of storytellers who, in the narration of a wrestling match, first describe the bodies of the contestants:

> Mos uero esse narrantium solet ut cum palaestrae certamen insinuant, prius luctantium membra describant quam latum ualidumque sit pectus, quam sanum, quam pleni tumeant lacerti, quam subterpositus uenter nec mole grauet, nec extenuatione debilitet. Vt cum prius aptos certamini artus ostenderint tunc demum magnae fortitudinis ictus narrent. Quia ergo athleta nostra contra diabolum fuerat certaturus, quasi ante arenae spectaculum, sacrae scriptor historiae in athleta hoc spiritales uirtutes enumerans, mentis membra describans ait. . . . (I.iii.4, p. 27)

> [But it is the custom of narrators, when a wrestling match is woven into the story, first to describe the limbs of the combatants, how broad and strong the chest, how sound, how full their muscles swelled, how the belly below neither clogged by its weight, nor weakened by its shrunken size, that when they have first shewn the limbs to be fit for the combat, they may then at length describe their bold and mighty strokes. Thus because our athlete was about to combat the devil, the writer of the sacred story, recounting as it were before the exhibition in the arena the spiritual merits in this athlete, describes the members of the soul.] (Vol. 1, p. 34)

Later, when Gregory comments on Job's successive tribulations, he again likens the hero's struggle to that of a wrestler in a theatrical contest:

> Quotiens in arenae spectaculum fortis athleta descenderit, ii qui impares uiribus exsistunt uicissim se eius expugnationi subiciunt; et uno uicto, contra hunc protinus alter erigitur. Atque hoc subacto, alius subrogatur, ut luctantis uires quandoque molliores inueniant quas ipsa sua crebres-cens uictoria fatigat; quatenus cum nouus quisque congreditur, is qui uinci uirium qualitate non ualet, personarum saltim mutatione superetur. Sic sic in hoc hominum angelorumque spectaculo beatus Iob fortis ath-leta prodiit, quantumque contra mutationes aduersantium ualeat con-tinuatione indefessi roboris ostendit. (X.I.1, p. 534)

> [As often as a mighty wrestler is gone down into the arena of the lists, those who prove no match for him in strength by turns present themselves

for the working of his overthrow, as fast as one is overcome another is directly raised up against him, and, he being subdued, another takes his place, that they may sooner or later find his strength in wrestling more yielding, in that his repeated victory by itself wears it out, so that as each fresh opponent comes to the encounter, he who cannot be overcome by the nature of their powers, may at least be got the better of by the changing of persons. Thus, then, in this theatre of men and angels, blessed Job proved himself a mighty wrestler, and how he prevailed against the charges of his adversaries, he shews by his continuance in unabated force.] (Vol. 1, p. 575)

Like Seneca in his description of the afflicted Sage, Gregory alternates between the images of the wrestler and the armed gladiator in characterizing Job's mental agon. Drawn into battle, Job meets the losses of his property, children, and health like enemies attacking him head-on: "quasi hostes contra faciem" (Preface, V.11, p. 16). He endures the words of his would-be consolers like foes attacking at his side: "quasi hostes ex latere." Defended by his shield, he vigilantly counters the swords of his attackers: "uenientibus gladiis uigilanter obuiauit." Armed with the swords and spears of love ("gladiis amoris," "amoris iacula") and defended by the shield of patience ("scutum patientiae," "patientiae clypeo"), the mind of the holy man draws strength to sustain his injuries: "ad perferenda mala sumit fortitudinem" (VIII.ii.2, p. 382). In the war of tribulation, saints like Job sometimes employ the shield of patience, at other times the darts of teaching, and thus display a marvelous skill of virtue that bravely endures exterior calamities and wisely counters perverse thoughts within themselves: "peruersa intus sapienter doceant" (III. xxi.39, p. 140). Thus our hero Job ("bellator noster"), wounded in body, stands erect in the fortress of his mind: "erectus intrinsecus munimine permanet mentis" (III.x.17, p. 126). Conquering himself through patience, he possesses his own soul, the inner victory that renders him invincible in adversity: "sese ad contraria inuictum parat" (V.xvi.33, p. 241).

Gregory's allegorical use of traditionally epic images betrays a clear Stoic influence. In his ninth-century biography of Gregory, John the Deacon calls him "arte philosophus,"[31] and F. Holmes Dudden

31. John the Deacon, *Vita* I.i, PL 75, c63.

rightly considers that title an indication of Gregory's mastery of moral philosophy.[32] Gregory himself observes that although Christ first chose the uneducated to confound the wise, he afterwards called philosophers as well to discipleship (XXXIII.xviii.34, p. 1705). As a Christian philosopher, Gregory makes what G. R. Evans has called an innovative and remarkably "confident use . . . of his borrowed philosophical ideas," introducing Stoic and Neoplatonic teachings into biblical contexts and altering their fundamental terms in the process.[33]

In the Senecan narrative, as we have seen, a personified Fortune, who is virtually identical with God (*Deus mundus*), puts the Wise Man to the test. When Gregory adopts the Stoic images of the wrestler and the gladiator in his exposition of Job, the part of the Adversary is redefined so that, as Villy Sørensen puts it, "*fortuna* in Seneca corresponds to Satan in Job."[34] The resemblances are readily apparent. Both Fortune and Satan act to deprive the Virtuous Man of exterior goods and measure their blows according to the moral stature of their human opponent. Both are unable to affect the inner disposition of the hero, whose fortitude displays itself in mental constancy (*constantia mentis*) and who grows in spiritual goods, especially self-knowledge, as a result of material loss.

There are, however, significant differences as well. When confronted with the problem of the innocent sufferer, Seneca defines the issue as a purely subjective one, dependent on the rational response of the Sage. Correctly perceived, nothing is evil, and "no evil can befall a good man" (p. 7) (*De Prov.* II.1: "Nihil accidere bono viro mali potest"). For Gregory and for the author of Job, however, evil is objective and the question centers on justice, God's and man's. Gregory, meditating on Christ and Job, insists that the just do suffer, but that that affliction in no way compromises the justice of God. Indeed, everything we suffer is just: "iusta sunt cuncta quae patimur" (II.xviii.31, p. 79).

32. F. Holmes Dudden, *Gregory the Great: His Place in History and Thought*, vol. 1 (New York: Russell and Russell, 1905, 1967), p. 76.

33. G. R. Evans, *The Thought of Gregory the Great* (Cambridge: Cambridge University Press, 1986), p. 65.

34. Villy Sørensen, *Seneca: The Humanist at the Court of Nero*, trans. W. Glyn Jones (Edinburgh: Canongate; Chicago: University of Chicago Press, 1984), p. 200.

Gregory finds a dramatic answer to this apparent self-contradiction in the person of the devil and his malicious intent. Inspired by such New Testament passages as 1 Peter 5:8, Gregory represents the Joban Adversary no longer as an actual member of the heavenly court, as the Book of Job implies, but rather as personified Evil, the Old Enemy of both God and humankind.[35] The devil exercises his terrible force against Job, but his real target is God; Job simply occupies the middleground of the conflict between God and the devil: "Inter Deum itaque et diabolum beatus Iob in medio materia certaminis fuit" (Preface III.8, p. 14). By driving a wedge between God and the scriptural Adversary and depicting the conflict between them as vehement and cosmic in proportion, Gregory avoids the problem of attributing injustice to God.

At the same time, as Carole Straw observes, Gregory avoids the Manichaean position of two gods, one evil and one good, by pointedly affirming "the omnipotence of God and the unity of the divine dispensation."[36] The devil has a kind of contract with God which allows him a limited freedom to gratify his own perverse desire to torment others. God, for his part, uses the devil's attacks to accomplish an entirely different, benevolent result. Thus the divine plan is implemented even as it is opposed: "Sic sic diuinum consilium dum deuitatur, impletur" (VI.xviii.29, p. 305). As Straw puts it, the devil paradoxically " 'fulfills' God's will by his very 'resistance' to it," and "the anger and evil of the devil bring to completion the kindness and mercy of God" (p. 62). The Lord therefore permits his brave soldier Job to be attacked again and again only to increase Job's glory as a conquerer in proportion to the repeated assaults of the defeated enemy (II.xi.19, pp. 71–72).

Pitted against such a malignant, invisible enemy, Job achieves a heroic stature greater than that of the Stoic Sage opposed to mundane Misfortune. Indeed, Job's passionate outcry becomes for Gregory the measure of his true fortitude. When Gregory comments upon Job's lamentation, he cites the Aristotelian doctrine of the Golden

---

35. See Neil Forsyth, *The Old Enemy: Satan and the Combat Myth* (Princeton: Princeton University Press, 1987), esp. pp. 107–23, for an excellent discussion of the changing biblical image of the *adversarius*.

36. Carole Straw, *Gregory the Great: Perfection in Imperfection* (Berkeley: University of California Press, 1988), p. 62.

Mean to refute the Stoic notion that true fortitude consists in *apatheia*, the absence of feeling. Job, he says, observes the rule of true philosophy (II.xvi.29, p. 77: "uerae philosophiae regulam tenuit"), which holds that the measure of true virtue is neither hardness of heart not irrational grief, but rather the submission of sorrow to a reason enlightened by faith (II.xvi.28, p. 77). Indeed, as we shall see, Gregory understands the felt experience of suffering, an actual share in Christ's passion and death, to be a necessary prerequisite for the attainment of true wisdom.

Gregory's exegetical expansion of the Senecan images of athlete and warrior is warranted by both Scripture itself and previous Christian treatments of Job.[37] A key verse in the Book of Job terms the earthly life of humankind a warfare: "Militia est vita hominis super terram" (Job 7:1), and a variety of New Testament texts (1 Corinth. 9:7, Phil. 2:25, 2 Tim. 2:3–4, Phil. 1:2, Eph. 6:11–17) describe the Christian as a soldier of Christ. Interpretation through concordance, moreover, inspired exegetes to associate martial images with other biblical passages that were read in parallel with Job.[38]

Cassiodorus (c. A.D. 480–575), for instance, reads Psalm 37 as an instance of ethopoeia in which David impersonates Job as the unconquered soldier of Christ.[39] The psalm, Cassiodorus observes, voices sentiments similar to those found in the Book of Job and has a similar structure, moving from a two-part narrative of affliction in body and soul to an expression of healing consolation ("consolatio medicinae salutaris") and trust in God, and ending with a praise of God as Savior. David playing the part of Job ("Iob este Dauidicus") becomes strong and triumphant in his spiritual mastery of misfortune (p. 353). Thus Job, the archetypal soldier of Christ and victor over mortal life, prefigures both the strife and the victory of all the Lord's warriors: "Domini milites" (p. 353).

Prudentius too takes the Book of Job as a key point of reference when he interprets the Abraham story in Genesis allegorically as a

37. Lewalski cites a variety of Christian commentators, including Prosper, Methodius, Tertullian, Cassiodorus, and Prudentius (*Milton's Brief Epic*, p. 22).

38. Explicit biblical references to Job occur in Ezechiel 14:14, Tobit 2:15, and James 5:11.

39. Cassiodorus, *Expositio Psalmorum*, ed. M. Adriaen, CCSL 97 (Turnhout: Brepols, 1958), p. 343. Subsequent citations are parenthetical by page.

spiritual battle between personified virtues and vices. Indeed, Prudentius' *Psychomachia* (A.D. 405) stands as the most important literary precedent for both Gregory's conversion of authoritative biblical
metaphor into bellicose allegory and his exegetical use of epic materials. In Prudentius' poem, Long-Suffering ("Patientia") endures the
vicious attack of Wrath ("Ira"). Unable to hurt Long-Suffering, who
is protected by a corselet, Wrath exhausts her strength in fury and
finally slays herself. Observing that Wrath is her own enemy, the
invincible Long-Suffering walks unharmed through the battlefield
accompanied by a noble man, her earthly exemplification, Job.[40]
Prudentius goes on to observe that all the other Virtues rely upon
Long-Suffering, because there is by definition no *virtus* without the
strength ("fortitudo") represented in patient endurance.

In his depiction of battle and especially in his portrayal of Wrath
("Ira"), Prudentius uses Virgilian language, echoing in particular
Book 12 of the *Aeneid*. As Macklin Smith phrases it, "Prudentius . . .
uses epic to compose allegory."[41] The procedure deliteralizes pagan
epic, exposing at once the falsity of its letter and the heroic ideal to
which it gives expression and revealing the truth of its Christian
allegory as an authentically "other" form of heroism.

Gregory's procedure in the *Moralia* is similar. To establish the
Book of Job as a heroic work, Gregory first calls attention to the epic
(especially Virgilian) question of the pious sufferer that informs the
Book: "cur tot flagella pertulit" (Preface III.7, p. 12). Gregory then
elaborates an allegory of Job that uses the battle scenes and athletic
games of classical epic; he incorporates the heroic topic of *fortitudo et
sapientia* in characterizing Job as a soldier of Christ, a *miles Christi*;
and he consciously rejects a grand style exposition of Job, refusing to
submit heavenly words to the rules of Donatus (*Ad Leandrum* 5, p. 7)
and choosing instead the humble style (*sermo humilis*) of a Christian
teacher. Epic thus becomes the allegory of Scripture, and epic truth
(as the Otherness of epic) becomes identified with the biblical Word
itself, understood typologically with reference to Christ, the Church,
and the individual Christian.

40. I use the Loeb Classical Library edition of the *Psychomachia* in *Prudentius*,
vol. 1, trans. H. J. Thomson (Cambridge: Harvard University Press, 1949, 1969).
41. Macklin Smith, *Prudentius' Psychomachia: A Reexamination* (Princeton:
Princeton University Press, 1976), p. 105.

The primary Christological reference, according to which Job's sufferings in body and soul foreshadow the redemptive passion of Christ, contributes more than any other cause to the Gregorian redefinition of heroic fortitude. Gregory observes that the name Job translates into Latin as *dolens*, so that the Redeemer's suffering might be signified by both Job's name and his wounds: "per eius et nomen et uulnera" (VI.I.1, p. 284). Job's bodily afflictions from head to foot also prefigure the persecutions endured by the members of Christ's Mystical Body, the Church.

In this context fortitude no longer qualifies the public action of a citizen-soldier seeking *fama*; it marks instead a person's heroic acceptance of God's Will in the form of the cross. Just as danger, especially the danger of death, occasions the fearlessness of natural fortitude, the boldness of divine fortitude originates in the Fear of the Lord (*Timor Dei*), the gift of the Spirit that strengthens the mind to regard the loss of temporal things as nothing in comparison to the loss of God Himself (see V.xvi.33, p. 241). In this way, Gregory avers, fear gives rise to fortitude, fortitude to patience, and patience to perfection.

The Hero's Sapience

The prudent man, according to Aristotle, is "able to deliberate well about what is good and advantageous for himself . . . as a means to the good life in general."[42] That pragmatic ability, in turn, depends upon his self-knowledge (including the knowledge of his own ignorance) and his knowledge of ultimate causes. Thus, as we have seen, the Neoplatonists considered it the greatest wisdom for a person to recall his true spiritual homeland and choose a course of earthly detachment in keeping with his soul's high destiny.

For Saint Paul, however, true wisdom is not the human achievement of a "wise man" (*sapiens*) exercising his understanding; rather, true wisdom is revealed in the person of Christ who is "the power of God and the wisdom of God" (1 Corinth. 1:24). According to Paul, this divine wisdom, which glories in the cross, seems foolishness to

---

42. Aristotle, *Nicomachean Ethics* VI.v.i, p. 337.

the Greek philosophers, and one attains to it not by one's own rational powers but by having instead "the mind of Christ" (1 Corinth. 2:16). Indeed, one can reason rightly about life's choices only if one first believes, if faith enlightens the *ratio*.

Gregory follows Saint Paul in making the sacred scriptures, as the revealed Word of God, the standard for a true moral philosophy. According to Gregory, we come to fulfill the Delphic oracle, to know ourselves, through reading the Bible: "Holy Writ is set before the eyes of the mind like a kind of mirror, that we may see our inward face in it; for therein we learn the deformities; therein we learn the beauties that we possess" (vol. 1, p. 67) (II.I.1, p. 59: "Scriptura sacra mentis oculis quasi quoddam speculum opponitur, ut interna nostra facies in ipsa uideatur"). As Gregory's dedicatory letter to Leander of Seville makes clear, he himself reads the Book of Job as a personal mirror. Sick for over a year with digestive ailments and burdened with pastoral responsibilities, Gregory muses over his commentary on Job: "And perchance it was this that Divine Providence designed, that I, a stricken one, should set forth Job stricken, and that by these scourges I should the more perfectly enter into the feelings of one that was scourged" (vol. 1, p. 10) (*Ad Leandrum* 5, p. 6: "Et fortasse hoc diuinae prouidentiae consilium fuit, ut percussum Iob percussus exponerem, et flagellati mentem melius per flagella sentirem").[43]

For Gregory, as for the Stoics and Neoplatonists, self-knowledge is fundamental to wisdom. According to the Gregorian understanding, however, human beings are lacking in self-knowledge, in wisdom, not because of a Platonic fall into bodily and sensory experience, but because of the original sin that separated humankind on earth from intimacy with God and thus precipitated a darkening of human nature in both body and soul (IX.xxxiii.51, p. 492). Having lost the light of invisible things that transfigured the visible things of paradise (V.xxxiv.61, p. 261), and being thus expelled from paradisal joys, humankind immerses itself in the love of exterior things that can be seen and touched. The soul is then blinded in its inner spiritual vision to the extent that it is distracted by exterior impressions, clouded with outward images: "tantoque ab interna speculatione

43. For biographical information, see Jeffrey Richards, *Consul of God: The Life and Times of Gregory the Great* (London and Boston: Routledge and Kegan Paul, 1980).

caecata est quanto foras deformiter sparsa" (V.xxxiv.61, p. 261). Only with great efforts does a person turn aside from his own bodily appearance and direct his soul to the knowledge of itself ("ad cognitionem suam") as a spiritual entity. Thinking of himself in spiritual terms, he can prepare a way for himself toward the consideration of the eternal Good: "ut semetipsam sine corporea imagine cogitet et cogitando se, uiam sibi usque ad considerandam aeternitatis substantiam paret."

God Himself aids humankind in its recovery of self-knowledge in various ways. First of all, the promptings of conscience, as the inner voice of God, recall the soul to the knowledge of itself (XVI.xxviii.35, p. 819: "ad cognitionem sui anima subtilius reuocetur") and allow it to behold within itself its own hidden judge. The elect thus remember that they are created in the image and likeness of the Creator and strive to live in accord with that perceived similarity: "ad auctoris sui imaginem ac similitudinem si condita meminit, et iuxta perceptae similitudinis ordinem incedit" (XXX.xvii.56, p. 1529).

That divine image and likeness gains a unique visible expression in the Incarnate God, in the Word-Made-Flesh. Scripture therefore allows for a typological self-knowledge. One's own humanity emerges in conformity with the pattern of Christ's life as an *imitatio*, even as Job, the Old Testament "homo verus," foreshadows the Christ who is True God and True Man. Gregory's emphasis on self-knowledge thus leads him to characterize Job according to a double image. As Lawrence Besserman observes, Job emerges "as a patient Christian saint" in Gregory's historical and moral readings; as a "type of Christ" in Gregory's allegory.[44]

Gregory's Christological approach to Job's suffering provides a basis for his redefinition of not only *fortitudo* but also *sapientia* as heroic virtues. Suffering is for Gregory both the means and the expression of true wisdom because, as Straw phrases it, "through life in the body, man comes to know himself and his Creator, to understand what it means to be human and, by contrast, to glimpse something more of divine perfection."[45] That comparative self-knowledge,

---

44. Lawrence L. Besserman, *The Legend of Job in the Middle Ages* (Cambridge: Harvard University Press, 1979), p. 55.
45. Straw, *Gregory the Great*, p. 127.

which "finds its center in man's carnal existence," depends on a number of characteristically Gregorian juxtapositions: Mutability and Immutability, Way and Destination, Body and Soul, Emotion and Reason.[46]

As Straw puts it, in Gregory's view the "sorrows of mutability come from Adam's rejection of stability in God."[47] Mutability, in short, marks our postlapsarian condition, making it a continuous, miserable alternation of prosperity and adversity, good times and bad: "mortalitatis lapsum per prospera et aduersa uariantem quam despicabilem" (IV.xii.23, p. 179). Thus Job, meditating on how human hope is raised by prosperous circumstances only to be dashed by troubles, recalls with regret the changeless state of happiness that humankind could have retained in paradise. Having lost its standing position in the cosmos through a falling away from God, humankind experiences time itself as slippery ("quasi lubrico temporalitatis") and suffers both exterior and interior change whenever it tries to raise itself up to better works: "Quam tamen mutabilitatem non solum exterius, sed interius quoque homo patitur, dum ad meliora exsurgere opera conatur" (XI.1.68, p. 625).

Thus life itself is a constant trial. The striving person discovers in himself only instability and the tendency to change, so much so that, despite his best intentions, he falls again and again and lacks the strength to maintain a contemplative stance: "vult in contemplatione stare, sed non ualet" (VIII.vi.8, p. 386). In this way he remembers what he has lost, the paradisal strength of contemplation and the firmness of original fortitude: "uim contemplationis perdidit, robur conditae fortitudinis amisit" (IX.xxxiii.50, p. 491). Only by embracing in humble obedience the trial and suffering that belong to fallen humanity does a person grasp and reconquer, albeit to a limited extent, his own unfallen condition and its original constancy rooted in God. He wills what God wills. Unlike the *constantia mentis* of the Stoics, however, Gregorian wisdom (to use Straw's phrase) "demands not *apatheia*, but *passio*" (p. 199), the willingness to suffer, the firm "yes" to one's own experience of weakness.

The changing nature of things, the painful instability of the fallen

---

46. Ibid.
47. Ibid., p. 109.

world, helps a person to remember that he is in motion himself, a pilgrim on a journey, an exile from his true homeland. Confused by the blindness of exile due to original sin, a person might mistakenly believe the place of exile to be his Fatherland: "ut exsilium patriam crederet" (VII.ii.2, p. 335).[48] Frequent perturbations, however, prevent us from loving the way instead of the destination, and the elect live out of the consciousness that the present life is a road leading to the Fatherland: "uia quippe est vita praesens, qua ad patriam tendimus" (XXIII.xxiv.47, p. 1179). The wayfarer does not desire to remain with transitory things but to arrive at eternal things (XV.lvii.68, p. 792). Similarly, the pilgrim people of God experience heartfelt longing for the supernal Fatherland (XVIII.xxx.48, p. 916). Indeed, it is the habit of the just to consider the transitoriness of the present life in order to perceive from the flight of passing external things the things that endure within us: "quae manentia intus" (Preface to Book XII, p. 628).

Corporeal mutability, even more than the exterior blows of fortune, teaches the Christian Wise Man to consider what is immutable in himself. Gregory therefore describes Job as a philosopher who purposely sits upon a dunghill in order to consider in that physical context his own bodily decay: "ut considerationem fragilitatis suae etiam ex circumstantibus traheret" (III.vii.10, p. 120). Job placed his ulcerous body there, Gregory says, in order to remind himself how quickly the body returns to stench: "quod festine corpus ad fetorem rediret."

Such a bodily positioning frees the mind and gives the body an instrumental share in the redemption of the soul. Thus, as an exemplum of the wise man (*consiliator*), a sorrowing Job (*dolens*) hastens in thought from temporal to eternal things and, although still in the world, mentally passes beyond it: "mente iam extra mundum surgit" (I.xxv.34, p. 44). To do so is to share paradoxically in the immutability of the angelic nature through the awareness of one's own mutability (V.xxxviii.68, p. 267). Unable to contemplate God steadfastly and directly like the angels, a human being can nonetheless consider the fragility of his own body and thus, loosened from its chain, rise up in spirit to the consideration of the God who is Spirit (IV.xxxiv.68, p. 213).

48. See also I.xxv.34, p. 43.

Gregory's own exegetical approach to the Book of Job exemplifies this kind of mental movement from the slippery body of the literal text to its abiding spiritual meaning. If we understand Job's words correctly, his superficially blasphemous outcry ("eius maledictio") actually expresses the right judgment of a man not stirred by wrath but rather tranquil with true teaching: "non est ira commoti sed doctrina tranquilli" (IV.i.3, p. 165). Outwardly ("foras") he speaks in sorrow, but allegorically ("intus") he administers the power of a healing medicine to the wounded: "uulneratis intus ostendit uirtutem medicaminis" (IV.i.3, p. 166). Through a polysemous discourse Job thus combines in his person both the instructed and the instructor, the patient and the physician, the Boethius who weeps and the Philosophia who consoles.

Job's Boethian Heroism

Using epic to construct his Joban allegory, Gregory presents Job as a warrior whose *fortitudo* surpasses that of his Iliadic counterparts, as a philosophical traveler whose *sapientia* exceeds that of Odysseus on his homeward journey. Job's human nature, perfected in wisdom and power through suffering, reflects Christ's own divine humanity and far surpasses in heroic virtue the excellence of even an allegorized Aeneas. The biblical hero who emerges from Gregory's *Moralia* grows in self-knowledge through his trials and finally comes face to face with a God like the one to whom Lady Philosophy directs her pupil Boethius. As G. R. Evans observes, Gregory's God, like that of *The Consolation of Philosophy*, is "one immortal, supremely good, tranquil and unchanging, supremely happy and reasonable being" who governs the world providentially according to a wise and omnipotent plan.[49]

It is likely that Gregory knew Boethius' *Consolation* and was inspired by it in his commentary on Job. Saint Thomas Aquinas, following both Maimonides and Gregory, was keenly aware of the

---

49. Evans, *Thought of Gregory the Great*, p. 57. Evans calls attention to the quest of Christian apologists like Hilary of Poitiers (c. 315–67) who sought "Scriptural evidence that the divine attributes were in fact those felt to be appropriate on philosophical grounds to the Supreme Being" (p. 56).

structural and thematic parallels between the Book of Job and Boethius' *Consolation* and called attention to them in his thirteenth-century commentary.[50] Indeed, as Aquinas interprets it, Job is virtually a biblical *Consolation*. The two books, one scriptural and therefore theological, the other philosophical, teach the same truth (*forma tractatus*) and employ a similar narrative and pedagogical method (*forma tractandi*).

Aquinas' Prologue to his Joban *expositio* begins with a refutation of early philosophers, such as Democritus and Empedocles, who attributed the majority of occurrences to chance. Aquinas cites "the diligence of later philosophers," who have argued "that natural things are controlled by providence," because the regular "movement of heaven and of the stars," as well as other predictable natural effects, point to the governance of things "by some supereminent intelligence."[51] Aquinas then raises the key issue (also central to Boethius' *Consolation*) whether "human affairs" are similarly governed "by some providence or superior ordinance" (pp. 67–68). The "whole intention" of the Book of Job is, he says, to show "through plausible arguments that human affairs are ruled by divine providence" (p. 68). Since the causeless affliction of the just "seems to undermine totally the foundation of providence," the Book of Job purposely raises and resolves the *quaestio* through a test case: "the many grave afflictions of a certain man, perfect in every virtue, named Job" (p. 68).

Job, like Boethius, is an innocent sufferer. When Job bitterly laments the loss of his property, his children, his health, and his good name, he lays bare his wound in the sight of God and men. Aquinas immediately draws the parallel: "So too Boethius in the beginning of *On the Consolation of Philosophy* disclosed his sadness to show how to mitigate it with reason, and so Job disclosed his sadness by speaking" (p. 100).

Like Gregory, who insists that Job observed "the rule of true philosophy" ("uerae philosophiae regulam") in his outcry by keeping a balance between his emotion and his reason, Aquinas attributes to

50. For a discussion of Aquinas' debt to Maimonides and Albert the Great see Beryl Smalley, *The Study of the Bible in the Middle Ages* (Oxford: Blackwell, 1952; Notre Dame: University of Notre Dame Press, 1964), p. 302.

51. Thomas Aquinas, *Literal Exposition on Job: A Scriptural Commentary Concerning Providence*, trans. Anthony Damico, ed. Martin D. Yaffe (Atlanta, Ga.: Scholars Press, 1989), p. 67. Subsequent citations are parenthetical by page.

Job "such moderate sadness that it was subject to reason" (p. 87). Following Gregory, Aquinas rejects the opinion of the Stoics, who said "that external goods are not the goods of man and that there could be no sadness in the spirit of the wise man over their loss." In opposition to them, he endorses the view of the Peripatetics, who held that "external goods are indeed a kind of goods for man," and therefore "the wise man is moderately saddened at the loss of external goods." As Aquinas observes, "reason cannot remove the condition of nature," and the "sensual nature" of human beings is naturally delighted by pleasant and useful things, "pained and saddened over harmful things" (p. 99).[52]

Whereas Gregory distinguishes between the literal and the allegorical levels of Job's words, between what is exposed to the outside ("foras") and hidden within ("intus"), Aquinas differentiates between the various levels of Job's psychological makeup. In his emotional outpouring, Job "speaks in the character of his sensual side, expressing his feeling, which has room only for the present corporeal goods and evils" (p. 107). Thus Job sometimes enacts "the role of an afflicted man" (p. 183), "the role of an embittered man" (p. 184). While allowing his sensual nature its due, however, Job still affirms and assents to the divine will in his rational nature, combining the steadfast patience of his mind and will with human feelings of sadness appropriate to the terrible losses he has experienced (see p. 140).

To be sure, powerful feelings can subvert the reason, even as emotional language can impair one's ability to think objectively. When Gregory and Aquinas treat that danger in their analysis of Job's rebuke of his despairing wife, the exchange between the couple becomes a biblical analogue to Lady Philosophy's dismissal of the strumpet Muses.[53] Job's unnamed wife speaks only once, encouraging her afflicted husband to curse God and die: "Benedic Deo et morere" (Job 2:9).[54] In that single enigmatic utterance, the commen-

---

52. Aquinas refers again and again to the opposed positions of the Stoics and Peripatetics on the grief of the Wise Man. See also pp. 115, 139, and 140.

53. For a discussion of this passage from the perspective of medieval mysogyny see my "Job's Wife, Walter's Wife, and the Wife of Bath," in *Old Testament Women in Western Literature*, ed. Raymond-Jean Frontain and Jan Wojcik (Conway: University of Central Arkansas Press, 1991), pp. 92–107.

54. The Latin euphemism, which substitutes "bless" for "curse," reflects the original Hebrew use of euphemism as a standard practice in this and similarly blasphemous passages.

tators find a reenactment of Eve's temptation of Adam: "uerba sua
Eua repetit" (*Moralia* III.viii.14, p. 123). When Job's wife at the
instigation of Satan leads Job into despair, she not only speaks words
of a bad persuasion (III.viii.14, p. 123: "male suadentis uerba"); she
also seduces Job with blandishments (III.viii.13, p. 122: "per uerba
blandiens loquitur") and, appealing to his sensuality, pierces his
heart with the force of love: "uis amoris cor perforat." Job, however,
resists her Siren-like temptation to suicide. Indeed, when he corrects
and instructs his erring wife, he offers a model for the exegetes who
either allegorize Job's own malediction (when, for example, he literally curses the day of his birth) as an articulation of dogma, or
consider it the expression of only his lower, sensual nature, his
carnal, feminine self, not his whole person.[55]

Job's carnal self, exteriorized in his weeping wife, can find no
meaning in his suffering. As Aquinas observes, however, when Job
speaks out of his rational nature "in the manner of a debater" (p. 156),
he answers his heretical would-be consolers, who interpret misfortune only as a divine punishment for wrongdoing, by pointing to
three possible causes for affliction: to protect people by restraining
the malice of the wicked, to manifest the exemplary virtue of the
good, and "to punish sinners" (p. 156). The second reason, as Aquinas
insists, applies to Job: "This was the cause of blessed Job's adversity—
that his virtue should be made manifest to all" (p. 83). God tests Job
by permitting Satan to test him, not that God might know "what kind
of man he is, but in order to have others know him and so that the
man may know himself" (p. 153). When Job, therefore, stripped of
his earthly goods, reflects on his own nakedness at birth and at death

---

55. According to Gregory, the word "woman" (*mulier*) in Scripture either literally designates a member of the female sex or figuratively names weakness: "In
sacro eloquio mulier aut pro sexu ponitur aut pro infirmitate" (XI.xlix.65, p. 623).
Gregory goes on to contrast the discretion of a strong man ("vir fortis") with the weak,
indiscreet mind ("mens infirma uel indiscreta") of a woman. Elsewhere (*Moralia*
XXX.xvi.54, p. 1528) Gregory interprets the creation of Eve during the sleep of Adam
in a way that associates woman's nature with a man's emotional sphere, his uncon-
scious, his "animal part." A man's reason should rule his emotions, Gregory says, even
as a man governs his wife. For a similar gendered distinction between the higher and
lower parts of the soul see Cicero, *Tusculan Disputations*, II.xxi, pp. 200–205. See my
"Translating Job as Female," forthcoming in *Translation Theory and Practice in the
Middle Ages*, ed. Jeanette Beer (Kalamazoo, Mich.: Medieval Institute Publications),
for a discussion of Job and gender symbolism.

(Job 1:21), he knows himself as a creature radically dependent in prosperity and adversity upon "the judgment of divine providence" (p. 89). Like the Stoics, Job "demonstrate[s] rationally" (p. 88) the right of God to dispossess him of goods and the injustice of human complaint.[56]

Rational argument alone, however, cannot resolve the *quaestio* of divine justice and providence—especially since Job's affliction does *not* manifest his virtue to his companions, but rather compromises it in their eyes. Eliphaz, Bildad, Zophar, and Elihu continue to defend God's justice by blaming Job himself for his troubles. In answer Job posits "another life in which just men are rewarded and evil men are punished" (p. 194) and prophetically declares his faith in eternal life (p. 224), in the resurrection of the dead (pp. 230, 270), and in the resurrected Christ as his Redeemer (pp. 268–69): "For I know that my Redeemer liveth" (Job 19:25).

Aquinas, therefore, reconstructs the Joban *disputatio* about divine providence on three levels of response correspondent to the threefold Boethian definition of human nature. Job responds as a sensual, mortal being with tearful lamentation, with the longing for death. As a rational being, he resigns himself virtuously to God's will. As a besouled, immortal being, he looks forward to a heavenly homecoming. The last and highest level of response, which makes Job an Old Testament Christian, has, as Aquinas notes, its closest analogue in the teaching of the Neoplatonists:

> For the Platonists have posited that the souls of men were derived from the souls of stars. Hence, when human souls preserve their dignity by living according to reason, they return to the splendor of the stars whence they have descended. Hence, one reads in the *Dream of Scipio* that "rulers and preservers" of cities "who have set out from here," namely, from heaven, "return there." In this work, too, the author gives one to understand that he was not placing the ultimate remuneration for virtue in temporal goods but in spiritual goods after this life. (p. 406)

56. Job's speech, "The Lord gave, and the Lord hath taken away" (Job 1:21), provides a biblical parallel to the speech of the Cynic philosopher Demetrius, quoted approvingly by Seneca in *De Prov.* V.5–6, p. 37: "I shall make no protest against your taking back what once you gave." As G. R. Evans notes (*Thought of Gregory the Great*, p. 31), Gregory the Great actually uses a formal syllogism to demonstrate logically the justice of human suffering (II.xviii.31, p. 79).

Whereas Gregory emphasizes that only a *vir*, heroic in wisdom and fortitude, can mirror the wisdom and power of God displayed in his providential plan, Aquinas stresses that only a *homo* who has fully realized his own hierarchical humanity in its sensual, rational, and divine dimensions can meet the God of Providence. That epiphanic encounter, like the concluding book of Boethius' *Consolation*, underscores at once the greatness of human nature and the radical insufficiency of human wisdom "to comprehend the truth of divine providence" (p. 415). The *homo* who is a hero (*vir*), however, can sustain the knowledge of his own limits and thus end his life's odyssey in a return home, both to himself and to God.

Indeed, the Christian hero is, by definition, at once an authentic human being and a saint. In an etymological discussion that succinctly summarizes the historical development of the idea of heroism from antiquity to the Middle Ages, John of Salisbury first derives the Latin adjective *verum* ("true") from the Greek word *heron* ("heroic"), meaning "secure and stable or certain and clear" and used to describe the mythological demigods who "attained a state of security and stability by being associated with the gods in ancient mythology."[57] He then goes on to translate both terms, *verum* and *heron*, with "a catholic word," *saint*. "'Confirmed' in virtue or glory," in fortitude and wisdom, the Christian saint achieves through grace a Boethian transfer "from this world's inconstancy and emptiness to the glory of true certainty and security," which is found in God alone. Such a saint, the commentaries aver, was Job.

57. John of Salisbury, *The Metalogicon: A Twelfth-Century Defense of the Verbal and Logical Arts of the Trivium*, trans. Daniel D. McGarry (Berkeley: University of California Press, 1955), 4.34, p. 255.

4 Hagiographic Romance

As the preeminent Old Testament type of the suffering and resurrected Christ, Job foreshadows all the saints, male and female, whose steadfast virtue, subjected to satanic testing through serial misfortunes, merits the reward of restored happiness. Allegorized as an Iliadic spiritual battle and an Odyssean spiritual journey back to the Fatherland, the history of patient Job, sorely tried and ultimately victorious, stands parallel to the heroic narratives of both pagan and Christian saints and mediates between them. It recalls, on the one hand, the afflictive adventures of Aeneas, Odysseus, and the virtuous young lovers in Hellenistic romance and inspires, on the other, imitation in the *legenda* of popular Joban saints like Eustace, Griselda, and Constance.[1] These *legenda*, as we shall see, mediate in turn between the books of Job and Boethius, using

1. Lawrence L. Besserman rightly observes that "an awareness of the various manifestations of Job in medieval culture puts us in a better position to appreciate works like Chaucer's "Man of Law's Tale," Gower's *Tale of Constance*, and romances like *Sir Isumbras, Robert of Cisyle, Amis and Amiloun*, as well as other stories of the Eustace-Constance-Griselda type—that is, stories of suffering, loss, trial, and reward at the hands of a merciful God" (*The Legend of Job in the Middle Ages* [Cambridge: Harvard University Press, 1979], p. 113). As Derek Pearsall notes, many Middle English chivalric romances—among them, *Octavian, Athelston, Sir Ysumbras, Sir Eglamour, Torrent of Portygale*, and *Sir Triamour*—exhibit a basic plot of trial, constancy, and reward. See "The Development of Middle English Romance," *Medieval Studies* 27 (1965): 92. Sometimes the exemplification of virtue in such romances verges on hagiography. See Ojars Kratins, "The Middle English *Amis and Amiloun*: Chivalric Romance or Secular Hagiography?" *PMLA* 81 (1966): 347–54.

Boethius' *Consolation* intertextually to qualify the world of (mis)fortune and human pain; Job to typify the realm of moral constancy, providential design, and happy endings.

Converting the story of Job into a romantic saint's legend necessarily required (1) a focus on the so-called frame narrative of initial prosperity, loss, testing, and miraculous restoration; (2) a reduction of the central dialogues to one more test in an expandable series of superhuman trials; and (3) a static characterization of the hero as one who remains unchanged in the midst of a mutable universe. We have already observed how the episodes of classical epic, interpreted as moral *exempla*, found a romantic retelling in the popular works of Chariton, Xenophon of Ephesus, Heliodorus, Achilles Tatius, and Apuleius. Similarly, the impulse to moralize the Book of Job, to make its hero exemplary for a wide Christian audience, led to its retelling as hagiographic romance.[2]

The ability of these romantic *legenda* to evoke multiple narrative parallels—from the Bible, from popular fiction and folklore, as well as from philosophical works like the *Consolation* of Boethius—enhanced their exemplary value and imaginative appeal for their medieval auditors, who were invited to draw analogies between the *legenda* and their own lives, extending the moral of each story from one application to another. The more parallels one could see, the better. Thomas Heffernan rightly observes that the medieval "hagiographer was especially concerned to use deliberate verbal reminiscences of earlier texts (principally biblical) in constructing his narrative."[3] Such echoes simultaneously define the saint as a follower and imitator of Christ and canonize him or her as imitable by others. Whereas saints' lives with a firm historical grounding tend to emphasize biblical parallels, the tales of hagiographic romance selfconsciously allude to both scriptural and secular stories, evoking

---

2. For pertinent discussions of hagiographic romance, see Diana T. Childress, "Between Romance and Legend: 'Secular Hagiography' in Middle English Literature," *Philological Quarterly* 57 (1978): 311–22; Andrea Hopkins, *The Sinful Knights: A Study of Middle English Penitential Romance* (Oxford: Clarendon Press, 1990), especially pp. 1–20. Following A. V. C. Schmidt and Nicolas Jacobs, Hopkins emphasizes the comic and didactic nature of romance in general, and religious romance in particular.

3. Thomas J. Heffernan, "An Analysis of the Narrative Motifs in the Legend of St. Eustace," *Medievalia et Humanistica*, n.s. 6 (1975): 68–69.

both simultaneously, if not equally. As Tomas Hägg has phrased it, "The hagiographic novel is the life of a saint in which the fictitious element has got the upper hand."[4]

According to Hägg, "the novelistic form" in late antiquity "was the means of attracting pagan readers."[5] Beginning in the second century with the emergence of the apocryphal Acts of the Apostles, "the same readership which provided a market for the Hellenistic novel was . . . devouring stories about apostles, martyrs, and saints."[6] Not only were the *Ethiopica* and *Leucippe and Clitophon* allegorized and attributed to Christian authorship and thus canonized;[7] original compositions—among them, the widely circulated *Paul and Thecla* (second century) and the popular Petrine *Recognitiones* of Pseudo-Clement (fourth century)—transposed the episodes of pre-Christian romances into new, explicitly Christian, apologetic contexts.[8] Finally, in the late fifth or early sixth century, possibly in the Vivarium of Cassiodorus, the *Historia Apollonii Regis Tyri*, based on a now lost pagan Greek romance,[9] appeared in a thoroughly Christian recension.[10]

These late antique Christian romances prepared the way for the medieval saints' lives of Joban figures like Eustace, Griselda, and

4. Tomas Hägg, *The Novel in Antiquity* (Berkeley: University of California Press, 1983), p. 164.

5. Ibid.

6. Ibid., p. 161.

7. See Hägg, *Novel in Antiquity*, p. 59; Heinrich Dörrie, "Die griechischen Romane und das Christentum," *Philologus* 93 (n.s. 47) (1938): 273–76.

8. For a treatment of *Paul and Thecla*, see Hägg, *Novel in Antiquity*, pp. 154–62; Gordon Hall Gerould, *Saints' Legends* (Boston and New York: Houghton-Mifflin, 1916), p. 33. For a discussion of the *Recognitiones*, see Ben Edwin Perry, *The Ancient Romances: A Literary-Historical Account of Their Origins* ((Berkeley: University of California Press, 1967), pp. 285–93; Hägg, pp. 162–64. According to Heffernan, there are over one hundred extant manuscripts of the *Recognitiones* ("Narrative Motifs," n. 45, p. 9).

9. Perry has suggested that the *Apollonius* was inspired by either "an earlier form of the Ps.-Clementine story, or by the same source on which the latter was built" (*The Ancient Romances*, p. 295). See also p. 286.

10. Commenting on that recension, G. A. A. Kortekaas notes: "The Christian linguistic elements, varying from the use of words with Christian overtones to borrowings from the Bible and phraseology incidentally concurring with Italian (perhaps even Roman) hagiography form an integrated component of its language" (*Historia Apollonii Regis Tyri*, ed. G. A. A. Kortekaas [Groningen: Bouma's Boekhuis, 1984], p. 106).

Constance. The conversion of pagan romance into hagiographic romance depended on the recognition of a parallel story or stories in Scripture to which the pagan narratives could relate as foreshadowing and the *legenda* as imitation. The Book of Job provided such a mediative biblical parallel, not only in the general outline of its plot, but also in its special character as a book of Gentile authorship providentially included in the Judeo-Christian canon.

Although the date and authorship of the Book of Job were debated by early exegetes, Gregory the Great and Isidore of Seville, following Saints Ambrose and Augustine, advanced the view that the Book was written by Job himself during the age of the patriarchs, before the time of Moses. After summarizing the views of others, Gregory concludes: "We nonetheless consider it more likely that the same holy Job who endured the battles of spiritual warfare also narrated the events of his own accomplished victory" (Preface I.3, p. 9: "Arbitrari tamen uerius possumus, quod isdem beatus Iob, qui certamina spiritalis pugnae sustinuit, etiam consummatae suae uictoriae gesta narrauit").[11]

Job, moreover, was not a Jew but a Gentile. In the Preface to the *Moralia*, Gregory explains that Divine Providence included the life of a righteous Gentile among the lives of Hebrews (Preface II.5, p. 11: "inter Hebraeorum uitas . . . uita iusti gentilis adducitur") for three reasons: first of all, because Christ came to save Jews and Gentiles alike; secondly, in order that the virtue of a Gentile not under the Law ("homo gentilis, homo sine lege") might confound the narrow-mindedness ("prauitas") of those under the Law; thirdly, that the example of a noble pagan might counter the impudence of Christians: "Vnde ad confutandam impudentiam nostram, gentilis homo ad exemplum deducitur" (Preface II.4, p. 10). Similarly, Isidore praises Job as a Gentile famous for his faith, great in his humility, outstanding in hospitality, gentle in correction, generous in almsgiving: "homo gentilis, fide clarus, humilitate summus, hospitalitate praecipuus, in disciplina mansuetus, in eleemosynis largus."[12]

This view of Job as a noble preredeemed pagan linked him in the

11. I quote from Gregory the Great, *Moralia in Job*, ed. M. Adriaen, CCSL 134 (Turnhout: Brepols, 1979). The translation is mine. Subsequent citations are parenthetical. See also Isidore of Seville, *Etymologiae* VI.ii.13–14, PL 82, c231.
12. Isidore of Seville, *De ortu et obitu Patrum* XXIV.37, PL 83, c136.

medieval imagination to *exempla* of other unbaptized men of good will, such as Cornelius, Trajan, and the emperor Constantine, whose virtue merited them faith and salvation. Job's authorship of an inspired book, moreover, tended to affirm the typological value of pagan works and sanction their conversion into Christian literary forms for the sake of converting their readers. It is not surprising, therefore, that the saints' legends generally recognized for their indebtedness to Greek romance are also marked by their explicit or implicit allusions to the Book of Job.

Popular throughout the Middle Ages, the Life of Saint Eustace provides the clearest example of this synthesis of scriptural and secular materials.[13] Scholars have commonly recognized resemblances in plot between the Life of Eustace, on the one hand, and the Pseudo-Clementine *Recognitiones* and the story of Apollonius, Prince of Tyre, on the other. Gordon Hall Gerould, for instance, notes in the Eustacian *vitae* "a marked likeness in manner and material to the late Greek romances."[14] In his edition of the Anglo-Saxon recension of the *Passio Sancti Eustacii Martyris* (tenth century), Walter W. Skeat observes that the legend, unlike the others included in Ælfric's saints' lives, is actually "a secular and romantic story" that is "turned into a 'saint's life' by the addition of the hero's martyrdom."[15] Skeat goes on to note that the story of the knight Placidas/Eustace actually appears in the English version of the *Gesta Romanorum* without the sequel of martyrdom, ending "happily, as it was clearly meant to do," given its strong orientation "on the story of Job." Following Skeat's lead,

---

13. After the first extant mention of Eustace by John of Damascus (A.D. 726), the Eustace legend became very popular in the West. According to Heffernan, "every century from the ninth to the fourteenth produced a Latin recension of the Legend" and versions abound "in virtually all European vernaculars" ("Narrative Motifs," pp. 65–66). For a discussion of the close relationship between *Sir Isumbras* and the Life of Eustace see Hopkins, *Sinful Knights*, pp. 119–43. During the Renaissance the story of Eustace was dramatized in (Nicholas Udall's?) *Play of Placidas, Alias St. Eustace* (1534), John Partridge's *The worthie Historie of the most Noble and valiaunt Knight Placidas, otherwise called Eustas, who was martyred for the Profession of Jesus Christ* (1566), and Henry Chettle's *Sir Placidas* (1599). See Gerould, *Saints' Legends*, pp. 300, 308, 316–17.

14. Gerould, *Saints' Legends*, p. 49. See also Heffernan, "Narrative Motifs," p. 72.

15. Walter W. Skeat, ed., *Ælfric's Lives of Saints*, vol. 2 (London: Kegan Paul, Trench, Trübner and Co., 1900), p. 452. Scholars now question the attribution of the legend to Ælfric.

Heffernan has extensively explored the influence of the Vulgate in the
narrative structure of the Eustace legend and termed the Book of Job
"the single most important biblical antecedent."[16]

In the Anglo-Saxon recension of the tale, Placidas is a military
tribune (p. 190: "sum cempena ealdor-man") like Job, whom the
church fathers had allegorized as God's warrior.[17] The story begins
with a listing of the good works of Placidas and his wife, even as the
Bible enumerates Job's virtues. Like the Gentile Job, Placidas, still a
heathen, draws the attention of the merciful and benevolent God ("se
mild-heorta and se welwillenda god") who wills the salvation of
all and finds acceptable the person "who worketh righteousness"
(p. 193), no matter what his race or origin: "þæt on ælcre þeode þe
riht-wisnysse wyrcð" (p. 192). One day while Placidas is hunting,
Christ appears to him in the form of a miraculous stag who speaks to
him, echoing the words of Christ to Paul on the road to Damascus. As
a result, Placidas and his wife and two sons are baptized, and he is
christened "Eustace."

The language of the narrative then plays with the famous nakedness of Job. Before his baptism, Placidas clothed the naked: "nacode
he scrydde" (p. 190). Through baptism, as Christ tells Eustace, he
has divested himself (p. 196: "ðu unscryddest") of the corruptible
man and vested himself ("gescryddest") with the incorruptible. As a
result he has angered the devil, who will strip him of worldly wealth
and thus allow him through suffering to gain spiritual riches in the
service of the King of Heaven. Appearing to Eustace in the stag,
Christ prophesies that he will be tried, even as His beloved servant
Job (p. 198: "swa min leofa ðeow iob") was tried, and eventually
vanquish the devil through patience, if he avoids cursing and mur-
muring in his thoughts: "warna huru þæt nan wyrgung and ceorung
astige on þinum geþohte" (p. 198).

The series of Joban trials begins. A pestilence kills Eustace's servants and livestock. When Eustace and his family temporarily flee
the property, thieves take all their goods. While in flight to Egypt, a
lustful captain demands Eustace's beautiful wife as ship-toll and,
separated from her, Eustace loses his two sons in rapid succession,

16. Heffernan, "Narrative Motifs," p. 72.
17. I quote from Skeat's edition, cited above, giving page references parenthetically.

one carried off by a lion, another by a wolf. Infused virtue strengthens Eustace in patience to keep him from suicide, but he begs God for an end to his trials, humbly observing that although Christ prophesied that he would be tested like Job (p. 202: "þæt ic sceolde gecostnod beon eall-swa iob"), he has actually suffered in some things even more than Job: "mare ic þolige þonne he."

After fifteen years alone in a foreign land, Eustace hears a heavenly voice promising him restored happiness on earth and an even greater reward in Heaven. An invasion prompts the Roman emperor Trajan to send men in search of his excellent tribune, Placidas. Through a series of remarkable events, they find Eustace, whom they identify through a tell-tale scar; Eustace's two sons, who have been raised separately as foundlings by shepherds and husbandmen, recognize each other as brothers and find their mother, whose chastity and beauty have been miraculously preserved. She, in turn, is reunited with Eustace. This blissful reunion after long separation, like the reunions in Greek romance, prompts feasting and thanksgiving to God—a jubilant ending cut short in the saint's legend by the martyrdom of the whole family as Christians.

The Life of St. Eustace almost effortlessly fuses the plot materials of Greek romance with the biblical story of Job, subordinating the fiction of the former to the truth of the latter. In a similar fashion, but with considerably more difficulty, the equally popular exemplary tale of Patient Griselda[18] joins a Beauty-and-the-Beast folktale with affinities to the Apuleian romance of Psyche and Cupid[19] to the providential themes of Job and Boethius.[20] In the tale of Griselda, the Book of Job does not simply mediate between folkloric romance and Christian saint's life; rather, a new textual triad forms at a higher level, wherein the saint's life mediates between scripture and philosophy, Job and Boethius.[21]

18. For an account of the various versions of the story, see Käte Laserstein, *Der Griseldistoff in der Weltliteratur* (Weimar: A. Duncker, 1926).

19. See Dudley David Griffith, *The Origin of the Griselda Story* (Seattle: University of Washington Press, 1931); Wirt Armistead Cate, "The Problem of the Origin of the Griselda Story," *SP* 29 (1932): 389–405.

20. For insight into the critical controversies surrounding the Griselda stories of Boccaccio, Petrarch, and Chaucer, see Mary J. Carruthers, "The Lady, the Swineherd, and Chaucer's Clerk," *Chaucer Review* 17.3 (1983): 221–34.

21. Charlotte C. Morse ("The Exemplary Griselda," *SAC* 7 [1985]) notes that Chaucer's "Clerk's Tale" seems "rarely to have been copied apart from *The Canter-*

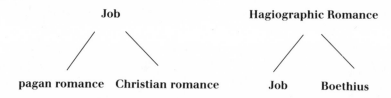

In the process, as we shall see, the conflict that is elided in the Eustace legend by silencing the saint's complaint (and thus letting the Joban frame narrative eclipse the central, disturbing Dialogue of Comfort) reemerges in a dialogic concordance of Boethian and biblical texts.

Griselda, Job, and Boethius

The medieval tendency to derive the same moral lesson, the same meaning, from the Book of Job and Boethius' *Consolation of Philosophy* established a powerful parallel between the two texts that served to relate them as *translationes*, one of the other. Alluding to both Job and Boethius, the Griselda story tests the limits of that *translatio* by bringing the two texts into conjunction and conflict. As Griselda's husband and tormenter, Walter resembles at once the mysterious but benevolent God of Boethius and the Satan of Job. Similarly, Griselda figures simultaneously as Lady Philosophy and Job in her patient endurance of a series of terrible domestic trials. Assimilated to Lady Philosophy, Griselda does not apostrophize her fate as did the heroines of Greek and Roman romance whose calamitous stories parallel hers. As a female *translatio* of silent Job, moreover, Griselda undermines the Gregorian distinction between the blasphemous and the pious Job, which uses the dialogue between Job and his despairing wife to label weeping, suffering, and complaint as feminine; fortitude and reasoned composure as masculine.[22] Thus the protagonists of the Griselda story, positioned between two closely related but subtly opposed Boethian and biblical interpretive grids, each have two faces,

---

bury Tales. It appears once with saints' lives and three times with romances, illustrating the tendency, particularly in the English tradition, to group saints' lives and romances" (n. 33, p. 66).

22. I address the issue of *translatio* and gender in a forthcoming essay, "Translating Job as Female," cited in n. 34 below.

divine and diabolic, masculine and feminine, the potential schizo-
phrenia of which Petrarch masks and Chaucer exposes.

In 1373 Petrarch wrote a Latin version of the Griselda story that
Boccaccio had used to conclude his *Decameron* (1353). Petrarch's
Griselda (*Epistolae seniles* 17.3) reflects his commitment to what
Charlotte C. Morse has termed "a heavily Stoic, practical moral philosophy."[23] As Morse observes, "Petrarch accommodates the story to
classical rhetoric," keeping "overt Christian references" to a mini-
mum.[24] Petrarch's only allusion to Job comes in his closing moralization of the tale, and there it is indirect, buried intertextually in a
citation of Saint James' Epistle: "Ut Jacobus ait Apostolus."[25] James
5:11 cites Job as an outstanding example of patience and a proof of
God's providential care. Petrarch, however, does not name Job but
rather paraphrases James 1:13 to assert that God only permits us to
be tested by evils, while he himself puts no one to the test: "et ipse
neminem temptet."[26]

Petrarch's Walter is enigmatic, his genuine benevolence toward
Griselda hidden from her as he tests her, removing from her first her
infant daughter, then her son, apparently to kill them; divorcing her
and then recalling her to prepare the hall for his new bride. Petrarch's Griselda is equally enigmatic, her feelings veiled in her
steadfast submission to Walter's will and God's: "Deo et tibi gratias
ago."[27] Thus Petrarch's rendition of the story makes it a Stoic and
Boethian allegory of God's providential action. As Chaucer's Clerk
explains, God, like Walter, "suffreth us, for oure exercise, / With
sharpe scourges of adversitee / Ful ofte to be bete in sondry wise"
(lines 1156–58), but "for oure beste is al his governaunce" (line
1161).[28] We, therefore, ought to live "in vertuous suffraunce" (line

23. Morse, "Exemplary Griselda," p. 57. See also Charles Trinkhaus, *The Poet as
Philosopher: Petrarch and the Formation of Renaissance Consciousness* (New Haven:
Yale University Press, 1979).

24. Morse, "Exemplary Griselda," p. 58.

25. William F. Bryan and Germaine Dempster, eds., *Chaucer: Sources and Analogues* (1941; New York: Humanities Press, 1958), p. 330.

26. After examining over sixty manuscripts of Petrarch's Latin story of Griselda,
J. Burke Severs found an explicit mention of Job in only one fifteenth-century manuscript. See "The Job Passage in the *Clerkes Tale*," *MLN* 49 (1934): 461–62.

27. Bryan and Dempster, *Chaucer: Sources*, p. 320.

28. Geoffrey Chaucer, "The Clerk's Tale," in Larry Benson, gen. ed., *The Riverside Chaucer*, 3d ed. (Boston: Houghton Mifflin, 1987). All quotations from the tale are
cited parenthetically by line number. Quotations from Chaucer's other works are also
taken from this edition and similarly cited.

1162) of God's wish and will and "be constant in adversitee / As was Grisilde" (lines 1146–47).

Petrarch clearly tells Griselda's story to inspire imitation. As Morse notes, however, "Petrarch never explains how anyone musters the spiritual or psychological strength to imitate Griselda."[29] Chaucer supplies that lack, represented in Petrarch's "comparative absence of Christian reference," by adding a series of biblical allusions in his tale of Griselda.[30] In the process, as J. Burke Severs observes, Chaucer makes "significant changes in characterization, in narrative technique, and in the tone and spirit which informs the tale."[31] The biblical allusions complicate and counter Petrarch's Boethian allegory by letting the revealed truth of theology answer to philosophy, the Bible to Boethius.[32]

In "The Clerk's Tale" Griselda is constantly described in an evocative manner that likens her to Christ; to the Virgin Mary at the Annunciation hour, in Bethlehem, at Cana, and at the foot of the cross; and, thirdly, to suffering Job. Whereas "Men speke of Job, and moost for his humblesse" (line 932), the Clerk sings the praises of Griselda, whose patience exceeds that of Job. Divorced, divested of her royal clothes, and dismissed from the palace, Griselda echoes Job's speech: " 'Naked out of my fadres house,' " quod she, / 'I cam, and naked moot I turne agayn' " (lines 871–72).

Griselda's Joban silence and pointedly controlled, two-edged speech (which hints at her true feelings) contrasts with the despair of her father who, like Job in the presence of his consolers, "curseth the day and tyme that Nature / Shoop hym to been a lyves creature" (lines 902–3).[33] Similarly, her heroic endurance of psychological torment contrasts with the emotive commentary of the male Clerk-

29. Morse, "Exemplary Griselda," p. 80.
30. Ibid., p. 58.
31. J. Burke Severs, "The Clerk's Tale," in Bryan and Dempster, *Chaucer: Sources,* p. 290.
32. Jane Chance notes a similar tension in Chaucer's lyrics. See "Chaucerian Irony in the Boethian Short Poems: The Dramatic Tension Between Classical and Christian," *Chaucer Review* 20.3 (1986): 235–245. Chance suggests that the contrast between the poems' "Boethian problem" and their "Christian (Augustinian) solution" actually extends the "doubleness . . . found in Boethius, given the double-nature of the protagonist, dispirited and desperate at the beginning of the *Consolation* and calm and rational at the end" (p. 243).
33. Cf. Besserman, *Legend of Job,* p. 112.

narrator, who sympathizes with Griselda in her plight and denounces Walter as diabolic, decrying his cruelty and needless testing of her virtue.

The biblical allusions and the narrative intrusion of Chaucer's Clerk accomplish two purposes. Chaucer not only creates in Walter's wife, Griselda, a Joban wife in answer to the clerical mysogyny that demonizes the biblical wife of Job and her counterpart, the nagging and seductive Wife of Bath. His version of the story also systematically undermines and redirects the Petrarchan allegory.[34] Griselda becomes the divine figure, Walter the demonic; Griselda, the redeemed and redeeming figure, Walter the one in need of redemption. Like the Gregorian Job, Griselda is "constant in adversitee" (line 1146), but hers is not the *constantia mentis* of a Stoic philosopher, but the *constantia amoris* of a saint. She suffers Christ's passion, converts her sadistic husband, and accomplishes genuine change in him and others through a divine (indeed, Incarnational) acceptance of mutability. Her patience, as Morse insists, has "positive power."[35]

The simultaneous confluence and opposition of Boethian and Joban themes that characterizes "The Clerk's Tale" also marks Chaucer's rendition of the Constance romance.[36] In "The Clerk's Tale" Chaucer signals the tension between philosophy and theology by the Clerk's self-conscious remarks about his indebtedness to and departure from his Petrarchan source. In "The Man of Law's Tale," as we shall see, a similar tension emerges from the teller's struggle with the mixture of romance and hagiography in the tale as his

34. I argue both propositions in "Job's Wife, Walter's Wife, and the Wife of Bath," in *Old Testament Women in Western Literature*, ed. Raymond-Jean Frontain and Jan Wojcik (Conway: University of Central Arkansas Press, 1991), pp. 92–107. See also my "Translating Job as Female," forthcoming in *Translation Theory and Practice in the Middle Ages*, ed. Jeanette Beer (Kalamazoo, Mich.: Medieval Institute Publications).

35. Morse, "Exemplary Griselda," p. 52. She cites Ralph Hanna, "Some Commonplaces of Late Medieval Patience Discussions: An Introduction," in Gerald J. Schiffhorst, ed., *The Triumph of Patience: Medieval and Renaissance Studies* (Orlando: University Press of Florida, 1978), pp. 67–70.

36. Margaret Schlauch surveys analogues of the Constance story in *Chaucer's Constance and Accused Queens* (New York: New York University Press, 1927). The tale of Constance has strong affinities to Hellenistic romance. See Elizabeth Archibald, "The Flight from Incest: Two Classical Precursors of the Constance Theme," *Chaucer Review* 20.4 (1986): 259–72; P. H. Goepp, "The Narrative Material of *Apollonius of Tyre*," *ELH* 5 (1938): 150–72.

"wisdom" falls short of the Pauline "foolishness" of his heroine.[37] Even as Chaucer splits the figure of Job in "The Clerk's Tale" to create the silent Griselda and her cursing father Janicula, he sets the Boethian apostrophe of the Man of Law, as he narrates the vagaries of fortune, against the Joban prayer of Custance, as she answers to Providence. Out of this juxtaposition Chaucer fashions a subtle satire that calls into question not only the wisdom of the Man of Law but also the impulse to romanticize sanctity.

Apostrophe, Prayer, and the Structure of Satire in "The Man of Law's Tale"

"The Man of Law's Tale" has figured prominently in the ongoing debate about the teller-tale relationship in *The Canterbury Tales*.[38] Is "The Man of Law's Tale" primarily a satire exposing the hypocrisy of its pilgrim narrator?[39] Or is it a pious legend about its saintly heroine,

37. The General Prologue portrait of the Sergeant of the Law emphasizes his wisdom. "[W]ar and wys" (*GP* 309), the Sergeant impresses the pilgrim Chaucer as a man of discretion and reverence: "his wordes weren so wise" (*GP* 313).

38. Pointing to the tenuous relationship between the headlink, the "poverty prologue," and the pious legend in rhyme-royal stanzas, Bernard F. Huppé and others have insisted that "the *Tale* must speak for itself without regard to its particular dramatic setting or its narrator." See Huppé, *A Reading of the Canterbury Tales* (Albany: State University of New York Press, 1964), p. 96. See also John Tatlock, "The Man of Law's Tale," in *The Development and Chronology of Chaucer's Works* (Gloucester: Peter Smith, 1963), pp. 172–88. Arguing on different grounds, David Lawton, in *Chaucer's Narrators* (Cambridge: D. S. Brewer, 1985), has insisted that "lines using a narratorial 'I' in the body of any of the tales cannot be used to demonstrate a point about the ostensible teller" (p. 104). Observing that the narrator's voice in all of Chaucer's "high-style" stories (including "The Man of Law's Tale") is virtually the same (pp. 76–105), Lawton restricts the applicability of speech-act theory to the prologues of tales, excluding the tales themselves (p. 4). C. David Benson makes an argument similar to Lawton's in "Their Telling Difference: Chaucer the Pilgrim and His Two Contrasting Tales," *Chaucer Review* 18 (1983): 61–76. H. Marshall Leicester, Jr., in "The Art of Impersonation: A General Prologue to the *Canterbury Tales*," *PMLA* 95 (1980): 213–24, was among the first to discredit the dramatic model by shifting emphasis away from the voices of pilgrims to the voicing of the tales themselves.

39. For excellent treatments of the appropriateness of the tale's assignment to the Man of Law as a satiric object, see Warren Ginsberg, *The Cast of Character: The Representation of Personality in Ancient and Medieval Literature* (Toronto: University of Toronto Press, 1983), pp. 144–51; Roger Ellis, *Patterns of Religious Narrative in the "Canterbury Tales"* (Totowa, N.J.: Barnes and Noble Books, 1986), pp. 119–68; Alfred David, "The Man of Law versus Chaucer: A Case in Poetics," *PMLA* 82 (1967): 217–

more properly called "The Tale of Custance"? The historical division of critics into two camps suggests that auditors are hearing two different voices in the tale, the narratorial "I" isolated as direct discourse and the oppositional "I" of Custance herself as a speaking subject.

Chaucer's additions to his source, Nicholas Trevet's Anglo-Norman *Chronique*, chiefly consist of (1) apostrophe, *exclamatio*, and rhetorical questions interjected by the narrator, and (2) prayers uttered by Custance.[40] I argue that Chaucer's additions effectively convert a saint's legend into a satire through the systematic opposition of two rhetorical figures—apostrophe (assigned to the narrator) and prayer (assigned to Custance)—that punctuate the unfolding plot line and provide a divergent commentary on the events being related.[41] Not only does Chaucer oppose the viewpoints of the tale's heroine and her pilgrim narrator in a *conflictus* of providential and fatalistic orderings of experience, but he assigns to each a characteristic *figura* that has its proper sign value, its power to define not only the individual *personae* as such, but also the differences between them. Custance's prayers do more than characterize her as a saint. As direct discourse they give Custance a voice and personal genre, allowing her to speak for herself and thus provide a counterinterpretation of events otherwise related to the audience only by the short-sighted narrator.

Apostrophic Narration

The tale itself is episodic, its story line punctuated by five sea voyages, its chronology spanning all of Custance's adult life, the setting for its action changing from Rome to Syria to England and

25; Chauncey Wood, "Chaucer's Man of Law as Interpreter," *Traditio* 23 (1967): 149–90.

40. The best source study is E. A. Block's "Originality, Controlling Purpose and Craftsmanship in Chaucer's 'Man of Law's Tale,' " *PMLA* 68 (1963): 572–616.

41. Satire derives from the word *satura*, "full plate," denoting a medley or mixture of fruits. The opposition of prayer and its converse, apostrophe, establishes a medley enabling the exposure of the Man of Law as a self-important *philosophus gloriosus*, a common target in the tradition of Menippean satire. See Northrop Frye, *Anatomy of Criticism: Four Essays* (New York: Atheneum, 1969), pp. 309–12; F. Anne Payne, *Chaucer and Menippean Satire* (Madison: University of Wisconsin Press, 1981). See also n. 2 above.

back again. The natural division of the tale into discrete episodes lends itself to narrative intrusion and provides ample opportunity for the teller to interject a stylized, pathetic, or moral-didactic commentary on Custance's long-suffering, which reflects, in turn upon his character and understanding of the story. He responds to the tale he tells in a series of sentimental outbursts typically beginning with a rhetorically charged "O": "O firste moevyng! Crueel firmament" (*MLT* 295–315); "O Sowdanesse, roote of iniquitee!" (lines 358–71); "O sodeyn wo" (lines 421–27); "O my Custance" (lines 446–48); "Who saved Danyel" (lines 473–504); "Allas! Custance, thou hast no champioun" (lines 631–37); "O queenes, lyvynge in prosperitee" (lines 652–58); "O messager, fulfild of dronkenesse" (lines 771–77); "O Donegild" (lines 778–84); "O my Custance" (lines 803–05); "O foule lust of luxurie" (lines 925–31); "How may this wayke womman" (lines 932–45); "But litel while it lasteth, I yow heete" (lines 1132–41). The apostrophe marks the narrator's distinctive style, defines his voice, articulates his worldview, and sets him apart (in the reader's awareness) from the tale he tells and its characters whose voices, recorded in direct discourse, remain distinct from the narrator's own.

Unlike prayer which, by definition, addresses itself to One unseen but intimately present, apostrophe invariably addresses the Absent One. As such, apostrophe is a rhetorical trope suited to a world view that is essentially anthropocentric, rather than providential. Indeed, absence and abandonment belong to the very definition of the form and explain its frequent occurrence in tragedy. In "The Man of Law's Tale" apostrophe is more than a figure of speech. Repeated and extended throughout the narrative, it becomes a figure of thought ("sic hoc schema faciat tropos ille textus") indirectly revelatory ("apparens magis quam confessa") of the speaker's whole perspective on things.[42]

While the narrator's speech generally (though not always) follows a horizontal line in his moral-didactic addresses to the audience and pathetic exclamations to his characters ("O my Custance"), the voice

---

42. Quintilian, *Institutio Oratoria* 9.2, vol. 3, trans. H. E. Butler, Loeb Classical Library (Cambridge: Harvard University Press, 1921, 1943), p. 400. Quintilian gives the example of Socrates, whose all-pervasive use of irony essentially defined his worldview "cum etiam vita universa ironiam habere videatur."

self-reflexive, the mark of his own "gentilesse," "pitee," and erudi-tion. In the context of his self-appointed status as a literary critic, the "O" of the Man of Law signals not only his *gravitas* as a judicial orator but also his ambition to rival Chaucer as an Ovidian imitator (lines 91–96):

> "Me were looth be likned, doutelees,
> To Muses that men clepe Pierides—
> *Methamorphosios* woot what I mene;
> But natheless, I recche noght a bene
> Though I come after hym with hawebake.
> I speke in prose, and lat him rymes make."

The Man of Law exposes the false *humilitas* of his disclaimer both by insulting Chaucer, who, he says, "kan but lewedly / On metres and on rymyng craftily" (lines 47–48), and by turning immediately "with a sobre cheere" (line 97) to his own apostrophic prologue: "O hateful harm, condicion of poverte!" (line 99).[47]

Apostrophic Irony

Chaucer proceeds to turn the narrator's use of the *figura* against him so that it signifies not his wisdom but his windiness. In *Poetria nova* (c. 1210) Geoffrey de Vinsauf follows the apostrophic lament on the death of Richard I (which he gives as an example of the form, and which Chaucer puts to mock-heroic use in "The Nun's Priest's Tale") immediately with a discussion of verbal irony used against the *philosophus gloriosus*—the "ape among the learned doctors" who "flaunts himself."[48] The inclusion of this kind of irony ("carried by ridicule against ridiculous men") under the heading of apostrophe

---

"The Word *Persona*," in *The Literary Persona* (Chicago: University of Chicago Press, 1982), pp. 19–32.

47. Ginsberg (*The Cast of Character*) remarks that "there seems to have existed a traditional animus between lawyers . . . and poets" (p. 149), citing Horace, Ovid, Virgil, and Boccaccio (see pp. 147–50). The inconsistency between the Man of Law's stated intent to speak in prose and the actual casting of the tale in rhyme royal stanzas may be an intentional Chaucerian allusion to *prosimetrum*, the mixed form traditionally associated with Boethius and Menippean satire.

48. Geoffrey of Vinsauf, *Poetria nova*, trans. Jane Baltzell Kopp, in James J. Murphy, ed., *Three Medieval Rhetorical Arts* (Berkeley: University of California Press, 1971), p. 50.

seems to indicate that the misuse of the trope by windy speakers inevitably exposes them to satiric treatment by others—that the form itself, as Geoffrey says, "may change her face."

Geoffrey's classification, at any rate, reflects the classical use of apostrophe as a satiric means. As Martin Winkler has shown, both Cicero (in his comic impersonation of Appius Claudius Caecus as a *gravis* persona) and Juvenal (in his Satire 14 *prosopopoeia* of an indignant ancestor) were well aware that an overuse of Grand Style tropes works to make a speaker ridiculous, and they used it accordingly, allowing the self-important objects of their satire to lay bare their own pomposity.[49] The Roman satirists clearly capitalize on the failure of their personae to heed the standard textbook recommendation to use it in its proper place ("loco"), rarely ("raro"), and only when the importance of the subject seems to demand it ("cum rei magnitudo postulare videbitur") for the sake of instilling indignation.[50]

Geoffrey's close association of apostrophe with irony directed against pretentious men of learning strongly enforces the idea that the exclamatory narrative voice we are hearing in "The Man of Law's Tale" is simultaneously creating the persona of the speaker and exposing his emptiness.[51] If, as Warren Ginsberg has shown us, "the foremost supposition of Roman rhetoric is that the style and tone of any speech reflect the character of its speaker" according to the principle "ut quasi mores oratoris effingat oratio," then the apostrophe as *figura* must be taken seriously as the character—literally, the mark ("notatio")—of the Man of Law.[52] In this context David Lawton is

49. Martin M. Winkler, "Juvenal's Attitude toward Ciceronian Poetry and Rhetoric," *Rheinisches Museum für Philologie*, vol. 131, no. 1 (Frankfurt am Main: J. D. Sauerlander, 1988), pp. 84–97. Winkler has argued more recently not only that "Grand Style is . . . one of the chief features of Juvenalian satire" but also that Juvenal's is "an epic satire, i.e., satire delivered largely in the epic style." See "The Function of Epic in Juvenal's Satires," *Studies in Latin Literature and Roman History*, vol. 5, ed. Carl Deroux (Brussels: Latomus Revue d'Études Latines, 1989), pp. 414–43.

50. Cicero, *Ad Herennium* 4.15.22, p. 284.

51. Eugene Vance rightly observes that the "rhetor" in Chaucer "is usually seen as a powerful and dangerous figure who subverts the well-being of society," citing as examples the Summoner, the Pardoner, and the Wife of Bath. See *Marvelous Signals: Poetics and Sign Theory in the Middle Ages* (Lincoln: University of Nebraska Press, 1986), p. 264.

52. Ginsberg, *The Cast of Character*, p. 17. See Cicero, *De oratore*, trans. E. W. Sutton and H. Rackham, vol. 1, Loeb Classical Library (Cambridge: Harvard University Press, 1942), II.xliii.184, p. 328.

right when he says that "the 'I' is integral of the *exclamatio.*"[53] The speech necessarily creates a speaker—in this case a speaker whose persona matches, even as it colors and qualifies, the third-person portrait of the lawyer in the "General Prologue." As Ginsberg has suggested, "The Canterbury pilgrims are twice-formed at least, once by the tales and once by their frame,"[54] but the techniques of characterization are different.[54] When narrative voice works to characterize the fictive speaker, the style literally makes the Man of Law.

Chaucer seldom uses the word "style," and when he does he associates it specifically with "heigh style."[55] "Manere," on the other hand, is a favorite expression of his, and he employs it frequently to mediate between a wide variety of literary and character types, linking them as *modus* and *mos.*[56] Chaucer assures us, for instance, that the Miller "tolde his cherles tale in his manere" (*MilP* 3169), while the Monk bewailed his histories "in manere of tragedie" (*MkT* 1991). Chaucer's conscious effort to harmonize the discourse and social behavior ("cheere") of his characters, "as techeth art of speche hem that it leere" (*SqT* 104), aligns him with a long rhetorical tradition that emphasized decorum in impersonation.[57] Whether that impersonation takes the form of *ethopoeia* (soliloquy), *prosopopoeia*, or *sermocinatio* (dialogue), the principle remains the same: "personae oratio accommodata ad dignitatem."[58]

Apostrophe and Prayer

The apostrophic voicing of "The Man of Law's Tale" must be considered a comment on its narrator. None of the other tales that most resemble it in plot (as some kind of female saint's legend)— "The Clerk's Tale" of patient Griselda, "The Second Nun's Tale" of Saint Cecilia, "The Physician's Tale" of Virginia—exhibits the in-

53. Lawton, *Chaucer's Narrators*, p. 92.

54. Ginsberg, *The Cast of Character*, p. 164.

55. The *Concordance* lists only four instances—three of them in "The Clerk's Tale" (lines 18, 41, 1148) and one in "The Squire's Tale" (lines 105–6).

56. There are six full columns of entries in the *Concordance*. The entries in both the *Middle English Dictionary* and the *Oxford English Dictionary* show that the sense development of "manner" reflects its assimilation to *modus* and *mos* as literary and social terms.

57. See Henrik Specht's magisterial article, " 'Ethopoeia' or Impersonation: A Neglected Species of Medieval Characterization," *Chaucer Review* 21.1 (1986): 1–15.

58. Cicero, *Ad Herennium* 4.43.55, p. 366.

trusive "O" of narratorial apostrophe or even assigns apostrophic speeches to their heroines. Indeed, the seeming busyness of the Man of Law contrasts sharply with the genuine industry of the Second Nun, who translates the Cecilia legend in plain style. The omission of apostrophe seems to reflect the Augustinian emphasis on *sermo humilis*, revived in Chaucer's own time by Wyclif, who generally counseled the avoidance of "heroic declamation" as a form inappropriate to the subject and aim of religious writing: "Sed non dubium quia plana locucia de pertinentibus ad salutem sit huius modi, ideo illa est eligenda declamatione eroyca postposita."[59] Indeed, Wyclif's well-known insistence on the plain style may help explicate the Host's call in the Epilogue for a Lollard ("Lollere") to tell a tale in answer to the Man of Law's apostrophic narrative.

Prayer and apostrophe, as converse *figurae*, remain at odds. Chaucer chiefly reserves apostrophic utterance for characters who are facing an experience of loss from a fortune-oriented perspective: Arcite's apostrophe to the absent (because imprisoned) Palamon and distant Emily (*KnT* 1223–74), Palamon's apostrophe to the absent (because released) Arcite (*KnT* 1281–1333), Dorigen's plaint to Fortune (*FranT* 1355–1456), Apollo's lament over his dead wife (*ManT* 274–91), Troilus' multiple plaints over Criseyde's exchange (*TC* 4.250–336), Criseyde's parallel apostrophe to Troilus (4.743–98).[60]

When Chaucer's narrators employ the figure, they invoke the tradition of the strumpet muses dismissed from Boethius' prison cell who "fedyn and noryssen" (*Boece* 1, pr. 1.52–53) his sorrow by inspiring "drery vers of wretchidnesse" (*Boece* 1, m.1.5–6). Boethius begins writing his *Consolatio* as a weeping narrator, his face wet with "verray teres" (line 6). His initial stance is replicated in the apostrophic narratorial commentary on tragedies provided by the weeping narrator of *Troilus*, the Monk ("O noble, O worthy Petro!" *MkT* 2375), the Merchant acquainted with "wepyng and waylyng" ("O sodeyn hap! O thou Fortune unstable!" *MerP* 1213, *MerT* 2057) and the tongue-in-cheek Nun's Priest with his mock-heroic *exclamationes*: "O false mordrour lurkynge in thy den! / O newe Scariot,

---

59. Quoted by Ginsberg in his discussion of "The Clerk's Tale" in *The Cast of Character*, p. 161.

60. For a general survey of Chaucerian apostrophe, see John Nist, "Chaucer's Apostrophic Mode in *The Canterbury Tales*," *TSL* 15 (1970): 85–98.

newe Genylon" (*NPT* 3226–27); "O destinee, that mayst not been eschewed!" (line 3338); "O Venus" (line 3340); "O Gaufred" (line 3347); "O woful hennes!" (line 3369).

The other two narrators of tales who call attention to themselves with apostrophic commentary are, of course, the Pardoner and the Prioress. The Pardoner prides himself on his theatrical performance and sophistic, oratorical skills, and his specific use of apostrophe— "O glotonye, ful of cursednesse!" (*PardT* 498), "O womb! O bely! O stynkyng cod" (line 534), "O cursed synne of alle cursednesse!" (line 895)—underscores his avaricious preoccupation with material goods. He apostrophizes avarice in its various forms to distance himself from it rhetorically and thus detach his audience from their money: "for to make hem free / To yeven hir pens, and namely unto me" (lines 401–2).

The Prioress, for her part, assimilates her apostrophic "O" to the vocative "O" of "O Alma Redemptoris Mater"—even as she represents her tale-telling in her prologue as a "song" (line 487). With the single exception of "O cursed folk of Herodes" (line 574), all of her apostrophes could superficially be considered prayers addressed, as they are, to God and his saints: "O martir, sowded to virginitee" (line 579); "O grete God" (line 607); "O yonge Hugh of Lyncoln, slayn also" (line 684). Indeed, the troubling thing about the Prioress' narration is that she uses the language of religious presence (prayer) in a way that makes God absent, her violent anti-Semitism negating the mercy she invokes. Blessing and curse mingle in her discourse. The "cursed folk" (line 574) of her single apostrophe becomes the "cursed" Jews of her echoic narrative (the epithet is repeated in lines 578, 599, 631, and 685), even as her story renders them absent through the vehicles of ghetto, death, and historical expulsion.[61] The Prioress' stance distances herself from both the Jews she curses and the God of Mercy she invokes. She, in effect, turns prayer (the address to One present but unseen) into apostrophe (the direct address of One who is not there), one figure merging into its converse.

Custance, on the other hand, never confuses the two. Her prayer dramatizes a perfectly appropriate response to her perilous circumstances and thus reifies the meaning of the figure. Medieval treatises

61. The murder of Hugh of Lincoln contributed to the expulsion of the Jews from England in 1290.

on prayer define the word in its root meaning: *precari,* "to beg," "to entreat"; *orare,* "to plead a case." Hugh of Saint Victor, for instance, insists that prayer arises out of the human heart with a primal force whenever a person experiences calamity: "Quid enim efficacius hominem orandi studium excitaret quam miseria et calamitas tantorum malorum, quibus addictus premitur?"[62] He prescribes, as a necessary preparation for prayer, meditation on the miseries of the human condition:

> Cogitemus quam brevis sit vita nostra, quam lubrica via, quam mors incerta. Cogitemus quod lugentes in hanc vitam intravimus, cum dolore pertransimus, cum luctu exituri sumus. Cogitemus quantis amaritudinibus admistum sit, si quid etiam dulce aut jucundum in via hujus vitae occursu suo nobis alludit.[63]

> [Let us consider how brief our life is, how slippery our way, and how unpredictable, death. Let us recall that we enter into this life wailing, pass through it with sorrow, and leave it with lamentation. Let us think about how mixed with bitterness everything is, if indeed we happen to experience anything sweet or pleasant on life's path.]

Chaucer's English contemporaries urge the same existentialist basis for prayer. The author of *A Pistle of Prayer* advises the person who prays to impress upon himself in graphic terms the immediacy of his own death so that every prayer has the force of the last: "it schuld be ful speedful to þee at þe first biginnyng of þi preier, what preier soeuer it be, longe preier or schort, for to make it ful knowen to þin hert wiþouten any feinyng þat þou schalt diȝe in þe ende of þi preier, and, bot þou spede þee þe raþer, er þou come to þe ende of þi preier."[64] Similarly, Walter Hilton encourages the subject of human need, suffering, and mortality as an appropriate topic for meditation, noting that the consideration of human misery typically culminates in a sincere prayer of petition: "Also for to þenke of þe wrecchidnesse, myscheues and perils, bodili and goostli, þat fallen in þis liyf, and aftir þat for to þenke of þe ioies of heuene, hou moche blisse þere

62. Hugh of St. Victor, *De modo orandi*, PL 176, c977.
63. Ibid. The translation is mine.
64. "A Pistle of Preier," in Phyllis Hodgson, ed., *The Cloud of Unknowing and Related Treatises* (Salzburg: Institut für Anglistik und Amerikanistik, 1982), p. 101.

and ioie . . . þe more þat þou þenkist and felist þe wrecchidnes of þis lijf, þe more feruentli schal þou desire þe ioie and þe reste of þe blisse of heuen."[65]

The process outlined in the manuals of prayer finds its narrative parallel in the story of Custance and in the reader who considers her misery. Her *vita* embodies the *miseria* of the papal text invoked by the prologue to the tale: Innocent III's *De contemptu mundi* (or, as Chaucer entitles it in his translation, "Of the Wretchede Engendrynge of Man Kynde"). The episodes of her perilous existence are punctuated with prayers of petition, entreaty, and self-surrender to God's will. The reader, drawn into her story—which reads like a Perils-of-Pauline summa of everything bad that can happen ("calamitas tantorum malorum")—is actually involved in a meditation on the very topic most conducive to prayer ("miseria") and thus stimulated to appropriate her utterance. The ego of the one who prays is, as Patrick Diehl would say, paradigmatic—an "open" ego inviting a communal voicing.[66] Custance, in short, is impersonated by prayer as a figure of speech and becomes herself personified prayer. To use a phrase from Eugene Vance, the "poetics" of Custance's sign (prayer) essentially defines her, even as it directs our response to her story.[67]

Custance's saintliness, her exemplary utterance, and her symbolic femininity (with its power to represent the soul in its relationship to God) exert a centripetal force on the auditors, who are drawn into identification with her as the embodiment of their communal ideal. As Alison Goddard Elliott has observed about the martyrs' *passiones*, and saints' legends in general, the direct discourse of the saints—whatever its simple locutionary force within the dramatic context—has an additional illocutionary power on its hearers as they appropriate the sentiments of their models in faith.[68]

This primary rhetorical movement into the text is opposed by the centrifugal, masculine impulse of the voice of the narrator, whose

65. S. J. Ogilvie-Thomson, ed., *Walter Hilton's "Mixed Life," Edited from Lambeth Palace MS 472* (Salzburg: Institut für Anglistik und Amerikanistik, 1986), pp. 58–59.
66. Cf. Patrick S. Diehl, *The Medieval European Religious Lyric: An Ars Poetica* (Berkeley: University of California Press, 1985), pp. 141, 158.
67. Cf. Vance, *Marvelous Signals*, pp. 258–63.
68. Alison Goddard Elliott, "The Power of Discourse: Martyr's Passion and Old French Epic," in Paul Maurice Clogan, ed., *Medievalia et Humanistica*, n.s. 11 (Totowa, N.J.: Rowman and Littlefield, 1982), pp. 39–60.

overt sympathy for Custace and expressed desire to intervene actively on her behalf oppose true identification with her, imitation of her action, and simple acceptance of her story at every step of its providential unfolding. Unlike Custance, who regards her own life story as a sequence of divine initiatives, of sendings on God's part and acceptance on hers, the lawyer regards the pattern of events to be an inevitable alternation of "wo" and "joy" based not on God's providential design but on the turning of fortune's wheel. Indeed, the Boethian distinction between providence and destiny essentially defines the differences between Custance's perception of things and that of the Man of Law. The strumpet muses of tragedy inspire the Man of Law, as a weeping narrator, to speak apostrophically, while Custance draws her inspiration elsewhere.

Custance and the Man of Law

Custance's first speech (lines 274–87), addressed to the Roman emperor, is more than a young girl's tearful farewell to her father, and more than an adolescent's worldly-wise acceptance of the facts of life—although the narrator interprets it as such (lines 267–73). Custance feels keenly the pain of parting from her parents, but she recognizes her lot as a consequence of original sin—"Women are born to thraldom and penance, / And to been under mannes governance" (lines 286–87)—and almost instinctively joins her suffering to that of "Crist, that starf for our redempcioun" (line 283). She subordinates destiny to providence, consenting to the marriage arranged by her father and the Sowdan as a way of obeying God: "So yeve me grace his heestes to fulfille" (line 284). At the beginning of the tale Custance already entrusts herself to the "devyne myght" (*Boece* 4, pr.6.337) who ultimately governs the world and who has the power to bring good even out of evil. Custance's "yes" to the will of God as revealed through secondary causes (in this case her father and the Sowdan) expresses her belief that "no thing nis withouten ordenaunce in the reame of the devyne purveaunce" (*Boece* 4, pr.6.349–51).

Custance's speech is followed almost immediately by three stanzas (lines 295–315), not found in Trevet, in which the narrator bewails the fact that Custance's departure coincides with an aberration in the ascendancy of the planet Mars. Unlike Custance, the Man of Law makes no distinction between providence and destiny. Instead he practically identifies God with fate, the First Mover with the "firste moevying" (line 295) of the *primum mobile*. His blasphemous address to the "crueel firmament" (line 295) directly contradicts the Christian belief, expressed by Lady Philosophy in Chaucer's *Boece*, that God's "love . . . governeth erthe and see, and hath also comandement to the hevene" (*Boece* 2, m.8.15–16). Indeed, the Man of Law's speech echoes the unenlightened complaint of Boethius before his instruction by Lady Philosophy: "O thow makere of the wheel that bereth the sterres" (*Boece* 1, m.5.1–2).

The narrator's commentary on the events in Syria, like his interpretation of Custance's farewell and departure, reveals a thoroughly fatalistic way of looking at things. In his exclamations against the Sowdaness he associates her so closely with Satan that she (like the Jews in "The Prioress's Tale") loses all humanity and, therefore, all freedom to make moral choices. Like Donegild, she becomes a "feyned womman" (line 362), evil by nature, who necessarily brings forth "iniquitee" (line 358). The massacre at the wedding feast is similarly glossed as a matter of necessity: "O sodeyn wo, that evere art successour / To worldly blisse, spreynd with bitternesse, / The ende of the joye of oure worldly labour!" (lines 421–23).[69]

Unlike the narrator, who is concerned with happiness in this life and who worships Good Fortune in the person of Christ "that is to every harm triacle" (line 479), Custance worships Christ as the "Flemere of feendes" (line 460). Her long prayer to the cross of Christ immediately follows the Man of Law's ejaculation to the "lord of Fortune" (line 448). She does not ask to be spared hardship and suffering; indeed, she clearly expects to "drenchen in the depe" (line 455). Her only concern is for her eternal salvation (line 454) and for the grace her "lyf t'amenden" (line 462). The sea reminds Custance not of the vagaries of fortune but of the "Lambes blood ful of pitee, / That wessh the world fro the olde iniquitee" (lines 452–53). She

---

69. As Robert Enzer Lewis has shown in "Chaucer's Artistic Use of Pope Innocent III's *De Miseria Humanae Condicionis* in the Man of Law's Prologue and Tale," *PMLA* 81 (1966): 485–92, the narrator quotes the papal text here and elsewhere very selectively, while alerting the reader to larger spiritual contexts that counterbalance and correct his point of view.

hopes that her own death by drowning will be a share in his victorious passion.

The narrator's commentary on Custance's time at sea consists of a series of rhetorical questions comparing her situation with that of Daniel, Jonas, Saint Mary of Egypt, and the five thousand fed in the desert, all of whom were helped by God. Not only are his citations less than accurate, but also they reflect a narrowly defined understanding of "purveiance" (line 483) as a provision for temporal welfare. Surely Chaucer uses the narrator's inept description of the working of God's providence and his appeal to authority—"as knowen clerkis" (line 480)—to remind his readers of Boethius' *Consolation*, where opinions like the lawyer's are specified and judged to be false (*Boece* 1, pr.4.283–88): "the jugement of moche folk ne loken nothyng to the desertes of thynges, but oonly to the aventure of fortune; and jugen that oonly swiche things ben purveied of God, whiche that temporel welefulnesse commendeth."

The Man of Law is incapable of understanding providence as God's plan for humankind's eternal salvation, a loving plan that stands behind all events, even the most painful ones. As Lady Philosophy tells Boethius, "Purvyaunce embraceth alle thinges to-hepe, althoghe that thei ben diverse and although thei ben infinit," while destiny, in dependence on providence, "departeth and ordeyneth alle thinges singulerly" (*Boece* 4, pr.6.67–71). The Man of Law consistently reduces the providential to the fortunate.

Custance, on the other hand, recognizes that God's providential plan often includes temporal suffering and injustice. Banished from Northumbria by Alla's (forged) decree, Custance calls her husband "routheless" (line 863) and "harde" (line 857); she speaks of the innocence of her babe, "that nevere wroghtest synne" (line 856) and yet must suffer. But Custance goes beyond this recognition. She recalls that humankind's salvation came about through the crucifixion and death of Christ, the innocent Sufferer, and that "Mooder Marie" (line 841), the purest of women, witnessed her son's torments, seeing her "child . . . on a croys yrent" (line 844) in atonement for the sins of others. Custance enters into her own passion "with an hooly entente" (line 867), embracing "the wyl of Christ" (line 825) and welcoming his "sonde" (line 826). She is prepared to die but also full of hope. She trusts not in the fateful stars but in the intercession of Mary, the "brighte sterre of day" (line 852), and in the power of

God: "In hym triste I, and in his mooder deere, / That is to me my seyl
and eek my steere" (lines 832–33). When Custance walks firmly
down to the ship, carrying her child in her arms, she becomes an
image of the inwardly free person described by Lady Philosophy
(*Boece* 1, m.4.1–7): "Whoso it be that is cleer of vertue, sad, and wel
ordynat of lyvynge, that hath put under fote the proude wierdes, and
loketh upryght upon either fortune, he may holden his chere un-
desconfited. The rage ne the manaces of the see . . . ne schal nat
moeve that man."[70]
If the memorable scene depicting Custance on the shore represents a certain climax in her development as a character and as a
symbol—for in her moral mastery of destiny she becomes what she is
literally called to be: Constance—there is no comparable development in the narrator. The rhetorical questions he interjects at lines
932–45 conform to the pattern of the earlier ones based on biblical
exempla. He continues to reduce God's saving activity to temporal
assistance, without seeing such interventions on the lower level as a
shadowing forth of the work of salvation in souls. The narrator's final
paraphrase of *De contemptu mundi* (lines 1132–38), like the earlier
ones, comments on the transitoriness of the "joye of this world" (line
1133) without reference to the lasting joy that is a fruit of the Holy
Spirit, and with scarcely an intimation of the "joye after wo" (line
1161) that the saints enjoy in heaven: "I ne seye but for this ende this
sentence, / That litel while in joye or in plesance / Lasteth the blisse
of Alla with Custance" (lines 1139–41). In denial of the Man of
Law's fatalistic assertion that earthly happiness "fro day to nyght . . .
changeth as the tyde" (line 1134), Custance's last years in Rome,
spent "in vertu and in hooly almus-dede" (line 1156), in the midst of
friends and family, seem like a pretasting of eternal happiness.

Disparate Voices

The primary verbal tension in "The Man of Law's Tale," then, is
not (as in many saints' lives) between the heroine's voice and the
voices of her pagan or diabolic persecutors but rather between the

---

70. V. A. Kolve has beautifully documented the medieval use of the turbulent sea
as an icon for the troubles and uncertainties of the human condition. See *Chaucer and
the Imagery of Narrative* (Stanford, Calif.: Stanford University Press, 1984), pp. 325–
40.

voices of Custance and the narrator with their subtly conflictive styles, genres, and points of view. A brief comparison of the trial scenes in "The Second Nun's Tale" and "The Man of Law's Tale" will illustrate the point. In Cecilia's trial before Almachius, she challenges him, speech by speech. When he asks about her " 'religioun and . . . bileeve' " (*SNT* 427), she corrects him for asking "lewedly" (line 430) for two answers in a single question. When he complains about her rudeness and accuses her of lawbreaking, she points to her " 'innocence' " (line 452), " 'good feith' " (line 434), and obedience to " 'conscience.' " His display of power prompts her reply: " 'Youre myght . . . ful litel is to dreede' " (line 437). When Cecilia laughs aloud at his demand that she deny Christ, Almachius accuses her of pride. Once again she insists on another interpretation: " 'I speke noght but stedfastly,' quod she; / 'Nat proudly' " (lines 474–75). She speaks " 'for my syde' " (line 475) against her accuser, acting as her own advocate. Her providential view of things opposes Almachius' so that crime becomes innocence; vice, virtue; power, weakness; pride, fortitude; learning, lewedness; sight, blindness; death, life.

A similar double perspective on things emerges in Custance's trial, but there the dialogue between Christian defendant and pagan accuser is transformed into a more subtle opposition between Custance and her narrator-advocate. When the Man of Law interprets the trial scene as the pathetic tragedy of an unfortunate gentlewoman—apostrophizing "queenes, lyvynge in prosperitee" (*MLT* 652) on behalf of Custance—he assumes a worldly point of view strangely akin to the idolatrous position taken by Cecilia's persecutor. The God who is present to Custance even in trial, even in death, is absent to him. He sees before him only an "Emperoures doghter" (line 655) standing alone and helpless, not the "doghter of hooly chirche" (line 675) vindicated by the Voice. Unlike Cecilia, Custance does not declare her innocence publicly before her judge; she prays instead privately to God: " 'If I be giltless of this felonye, / My socour be' " (lines 643–44). Her prayer belies the narrator's claim: "She hath no wight to whom to make hir mone" (line 656). Indeed, in the very scene where he defends her innocence with pathetic appeals underscoring the absence of help—"no champioun" (line 631), "no grace" (line 647), no "freendes at . . . grete nede" (line 658)—Custance's recourse to a God present to her in prayer quietly prepares the way for miracles and conversion.

By putting Custance's story on the lips of a sentimental (albeit sympathetic) narrator, Chaucer makes a powerful comment on the popular piety of his time that, with its misdirected veneration of the saints, threatened to obscure the true, exemplary power of their holy lives through "*golden legends*" and sensational display.[71] The Wycliffite treatises are full of complaints that popular preachers are making "longe talis of fablis, or cronyclis," instead of preaching "schortly" and "plenerly þe gospel,"[72] and misrepresenting the saints to justify their own worldly life styles: ". . . for þei louen welle to telle hou þis seynt or þis lyuede in gay and costly cloþis & worldly aray, & ʒit is a grete seynt."[73] In appealing for donations, moreover, they are using fabulous miracle stories to exploit people's desire for temporal well-being—even though, as the reformer insists, "bileue of hooly writ passiþ alle þes clepid myraclis."[74]

The epilogue to the tale, which appears in 35 of the 57 manuscripts, suggests the kind of associational ambivalence surrounding exotic legends like that of Custance when Harry Bailey calls upon the Parson to follow the Man of Law's "'thrifty tale'" (*MLT* 1165) with a reformist, Lollard "'predicacioun'" (line 1176). Chaucer's satire, with its disparate voices, makes its own call for reform without preaching simply by permitting Custance to speak, despite the windiness of her self-appointed spokesman. And that quiet voice, articulating a practical belief in divine providence, manages to be heard.

The lives of the three saints—Eustace, Griselda, and Custance—which we have examined all conform to the pattern of Job's life. As a scriptural hero, Job mediates typologically between the old heroes of pagan romance and the new heroes of Christian hagiography. The truth of Job's story thus verifies the extravagance of legend as in each case the exemplary virtue of the hero or heroine is tested, proved, and rewarded. The extraordinary trials which constitute the exterior action of the tales are matched by the equally remarkable

71. Sherry L. Reames charts the reaction against this sort of piety in *The Legenda Aurea: A Reexamination of Its Paradoxical History* (Madison: University of Wisconsin Press, 1985). See also William C. Johnson, Jr., "'The Man of Law's Tale': Aesthetics and Christianity in Chaucer," *Chaucer Review* 16.3 (1982): 201–21.

72. "The Rule and Testament of St. Francis," in John Wyclif, *The English Works of Wyclif*, ed. F. D. Matthew, EETS, vol. 74 (London: Trübner, 1880), p. 50.

73. "The Office of Curates," in ibid., p. 153.

74. "De Papa," in ibid., p. 469.

long-suffering of the protagonists, whose patient endurance and self-control constitute the heroic inner action, the static center, of the legends.

Whereas the relatively straightforward didacticism of the Eustace legend encourages the acceptance of passive purification and the exemplum of Petrarch's Griselda similarly teaches patience in adversity, the Chaucerian romances of Griselda and Constance complicate the plots of serial suffering, fortitude, and final reward through biblical concordance and Boethian allusion. As a result the fundamental synthesis of hagiography and romance becomes a fertile meeting ground for philosophy and theology. The Old Testament story of Job no longer mediates simply between parallel secular and sacred stories. Instead the saintly lives of Griselda and Constance mediate between Job and Boethius. Superimposed allusively on Chaucer's *legenda*, the pathetic outcry of Job merges with the apostrophic weeping of the Boethian prisoner, the suffering of Job with the suffering of Christ, the silence of Job with the wisdom of Lady Philosophy, demonic attack with the blows of misfortune and injustice, happy endings with divine intervention and providential design.

5 Boethian Lovers

The heroes and heroines of romantic Joban *legenda* are, as we have seen, fairly static in their characterization, the constancy of their virtue proven under trial, their stories ending even more happily than they began. Subordinated to this biblical pattern, Boethian laments function intertextually to indicate the cruelty of fortune and the inconstancy of the world and thus, by contrast, the degree of the saints' moral mastery of calamity, steadfastness, and dependence on Providence. A very different sort of story emerges in the Middle Ages when the intertextual relationship is reversed, when Job (as a type of Christ) becomes a background to Boethius. The Boethian hero sets the static Joban protagonist in motion, as it were, and the Christological allegories applied to Job extend the stages of Boethius' philosophical progress into religious conversion.

Unlike Job, whose godlike virtue is steadfast, the prisoner of the *Consolation* makes marked spiritual progress under the tutelage of Lady Philosophy, his positive development as a person intertwined organically with the changed circumstances of his life. Subordinated to this Boethian paradigm, the Book of Job radically alters its fundamental terms by providing a new context for their recuperation in which the hero's affliction becomes redemptive and Christlike; his feminine tutor, Theologia; his healer, grace; his wisdom, charity. A Joban hermeneutic grid, in short, leads to the reading and rewriting of Boethius' *Consolation* as a salvific love story in which the suffering hero advances from and through a passionate love of creatures to the love of the Creator.

The medieval interpretation that first configures and then extends the plot of the *Consolation of Philosophy* as a love story rests upon a double basis: the first, iconographic; the second, mythical. The lovers' triangle formed in the opening scene by the meretricious Muses, the male sufferer, and Philosophia appears again and again in manuscript illuminations of the *Consolation*, which serve to represent Boethius' work as a whole iconographically and thus determine its narrative pattern in the mind, in the book of memory.[1] This allegorical constellation finds its mythic mirror in the metrum (III.m12) of Orpheus and Eurydice.

As we have seen, midway through the *Consolation* the weeping Boethius sees himself reflected in the person of the grief-stricken Orpheus, whose backward glance at Eurydice inspires his own upward glance at Lady Philosophy. As a figure of death and darkness, the fallen Eurydice recalls the strumpet Muses of the first book; turned toward the light, she anticipates the ascent of Philosophia herself. Thus, along opposed narrative lines of descent and ascent, Eurydice joins in her person the negative and positive female *personae* widely separated in the iconography of the opening scene. Her features alter, depending on how Orpheus (and Boethius) look at her. As the myth unfolds, Eurydice mysteriously embodies the abstract double potentiality of temptress and guide in a diachronic fashion that displaces the synchronic opposition of the Sirens and Philosophia into a developmental continuum of "before" and "after" correspondent to the psychological stages in the unfolding and purification of love.

In their exploration of the psychology of love, medieval writers derived from Boethius' iconographic lovers' triangle and its Orphic mirror two distinct but closely related traditions of amatory romance: the first, parodic and reductive; the second, religious and expansive. At first sight the literary imitation of Boethius' work as a love story seems strange because, as Katherine Heinrichs observes, "the *Con-*

---

1. For reproductions of various illuminations, see Pierre Courcelle, *La consolation de philosophie dans la tradition littéraire* (Paris: Études Augustiniennes, 1967). For treatments of the medieval memory, see V. A. Kolve, *The Imagery of Narrative: The First Five Canterbury Tales* (Stanford, Calif.: Stanford University Press, 1984; Mary J. Carruthers, *The Book of Memory: A Study of Memory in Medieval Culture* (Cambridge and New York: Cambridge University Press, 1990).

solation itself, on the face of it, has nothing to do with love *par amours.*[2] Indeed, as Donald W. Rowe once remarked to me, the very expression "Boethian lovers" sounds like an oxymoron. Boethius actually makes love-service "a subcategory of servitude to Fortune" when he lists bodily pleasure as a transitory good (III.p2), and he images it as such when he describes himself as a poet, weeping and sick, in the company of the strumpet Muses.[3]

Boethius' pairing of the sufferer and the Sirens, however, and the related pairing of blind Love and blind Fortune, worked so powerfully in the medieval imagination that, according to Heinrichs, "parodies of *The Consolation of Philosophy* are conventional in medieval love poetry from the time of the *Roman de la Rose*."[4] In these parodies the lover does not merely echo Boethius in his complaints about the instability of love and the fickleness of fortune; he also allows a guide-figure (often a personification of Love) to replace Lady Philosophy and instruct him in amatory Ovidian remedies rather than philosophical ones. These parodies, in short, define "Boethian lovers" reductively, rewriting the *Consolation* as a love story based on only the initial pairing of the poet and the poetical Muses and adding a pseudo-Philosophia—Chaucer's Pandarus, for instance—as a go-between.

There is, however, another tradition of "Boethian lovers" in the Middle Ages which expansively parallels rather than reductively parodies the *Consolation* as a love story, using its triangle of lovers, and the myth of Orpheus and Eurydice in particular, to explore the polar relationship between the carnal and the heavenly Venus, both of whom attract the lover and thus direct his heroic spiritual quest, his growth in self-knowledge, and his movement toward the Eternal Fatherland. In these love stories, as we shall see, the lover's fidelity to a single beloved woman enables him to reach his final goal. Paradoxically, this continuity in love and attachment depends on a series of

2. Katherine Heinrichs, " 'Lovers' Consolations of Philosophy' in Boccacio, Machaut, and Chaucer," *SAC* 11 (1989): 109.

3. Ibid., p. 110.

4. Ibid., p. 93. Heinrichs points to Jean de Meun's *Roman de la Rose*; Machaut's *Fonteinne Amoureuse, Remede de Fortune*, and *Jugement dou Roy de Behaingne*; Froissart's *Paradis d'Amour*, Boccaccio's *Elegia di Madonna Fiammetta*, and Chaucer's *Troilus and Criseyde*.

conversions, radical breaks in which the face of the beloved changes before the lover's eyes, and he is forced to detach himself from false images of her, only to see her again in a more beautiful form. Each change in the beloved prompts conversion in the lover, transforming his cupidity into charity, as she, Eurydice-like, appears before him alernately in light and darkness, darkness and light, as an image of both the mutable and the eternal realms, the lover's way and his destination, his temptress and teacher. Such a beloved is Abelard's Heloise, Dante's Beatrice, and the Criseyde of Chaucer's Troilus.

Abelard: Calamity and Consolation

Although Jean de Meun's *Roman de la Rose* summarizes Peter Abelard's *Historia calamitatum* (c. 1125–32) in a truncated form that serves the parodic tradition,[5] the full Abelardian text deserves to be recognized as the first example of a love story whose emplotment takes a specifically Boethian and Joban form.[5] As Hayden White and others have taught us, the mode of emplotment reflects the historian's interpretation of events as he reconstructs them according to a literary paradigm.[6] While, as Mary Martin McLaughlin puts it, Abe-

5. See *The Romance of the Rose*, trans. Charles Dahlberg (Princeton: Princeton University Press, 1971), lines 8759–832, pp. 160–61. Chaucer, who translated the French *Roman* into English, includes a reference to "Helowys, / That was abbesse not fer fro Parys" (lines 677–78) in the Wife of Bath's Prologue, where she catalogs the wicked wives in her fifth husband's book. Married to a clerk, the Wife superficially resembles both Heloise, married to Abelard, and the wife of philosophical Job (cf. lines 434–36).

6. My analysis extends the view of D. W. Robertson, Jr., that "the *History* is a tightly constructed literary work . . . reinforced by Boethian themes" (*Abelard and Heloise* [New York: Dial Press, 1972], p. 110). I do not, however, find its literariness incompatible with authorship by Abelard. The sharp opposition between history and fiction in the critical debate about authenticity overlooks the importance of typology in medieval historiography. For a review of the scholarly controversy, see Jacques Monfrin, "Le problème de l'authenticité de la correspondance d'Abélard et d'Héloïse," pp. 409–24, and John F. Benton, "Fraud, Fiction, and Borrowing in the Correspondence of Abélard and Héloïse," pp. 469–511, in *Pierre Abélard, Pierre le vénérable* (Paris: Éditions du Centre National de la Recherche Scientifique, 1975). See Hayden White, *Metahistory: The Historical Imagination in Nineteenth-Century Europe* (Baltimore: Johns Hopkins University Press, 1973). On the fluid boundary between fact and fiction in medieval historiography and the typological representation of events, see Stephen G. Nichols, Jr., *Romanesque Signs: Early Medieval Narrative and Iconography* (New

lard's "lens of calamity . . . may seem to have forced upon his experience a unity and coherence that does violence to its realities," his very "selectiveness" allows him to define himself anew, and give shape and meaning to his shattered life, bringing together the past and the present.[7]

Abelard tells the history of his misfortunes using the literary genre of a letter of consolation ("epistola consolatoria") addressed to an unnamed friend.[8] It may well be, as McLaughlin says, that "Abelard himself was the friend whom he wanted to console," much as Boethius addressed himself through Lady Philosophy.[9] At any rate, in the collected *Letters* as we know them, Abelard's *Historia* occasions an exchange of letters between Heloise and himself, the epistolary series approximating the dialogue form of Boethius' *Consolation* and its psychological progression from distress (in the Personal Letters, 1–5) to self-transcendence (in the Letters of Direction, 6–7).

In the *Historia calamitatum*, as we shall see, Abelard casts Heloise in the triple role of strumpet Muse, Philosophia, and Paraclete as his own spiritual state (and relationship to her) changes. The subsequent letters record Heloise's own struggle with the double role Abelard assigns to her as she positions herself variously in relation to him as handmaid, daughter, lover, wife, lady, and sister. Abelard, assuming the part of Lady Philosophy, attempts to console Heloise and form her into his own likeness as a true philosopher and comforter. In the words of Etienne Gilson, the dialogue "ends with Abélard's Christian submission to Providence in the joy of sacrifice, and with Héloïse's acceptance of the Stoic principles which she found in Seneca and Lucan."[10]

Haven: Yale University Press, 1983); Ruth Morse, *Truth and Convention in the Middle Ages: Rhetoric, Representation, and Reality* (Cambridge: Cambridge University Press, 1991).

7. Mary Martin McLaughlin, "Abelard as Autobiographer: The Motives and Meaning of his *Story of Calamities*," *Speculum* 42 (1967): 472–73.

8. For a thorough study of the literature of consolation, see Peter Von Moos, *Consolatio: Studien zur Mittellateinischen Trostliteratur über den Tod und zum Problem der Christlichen Trauer*, 4 vols. (Munich: W. Fink, 1971–72). See also Michael H. Means, *The Consolatio Genre in Medieval English Literature* (Gainesville: University of Florida Press, 1972).

9. "Abelard as Autobiographer," p. 469.

10. Étienne Gilson, *Heloise and Abelard* (1938), trans. L. K. Shook (Ann Arbor: University of Michigan Press, 1960, 1972), p. 86.

Using Boethius' *Consolation* as a literary model for his *Historia*, Abelard constructs his "self," as Mary Carruthers phrases it, "out of bits and pieces of great authors of the past," echoing a major text "in the public domain."[11] He presents himself at the outset as a sick man "wholly enslaved to pride and lechery" (p. 65): "totus in superbia atque luxuria laborarem" (p. 182).[12] God's grace works to cure him, he says, using two remedies, one weaker and one stronger. The first remedy, Abelard's castration by Heloise's uncle, Fulbert, and his friends, heals him of lechery. The second remedy, the burning of his treatise on the Trinity by order of the Council of Soissons, cures him of intellectual pride. Behind "perverse Fortune" (p. 66) Abelard sees "God's compassion," beginning with his falling in love with Heloise, the affair which sent him "toppling down from [his] pedestal" and humbled him: "facilius de sublimitatis huius fastigio prosterneret" (p. 182).

At the beginning of the *Consolation*, Boethius too is a sick man in need of a twofold remedy. Like Abelard, who pridefully styles himself "the only philosopher in the world" (p. 65) (p. 182: "me solum in mundo . . . philosophum"), Boethius considers himself Philosophia's devotee, even though, as Lady Philosophy reminds him, he lacks the self-knowledge of a true philosopher. Boethius needs to remember who he is, even as Abelard requires humbling.

Lady Philosophy discovers the prisoner Boethius in his study, surrounded by Siren-like Muses who inspire him to write self-indulgent complaints, weeping as he writes. In the *Historia calamitatum* Abelard transposes the scene to depict Heloise and himself reading books as they textualize their romance:

> et secretos recessus quos amor optabat studium lectionis offerebat. Apertis itaque libris, plura de amore quam de lectione verba se ingerebant; plura erant oscula quam sententiae; saepius ad sinus quam de libros

11. Carruthers (Book of Memory, pp. 180–81) refers specifically to Heloise's quotation of Lucan, but the principle applies equally well to Abelard's adaptation of Boethius.

12. I use Betty Radice, trans., *The Letters of Abelard and Heloise* (New York: Penguin Books, 1974). Latin quotations are from J. T. Muckle, ed., "Abelard's Letter of Consolation to a Friend *(Historia calamitatum)*," *Mediaeval Studies* 12 (1950): 163–213; "The Personal Letters between Abelard and Heloise: Introduction, Authenticity, and Text," *Mediaeval Studies* 15 (1953): 47–94.

reducebantur manus; crebrius oculos amor in se reflectebat quam lectio in scripturam dirigebat. (p. 183)

[Her studies allowed us to withdraw in private, as love desired, and then with our books open before us, more words of love than of our reading passed between us, and more kissing than teaching. My hands strayed oftener to her bosom than to the pages; love drew our eyes to look on each other more than reading kept them on our texts.] (p. 67)

The beautiful and learned Heloise is Abelard's poetical Muse, inspiring him to write love letters and popular "love songs, not the secrets of philosophy" (p. 68): "carmina . . . amatoria, non philosophiae secreta" (p. 184). (See also Letter 1, pp. 115–17.)[13] Indeed, the "power of love" (p. 70) so constrains him that he has little time or interest in philosophical pursuits.

Like the opposition between the strumpet Muses and Philosophia in the *Consolation*, the Abelardian opposition between Heloise and philosophy seems to brook no compromise. When Abelard tries to convince Heloise, pregnant with their son, to marry him, she presents an extended argument against marriage, citing the epistles of Saint Paul and Seneca and Saint Jerome's *Contra Jovinianum*. She urges Abelard to recall the example of Cicero, who "could not devote his attention to a wife and philosophy alike" (p. 71): "non posse se et uxori et philosophiae operam pariter dare" (p. 186). She begs Abelard "not to put base pleasures before his sacred duties" (p. 73) as a scholar and canon: "ne divinis officiis turpes praeferas voluptates" (p. 188). Finally she makes her famous declaration "that the name of mistress instead of wife would be dearer to her and more honorable" (p. 74) for Abelard: "et quam sibi carius existeret mihique honestius amicam dici quam uxorem" (p. 189).

In Letter 3, Heloise elaborates on Abelard's remark in the *Historia* that women, from the very beginning, have ruined the noblest of men (see p. 70). She includes herself in a long list of temptresses, begin-

---

13. A fifteenth-century manuscript includes a set of love letters between a man and a woman (V[ir] and M[ulier]), written in the first half of the twelfth century in France by "ein Paar wie Abaelard und Heloise waren" (p. 103). The letters, in prose and verse, are full of learned allusions, including quotations of Boethius, Job, and the Song of Songs. See *Epistolae Duorum Amantium: Briefe Abaelards und Heloises?* ed. Ewald Könsgen (Leiden and Cologne: E. J. Brill, 1974).

ning with Eve and Delilah and concluding with Job's wife: "Job, holiest of men, fought his last and hardest battle against his wife, who urged him to curse God" (p. 131) (p. 80: "Iob sanctissimus in uxore novissimam atque gravissiam sustinuit pugnam, quae eum ad maledicendum Deo stimulabat"). The comparison to Job's wife is, in Heloise's view, especially apt, because Abelard's troubles, beginning with his cruel castration, date from the time shortly after their marriage, and because he, like Job, is a holy man, a true philosopher, tested by misfortune and persecuted by the devil.[14]

Paradoxically, when Heloise herself insists upon the incompatibility of sensual pleasures and philosophy, she simultaneously depicts herself as a strumpet and speaks on behalf of Philosophia, combining suasion with truth. Abelard's destiny and the greatness of his vocation, she says, precludes the "base servitude" (p. 70) of an exclusive bond to her. Abelard, however, insists upon the marriage. Only afterward does he recall her arguments and try to achieve the philosophical ideal which Heloise has held up to him and which he continues to associate with her image.

In Abelard's view, his castration marks his conversion from a false to a true love of wisdom:

> et ob hoc maxime Dominica manu me tunc tactum esse cognoscerem quo, liberius a carnalibus illecebris et tumultuosa vita saeculi abstractus, studio litterarum vacarem, nec tam mundi quam Dei vere philosophus fierem. (p. 191)

> [The hand of the Lord . . . touched me for the express purpose of freeing me from the temptations of the flesh and the distractions of the world, so that I could devote myself to learning, and thereby prove myself a true philosopher, not of the world but of God.] (p. 77)

Castrated like Origen, "the greatest of Christian philosophers" (p. 77), Abelard devotes himself as a religious to interpreting Sacred Scripture, "the study of true philosophy," while Heloise takes the veil of a nun.

As Abelard becomes a true philosopher, he endures a series of

14. Heloise goes on to compare her unrepentant confession of continued desire for Abelard to the bitter self-accusation of Job (Letter 3, p. 132). Similar passages from Job (Job 3:20: "in amaritudine animae"; Job 7:11: "confabulor cum amaritudine animae") are incorporated into the epistolary love complaints of the two lovers in the *Epistolae Duorum Amantium*, p. 40.

trials and slanderous attacks, Joban afflictions which he likens repeatedly to the sufferings of Jesus.[15] Comforted by the grace of God
in the wilderness, he and his students build there an oratory, which
Abelard names the Paraclete. In its solitude Abelard achieves a new
reconciliation of his ascetic vocation and intellectual aspirations and
experiences the consoling presence of the Holy Spirit.

When Abelard hands over the Paraclete to Heloise and her nuns
to be their convent in 1131, she becomes for him a feminine image of
the Wisdom and Consolation he seeks. No longer a strumpet Muse
who seduces him away from philosophy, Heloise now surpasses Lady
Philosophy herself. Abelard reports that "all alike admired her piety
and wisdom, and her unequalled gentleness and patience in every
situation" (p. 97) (p. 206: "et omnes pariter eius religionem, pruden-
tiam, et in omnibus incomparabilem patientiae mansuetudinem ad-
mirabantur"), and that the general longing for her "presence and her
spiritual conversation" increased the more she withdrew for prayer
and meditation.

Recalling the holy women who accompanied Christ on his travels, Abelard hopes to find among Heloise and the sisters "a haven
of peace and safety from the raging storms" (p. 102): "ad eas de
aestu huius tempestatis, quasi ad quemdam tranquillitatis portum"
(p. 209). Indeed, he makes his physical safety and his spiritual well-
being dependent on their prayers, especially the prayers of Heloise,
his sister and wife (see Letter 2, pp. 120–24). As Abelard and Heloise
jointly strive for sanctity, his indissoluble marriage with her becomes
an image for his own union with God, her name "Heloise" recalling
the very name of God, "Elohim" (see Letter 4, p. 149). As McLaughlin rightly observes, Abelard, reunited with Heloise after a long separation, finds in her "as abbess of the Paraclete, the sharer and, in a
sense, the agent of his vocation."[16]

In the transformation of his relationship with Heloise, Abelard
finds a proof that "everything is managed by divine ordinance"
(p. 105) (p. 211: "omnia divina dispositione geruntur"), and that God
Himself brings everything "to the best conclusion" in accord with

15. See Donald K. Frank, "Abelard as Imitator of Christ," *Viator* 1 (1970): 107–
13.
16. McLaughlin, "Abelard as Autobiographer," p. 483. She notes that a "re-
surgence of creativity" (p. 485) marked the last decade of Abelard's career, during
which he wrote his *Ethica seu Scito te ipsum,* a work whose title recalls the Delphic
oracle.

His plan: "optimo fine ipse terminat." Our sufferings, deserved and undeserved, also serve a good and merciful end as they "contribute to the expiation of our sins." Therefore, Abelard concludes, we should always pray to God, "Thy will be done," embrace the suffering that is ours, and not rebel in our hearts against the injuries "laid on [us] by divine dispensation" (p. 106). To do so, Abelard warns, is "to leave the path of righteousness" and charity.

Dante's Boethian Beatrice

Abelard's "epistola consolatoria" organizes the events of his life according to a providential pattern informed by Boethius' *Consolation*, in which his beloved Heloise first leads him away from philosophy, then speaks for philosophy, and finally transcends philosophy as a symbol of divine grace. Dante's *Vita Nuova* (c. 1296) has a similar double basis in history and Boethius and, although very different in style and subject matter from Abelard's *Historia*, chronicles a similar progression in the sufferer's life of love from ego-centered lust to you-centered benevolence to God-centered charity.

A prosimetric composition, the *Vita Nuova* presents a series of scenes in which a sorrowful Dante finds comfort and instruction in solitude through the appearance of visionary guides. At first Dante finds his happiness in Beatrice's salutation (*Vita* XI, pp. 30–31).[17] When she denies him her greeting, he weeps and laments in his chamber like a beaten, sobbing child: "come un pargoletto battuto lagrimando" (*Vita* XII.3, p. 32). Love then inspires him to find his happiness, not in anything that comes to him from the outside, but rather within himself, in an inner attitude that cannot fail him: the praise of his lady (*Vita* XVIII, p. 54). The subject matter of Dante's poems changes accordingly. As Charles S. Singleton notes, Dante ceases to "focus upon himself and the effects of love on him" in the style of a troubador; instead he sings in praise of Beatrice, who leads him out of his ego-centric interest in reward.[18]

17. I use Dante Alighieri, *La Vita Nuova*, ed. Tommaso Casini, 3d ed. rev. by Luigi Pietrobono (Florence: G. C. Sansoni, 1968).

18. Charles S. Singleton, *An Essay on "The Vita Nuova"* (Cambridge: Harvard University Press, 1949), p. 83. As Mark Musa observes, "In the picture of the lover

When Beatrice dies, Dante at first seeks happiness in Boethian philosophical consolations, represented in the compassionate gaze of the young lady in the window, who reminds him of Beatrice but who cannot substitute for her.[19] That, however, does not satisfy him. Finally, a vision which allows him to see Beatrice among the blessed ones in heaven gives him a new, divine source of happiness: in what is above himself, in Beatrice joined to God. At every stage in the progress of Dante's development, Beatrice is another name for love (*Vita* XXIV.5, p. 87), the love of God that Dante experiences in various degrees, according to his capacity.

In the *Commedia* Dante retells the tripartite story of his conversion as a salvific love story, repeatedly revising the part of the Boethian Orpheus to represent himself as a lover whose carnal nature at first yields to the strumpet Muse, whose reason is then attracted to Philosophia, and whose immortal soul finally clings to Divine Wisdom. The Siren and Lady Philosophy figure in succession as rivals to the beauty and wisdom embodied in Beatrice, each of them in turn falling back, Eurydice-like, into darkness as Dante directs himself toward heavenly light. Paradoxically, Dante's single-hearted devotion to Beatrice from beginning to end depends on his first seeing her and celebrating her in her rivals, joining together what he later learns to separate. Through what Albert L. Rossi has called "a series of complementary non-reenactments of Orpheus' drama," these moments of detachment mark the steady progress of Dante's ascent in the *Commedia*.[20] He succeeds where Orpheus fails, rises when Eurydice falls, as Dante uses the Orphic myth to structure three widely separated scenes, each a palinodic passage where the figure of Orpheus, the archetypal poet and philosopher, recalls the love poetry of Dante's own past.

---

there is offered a condemnation of the vice of emotional self-indulgence and an exposure of its destructive effects on a man's integrity" (*Dante's "Vita Nuova": A Translation and an Essay* [Bloomington: Indiana University Press, 1973], p. 171).

19. See Etienne Henry Gilson, *Dante and Philosophy*, trans. David Moore (Sheed and Ward, 1949; New York: Harper and Row, 1963), pp. 86–98, for a discussion of Philosophy as the *donna gentile* of the *Vita Nuova* and the *Convivio*.

20. Albert L. Rossi, "*Miro gurge* (*Par.* xxx,68): Virgilian Language and Textual Pattern in the River of Light," *Dante Studies* 103 (1985): 79–101, p. 86. Rossi finds "the first of these circumventions" in *Purg.* xxx,40–48, where Dante "plays out the tragic loss of Virgil in terms of Orpheus' loss of Eurydice."

The first scene is Dante's encounter with Francesca and Paolo in the second circle of hell, among the "carnal sinners, who subject reason to desire" (p. 49).[21] Francesca paraphrases the *Consolation* (II.p4,2) and thus names Boethius Dante's teacher: "There is no greater sorrow than to recall, in wretchedness, the happy time; and this your teacher knows" (p. 55) (*Inf.* V.121–23: "Nessun maggior dolore / che ricordarsi del tempo felice / ne la miseria; e ciò sa 'l tuo dottore").[22] Dante twice associates Francesca with Dido (lines 61–62, 85) while he places Aeneas and Orpheus above them in Limbo, the first circle of hell. Dante's encounter with Francesca thus recalls not only Aeneas' meeting with Dido in *Aeneid* 6, but also the story of Orpheus' descent in *Georgics* 4 and *Consolation* III.m12. Francesca's story causes a momentary stillness in the restlessness of hell and inspires Dante to weep for grief and pity, even as Orpheus' music suspends the torments of Hades and moves its denizens to compassion. Her anaphoric description of Love as the cause of her adultery and death, moreover, recalls the Virgilian and Boethian treatment of Love as the higher law given to lovers (*Cons.* III.m12,48: "Maior lex amor est sibi") that compels Orpheus to look back at Eurydice and lose her. Dante's bewildered pity, tears, and swoon at hearing Francesca's tale (*Inf.* V.72,116–17,139–42) parallels Boethius' troubled response to the myth of Orpheus (see *Cons.* IV.p1,1), even as Francesca's poetry in praise of Love and her reading of seductive romances recalls simultaneously Dante's own love poetry in the *dolce stil nuovo*, Abelard's bookish seduction of Heloise, and Boethius' sojourn with the strumpet Muses.[23]

The second scene shows an ascendant Orpheus in the figure of the singer Casella, whose shade Dante embraces three times at the

---

21. Unless otherwise indicated, I use Charles S. Singleton's edition and translation of Dante's *The Divine Comedy: Inferno*, vols. 1 and 2, Bollingen Series 58 (Princeton: Princeton University Press, 1970, 1977); *Purgatorio*, vols. 1 and 2, 1973, repr. 1977; *Paradiso*, vols. 1 and 2, 1975, 1977.

22. See Singleton's *Commentary*, p. 93; Edward Moore, *Scripture and Classical Authors in Dante*, Dante Studies, 1st series (Oxford: Clarendon Press, 1896; New York: Greenwood Press, 1968), pp. 282–83. Dante's acknowledged debt to Boethius is great. In *Par.* X,124–29 he numbers him among the Doctors of the Church.

23. The similarity between Paolo's seduction of Francesca da Rimini and Abelard's of Heloise has been noted. See Peter von Moos, "Le silence d'Héloïse et les idéologies modernes," in *Pierre Abélard, Pierre le vénérable*, pp. 461–62. Dante's response to Francesca anticipates his dream of the Siren in *Purg.* xix,19.

entrance to Purgatory. In a phrase evocative of Boethius, Dante begs Casella to "comfort [his] soul somewhat" (p. 21)—"consolare alquanto / l'anima mia" (*Purg.* II.109–10)—with a song of love. Casella responds by singing Dante's own *canzone* (II, *Convivio* III), "Amor che ne la mente mi ragiona" (*Purg.* II.112), in praise of Lady Philosophy. "Rapt and attentive" (p. 21) like feeding doves, Dante, Virgil, and the souls gathered there around Casella listen spellbound to his singing, until Cato's rebuke startles them into action. The image recalls the music of Orpheus, which hushed the wild animals; the singing of Philosophia herself, which consoled Boethius; and Boethius' prosimetric *Consolation*, which comforted Dante after Beatrice's death. As John Freccero insists, the philosophical *amor* of Casella's song represents a definite advance over the carnal *amor* of Francesca, but it nevertheless clearly falls short of the divine *amor* of Beatrice. Therefore, "just as Boethius' *Philosophia* had cast out the Muses of secular poetry, she in turn is 'cast out' in Dante's text by Cato's rebuke."[24]

The third Orphic scene shows Dante in the Earthly Paradise. As Singleton and others have noted, Dante's "triune farewell to Virgil" in a single tercet (*Purg.* XXX.49–51) recalls Orpheus' thrice-repeated call to Eurydice as she vanishes from his sight at the very threshold of the upper world (*Georg.* 4.525–27).[25] At the same time the Virgilian words with which Dante greets Beatrice's presence, "I know the tokens of the ancient flame" (p. 329) (*Purg.* XXX.49: "conosco i segni de l'antica fiamma"), represent his backward glance at Dido, Francesca, and the Eurydice-like Beatrice he served as a courtly lover. That backward glance both precipitates the loss of Virgil, who disappears from Dante's sight, and necessitates the intervention of the heavenly Beatrice. Like Lady Philosophy at the close of the Orpheus metrum (*Cons.* IV.p1), Beatrice promises Dante the means of ascent to his true, paradisal homeland, but first, her eyes ablaze, she demands his renunciation of the strumpet Muses who have enslaved him—both the false pleasures of *temporalia* (XXXI.

24. John Freccero, *Dante: The Poetics of Conversion*, ed. Rachel Jacoff (Cambridge: Harvard University Press, 1986), p. 190. Singleton, on the other hand, downplays the importance of the reference to Philosophia and treats the *canzone* as "simply a love song" (*Commentary*, p. 40).

25. Singleton, *Commentary*, p. 741.

34–36) and the seductions of secular philosophy (XXXIII.85–87).[26] Only when a chastened Dante confesses his twofold failings can he look into Beatrice's eyes and understand what she reveals to him.

The critical moment at the end of the *Purgatorio* when Dante looks backward and forward at Beatrice, losing her as a carnal Muse and gaining her as a celestial guide, provides a gloss for the double perspective on Criseyde in Chaucer's *Troilus* and for the poem's participation in two opposed traditions of Boethian lovers, parodic/reductive and religious/expansive. Pandarus, who represents the poet from within the poem as a go-between, works to construct a parodic narrative in which he, playing the part of a worldly-wise Lady Philosophy, heals a lovesick Troilus with erotic remedies.[27] Troilus, on the other hand, represents the poet as an Orpheus-figure who constructs an ascendant love-narrative out of the same set of events. Troilus' view of things, as we shall see, collaborates with Pandarus' version of the story, competes with it, and finally displaces it. Not only do allusions to the myth of Orpheus and Eurydice color the whole of Chaucer's *Troilus*; the literal action and moral interpretation of the myth as told by Lady Philosophy provide an important intertextual key for the two-part narrative structure of the *Troilus* and its epilogue.

Orpheus, Eurydice, and the "Double Sorwe" of Chaucer's *Troilus*

Chaucer's "litel bok" has a clear two-part structure.[28] Chaucer himself makes the *divisio* of his *tractatus* explicit when he, in the person

26. For a comment on Beatrice's rebuke and Dante's "exaggerated philosophism" (p. 111), see J. F. Took, *Dante: Lyric Poet and Philosopher: An Introduction to the Minor Works* (Oxford: Clarendon Press, 1990), p. 111.

27. For a discussion of Geoffrey of Vinsauf and Pandarus as poet, see Paula Neuss, "Images of Writing and the Book in Chaucer's Poetry," *Review of English Studies* 32 (1981): 385–97. For Pandarus as Lady Philosophy, see Martin Camargo, "The Consolation of Pandarus," *Chaucer Review* 25.3 (1991): 214–28.

28. Geoffrey Chaucer, *Troilus and Criseyde*, in *The Riverside Chaucer*, 3d ed., ed. Larry D. Benson (Boston: Houghton Mifflin, 1987), V, 1786. I use this edition of Chaucer's works throughout, giving parenthetical citations. The two-part structure is reflected in the critical division on the poem's interpretation. C. S. Lewis's definition of the *Troilus* as "a great poem in praise of love" (*The Allegory of Love* [New York: Oxford

of the poet/narrator, announces his intention the "double sorwe of Troilus to tellen" (I.1). The delayed modifier "in lovynge" (I.3) is positioned in such a way that it modifies both the "double sorwe" and the binary course of the dramatic action "fro wo to wele, and after out of joie." Directly before the narrative proper begins, the narrator reiterates the program of the poem from the audience's point of view: "ye may the double sorwes here / Of Troilus in lovynge of Criseyde"—the added clause "And how that she forsook hym er she deyde" modifying the second of Troilus' sorrows rather than indicating a third part of the narrative (I.54–56).

Despite the obvious structural significance of the "double sorwe" and the symbolic importance the Middle Ages generally attached to numbers and *divisiones*, little critical attention has been given to the phrase as a key to the poem's meaning.[29] Thomas E. Maresca is, I believe, the only critic to note a concordance between the "double sorwe of Troilus . . . / In lovynge" and the love "that doublide [the] sorwe" (*Boece* III.m12:26) of Orpheus in Lady Philosophy's version, and Chaucer's translation, of that myth.[30] Maresca, however, only

---

University Press, 1938, 1958], p. 197) leads him to discount not only the moralitee in the epilogue, but also the pain and suffering of the last two books. D. W. Robertson, Jr., John P. McCall, and Theodore A. Stroud, on the other hand, all tend to dismiss as illusory the movement "fro wo to wele" (I,4) in the first three books. See Robertson, "Chaucerian Tragedy," *ELH* 19 (1952): 1–37, repr. in *Chaucer Criticism*, vol. 2, ed. Richard J. Schoek and Jerome Taylor (Notre Dame: University of Notre Dame Press, 1961), pp. 86–121; McCall, "Five-Book Structure in Chaucer's *Troilus*," *MLQ* 23 (1962): 297–308; Stroud, "Boethius' Influence on Chaucer's *Troilus*," *MP* 49 (1951–52): 1–9, in Schoek and Taylor, pp. 122–35.

29. Judson B. Allen has emphasized that any satisfactory approach to a medieval narrative as an allegory of event must include a recognition of the discrete parts of its *forma tractatus*, as outlined in the plot sequence, and a discovery of a parallel text with analogous divisions or distinctions. See Allen, *The Ethical Poet of the Later Middle Ages* (Toronto: University of Toronto Press, 1982). Robertson, Stroud, McCall, and Thomas E. Maresca all imply that Troilus really has only a single sorrow: the unhappiness that belongs to living in a state of sin or cupidity as a slave of Fortune. Indeed, Maresca goes so far as to equate Troilus' "double sorwe" with the "duplex poena" of body and soul endured by the damned in hell—a gloss that does little to illuminate the two-part rising and falling action of the poem "fro wo to wele, and after out of joie." See Maresca, *Three English Epics* (Lincoln: University of Nebraska Press, 1979), p. 157. F. N. Robinson finds a possible source for Chaucer's phrase in the "doppia tristizia di Jocasta" in Dante's *Purgatorio* XXII.56, but admits that the context in which the phrase appears there does not seem applicable to the *Troilus*. See Robinson, ed., *The Works of Geoffrey Chaucer*, 2d ed. (Boston: Houghton Mifflin, 1957), pp. 813–14.

30. See Maresca, *Three English Epics*, p. 160.

regards the verbal echo as one of the many classical allusions to the underworld in Chaucer's poem, whose action he construes as an unbroken, vicious descent into corporeality. He fails to draw any systematic structural parallel between the action of the myth and the action of the *Troilus*. Indeed, even though Criseyde directly compares Troilus and herself to Orpheus and Eurydice in a speech (IV.785–91) that echoes Troilus' earlier one (IV.470–76), practically no scholarly attention has been given to the parallelism of the two stories.[31]

If, as the scholarly consensus affirms, the *Troilus* derives its philosophical tenor from Boethius' *Consolatio*, then Chaucer certainly had the story of Orpheus in mind as he composed his "litel bok." Chaucer's witty short poem addressed to "Adam Scriveyn" indicates that he was translating the *Consolatio* at the same time that he was writing *Troilus and Criseyde* (probably 1380–85), and paraphrases of *Boece* which occur in two key passages of the *Troilus*, III.1744–71 and IV.953–1085, confirm the close connection between the two works. Like Chaucer's *Troilus*, the tale of Orpheus and Eurydice is a love story—indeed, the only love story contained in the *Consolatio*. It is, moreover, a story which has a central symbolic importance for Boethius' work as a whole. Book III begins with Lady Philosophy's stated intent to guide the prisoner until he has first beheld the "false goodes" of this world and then turned his "eighen to the tother syde," where he may "knowe the cleernesse of verray blisfulnesse" (*Boece* III.p1.48–50); it concludes with the tale of Orpheus, whose backward glance upon Eurydice ends his upward progress into light, and whose failure offers a warning to every man to avoid looking "into lowe thinges of the erthe" if he wishes to behold the "sovereyn good" (III.m12.70,63).

---

31. Donald W. Rowe observes that the "myth and Boethius' interpretation of it is relevant to the *Troilus*," but he himself does not explain that relevancy. See Rowe, *O Love! O Charite! Contraries Harmonized in Chaucer's "Troilus"* (Carbondale: Southern Illinois University Press, 1976), n. 24, p. 192. Monica E. McAlpine (*The Genre of "Troilus and Criseyde"* [Ithaca: Cornell University Press, 1978], pp. 67–68) offers a psychological interpretation of Boethius' metrum, but fails to apply it to the *Troilus* directly. Ida L. Gordon tersely responds to the "ineptitude of [Criseyde's] choice of Orpheus and Eurydice as an analogy for the eternal reunion of her spirit with Troilus," given her subsequent betrayal of her lover, without considering the larger implications of the reference for the work as a whole. See *The Double Sorrow of Troilus: A Study of Ambiguities in "Troilus and Criseyde"* (Oxford: Clarendon Press, 1970), p. 105.

The tale of the Thracian bard, then, is a tragic love story used to convey the central moral lesson of Boethius' *Consolatio*, a lesson correspondent to the moralitee spelled out in the epilogue to Chaucer's *Troilus*, a poem recounting "Swich peyne and wo as Loves folk endure" (I.34). Chaucer clearly understood both stories to be teaching the same lesson. Moreover, both the Orpheus metrum and Chaucer's poem have a decided two-part structure based on the lover's winning, and then losing, his beloved. I hope to make explicit the larger implications of such correspondences by systematically exploring the parallelism in plot between the two tales, using the twofold *distinctio* that emerges from the commentary tradition on the Orpheus myth to explain Chaucer's *divisio* of the narrative action of the *Troilus* into two parts.

Medieval commentators typically located the Orphic descent within the fourfold *distinctio* of descents provided by Bernardus Silvestris in his twelfth-century *Commentum Super Sex Libros Eneidos Virgilii*.[32] According to Bernardus, all human beings accomplish the first descent at the moment when the soul leaves the realm of pure spirits and joins with the body in a kind of marriage. The other three descents that he names specify the range of possible spiritual responses to the material universe. If spirit dominates over matter through contemplative exercise, man makes a virtuous descent to creatures. If sensual desires subjugate the soul, the descent is a vicious one. Finally, if the mind exercises a magical rather than a moral control over creatures through the conjugation of spirits, the *descensus* is an artificial one.

While the first pattern of descent necessarily has a universal application, the second and third varieties of *descensus* have a particular application to the myth of Orpheus and Eurydice in the writings of Bernardus, Boethius, Guillame de Conches, Nicholas Trevet, and other commentators interested in its moralization. According to Bernardus, Orpheus and Hercules, whom everyone considers to have been wise men (*sapientes*), made a virtuous descent to creatures,

32. See *The Commentary on the First Six Books of the "Aeneid" of Vergil Commonly Attributed to Bernardus Silvestris*, ed. Julian Ward Jones and Elizabeth Frances Jones (Lincoln: University of Nebraska Press, 1977), p. 30; Earl G. Schreiber and Thomas E. Maresca, trans., *The Commentary on the First Six Books of Virgil's "Aeneid" by Bernardus Silvestris* (Lincoln: University of Nebraska Press, 1970), pp. 32–33.

meditating on their frailty in order to turn from them and recognize more clearly the greatness of the Creator. Eurydice, on the other hand, made an irreversible, vicious descent to the underworld. This exegetical tradition of a double, positive and negative descent certainly influenced Chaucer's understanding of the Orpheus myth, given the evidence of the parenthetical glosses in his translation of Boethius.[33] As I hope to show, the *descensus virtutis* and the *descensus vitii* apply respectively to the rising and falling action of Chaucer's *Troilus* in much the same way that they do to the pattern of events in the Orphic myth.

Briefly put, Troilus' falling in love with Criseyde and his efforts to gain her affection which culminate in the rhapsodic "marriage" of Book III correspond to the virtuous descent of Orpheus into the underworld to rescue Eurydice, an attempt which terminates in the near-victory of an ascent into the light. Both stories, then, have an initial movement "fro wo to wele." Similarly, the high point of both stories is followed abruptly by a falling action leading the protagonists "out of joie"—Criseyde's leaving Troy and forsaking Troilus corresponding to Eurydice's vicious descent into Hades, and Troilus' despair at her loss corresponding to Orpheus' intense grief at his failure to retrieve and keep his wife.

These broad parallels become an important interpretive tool, given the meaning the medieval commentaries on the myth attached to the double *descensus* into *temporalia*. Chaucer's *Troilus* relates intertextually to Boethius' *Consolatio* as a whole in much the same way that the poetical myth of metrum 12 does. Both poems affirm the paradoxical necessity of attaching oneself to earthly things, and then detaching oneself from them, and give expression to the human pain that comes from these two contrary movements of love. One comes to know the perfect only through an affective knowledge of the imperfect. As Lady Philosophy tells the prisoner, "yif ther be a blisfulnesse that be freel and veyn and imparfyt, ther may no man doute

33. Chaucer certainly used Trevet's commentary on Boethius. See Kate O. Petersen, "Chaucer and Trivet," *PMLA* 18 (1903): 173–93; Mark J. Gleason, "Clearing the Fields: Towards a Reassessment of Chaucer's Use of Trevet in the 'Boece,' " in *The Medieval Boethius: Studies in the Vernacular Translations of "De Consolatione Philosophiae,"* ed. Alastair J. Minnis (Cambridge: D. S. Brewer, 1987), pp. 89–105; Alastair J. Minnis, " 'Glosynge Is a Glorious Thyng': Chaucer at Work on the 'Boece,' " in *The Medieval Boethius,* pp. 106–24.

that ther nys som blisfulnesse that is sad, stedefast, and parfyt" (*Boece* III.p10.31–35).

While the story of Troilus and Criseyde, as Chaucer tells it, belongs mainly to the set of stories dramatizing the Boethian moral and philosophical position with regard to the love of creatures, the Orphic myth belongs simultaneously to other intersecting sets of stories— notably the tales of courtly love and the pagan typologies of Christ— which, in turn, color Chaucer's treatment of the Troilus legend. Troilus-as-Orpheus is a poet whose limited lyric transformation of his own history allows Chaucer, through his narrator, to comment self-reflexively on the relationship between art and life, harmony and history, poetry and philosophy.

Chaucer's *Troilus and Criseyde* begins with two allusions to the Orpheus-Eurydice myth. After the narrator announces his intention to tell about "the double sorwe of Troilus," he invokes Thesiphone, whom he describes as a "cruwel Furie, sorwynge evere in peyne" (I.9). According to the account in Ovid's *Metamorphoses*, the Furies wept for the first time when Orpheus sang his love song in Hades: "Tunc primum lacrimis victarum carmine fama est / Eumenidum maduisse genas."[34] Similarly, Chaucer's translation of Boethius reads: "And the thre goddesses, furiis and vengeresses of felonyes, that tormenten and agasten the soules by anoy, woxen sorweful and sory, and wepyn teeris for pite" (*Boece* III.m12.33–36). The sorrowing Fury, then, is a figure especially associated with the Orpheus myth, and the narrator's invocation of Thesiphone serves to establish a certain parallel between the two stories.

Even as the Orphic story in Chaucer's *Boece* begins with the "ryght greet sorwe" Orpheus had "for the deth of his wyf" (*Boece* III.m12.5), so too, Chaucer's *Troilus and Criseyde* begins with the first of Troilus' "sorwes": his abrupt falling into love with Criseyde, who, as a widow, is a wife shadowed over by death: "a widewe was she and allone" (I.97). When, after Calkas' defection, Criseyde falls to her knees to plead for Hector's protection, she wears a "widewes habit large of samyt broun" (I.109). When Troilus first feels attracted to Criseyde, he sees her clad "in widewes habit blak" (I.170). The initial description of Criseyde associates her with death, with bereavement, and

---

34. Ovid, *Metamorphoses*, vol. 2, ed. and trans. Frank Justus Miller, Loeb Classical Library 2 (New York, 1916), 10:45–46.

with the realm of spirits. She is, we are told, "aungelik" and "lik a thing immortal," "an hevenyssh perfit creature, / That down were sent in scornynge of nature" (I.102–5). In short, Criseyde resembles the beautiful young wife Eurydice, cast down by Death among the shades.

At the beginning of the story Criseyde has already made her descent from the realm of pure spirits into the underworld of corporeality, love, and death. Troilus' sudden falling into love with her is described as an abrupt *descensus*: "This Troilus is clomben on the staire, / And litel weneth that he moot descenden" (I.215–16). Having never felt sexual attraction before, and having roundly mocked the young lovers in his acquaintance, Troilus is confused by the force of his own emotions when he looks upon Criseyde, "so gret desir and such affeccioun" (I.296) does he feel for her.

Troilus' passion for Criseyde brings him metaphorically, if not literally, into the shadow of death: "For hote of cold, for cold of hote, I dye" (I.420). Obsessed with the thought of her, Troilus grows feverish and pale with the "hote fir" (I.445) of longing—so much so that he calls his affliction by the name of some "other siknesse, lest men of hym wende / That the hote fir of love hym brende" (I.489–90). Love for Criseyde burns in Troilus' heart, even as "the most ardaunt love of his wif brende the entrayles of [Orpheus's] breest" (*Boece* III.m12: 13–15) and drew him into the underworld.

Maresca, Robertson, and others insist that Troilus' falling into love in Book I is the first step in a continuous process of moral abasement. Indirectly they associate his *descensus*, from the beginning of the poem to the end, with the third descent defined by Bernardus:

Est vero tercius vitii, qui vulgaris est, quo ad temporalia pervenitur atque in eis tota intentio ponitur eisque tota mente servitur nec ab eis amplius dimovetur.

[And truly there is a third, vicious descent, which is common, by which one is completely oriented toward the things of this world so that one's whole desire is fixed on them, one's whole mind is enslaved to them, and cannot anymore be removed from them.][35]

35. *Commentary*, p. 30; translation mine.

This interpretation of the action necessarily dismisses as illusory the movement "Fro wo to wele" in Books I-II-III, and renders Chaucer's own two-part *divisio* meaningless.

There are, however, considerable grounds for associating the course of Troilus' love for Criseyde in the first books with the virtuous, rather than the vicious, descent in Bernardus' schema. As we have seen, Bernardus illustrates the *descensus virtutis* with Orpheus' attempt to retrieve Eurydice from the underworld—"Sed hoc modo Orpheus et Hercules qui sapientes habiti sunt descenderunt"—and explains that a descent of this kind is undertaken by the lover of wisdom who desires to come to know God more clearly through the knowledge of His creatures: "ut per creaturarum cognitionem creatorem evidentius cognoscat."[36]

The *Canticus Troili*, the song Troilus intones immediately after his decision "Criseyde for to love" (I.392), directly connects his understanding of his own affective life with his understandng of the nature of God: "If no love is, O God, what fele I so? / And if love is, what thing and which is he?" (I.400–401). Interiorly he surrenders himself to the God of Love in words echoing Christ's on the cross—"O lord, now youres is / My spirit, which that oughte youres be" (I.422–23)—and only then, in dependence on this God's will, does he give himself to Criseyde to "bicome hir man" (I.434). Like Orpheus taking Eurydice by the hand, Troilus' efforts to love and serve Criseyde symbolize his desire "to lede his thought into the soveryn day (*that is to seyn, into cleernesse of sovereyn good*)" (*Boece* III.m12:61–63). Nor is Troilus' meditative descent without success. At the end of Book III, as a result of loving Criseyde, he can speak the words Boethius attributes to Lady Philosophy, celebrating the bond of love that sustains and orders the cosmos, praising "Love, that of erthe and se hath governaunce" (III.1744).

The text suggests that Troilus' love for Criseyde ennobles him and that, as Rowe says, his is a "fortunate fall," a genuine conversion, a turning away from "surquidrie and foul presumpcioun" (I.213) toward a love that is "vertuous in kynde" (I.254).[37] While we may be

36. Ibid.
37. Rowe, *O Love!*, 71. Rowe's discussion of the *descensus* pattern in the *Troilus* essentially reinforces mine, even as his treatment of creation's dissimilar similitude to God provides a philosophical and theological explanation for the ascetical movement

dubious when Pandarus tells Troilus, "Love, of his goodnesse, / Hath the converted out of wikkednesse" (I.998–99)—given Pandarus' ability to speak "for the nones" (I.561)—we can hardly dismiss the repeated testimony borne by the narrator to Troilus' moral transformation.

Already at the end of Book 1 the narrator reports that Troilus' valor in battle increased, and that his social behavior "Soo goodly was . . . / That ecch hym loved that loked on his face":

> For he bicom the frendlieste wight,
> The gentilest, and ek the mooste fre,
> The thriftiest and oon the beste knyght,
> That in his tyme was or myghte be.
>
> (I.1077–82)

Later Pandarus' description of Troilus as "worthi Ector the secounde" (II.158) gains support when the people gather in the streets to acclaim him: "Here cometh oure joye, / And, next his brother, holder up of Troye" (II.643–44). The narrator, too, joins in the general approbation and declares, "It was an heven upon hym for to see" (II.637). At the end of Book III the narrator is even more emphatic about the transformation wrought in Troilus through the power of love. He attributes to Love's influence the "encrees of hardynesse and myght" (III.1776) in Troilus the warrior; the perfection of Troilus' social graces; and his conscious, resolute avoidance of "Pride, Envye, and Ire, and Avarice /. . . and everich other vice" (III.1805–1806). Indeed, the narrator considers every good quality in Troilus "th' effect and joie of [his] servise" of Love (III.1815). Criseyde also offers her testimony that she loves Troilus because of his "moral vertu, grounded upon trouthe" (IV.1672).

Troilus' own words and actions, moreover, testify to his inward transformation. Not even Pandarus' busyness and Troilus' collaboration in his reprehensible scheme can nullify the impression that God somehow reveals Himself to Troilus through Criseyde on that rainy night when they first make love. Troilus' sense of personal unworthiness, of guilt, and of gratefulness at being forgiven and accepted by

---

of attachment and detachment I see informing the rising and falling action of the plot sequence.

Criseyde gains beautiful expression in hymns and prayers directed to Venus, Hymen (Imeneus), and Cupid. Troilus calls aloud, "O Love! O Charite!" and addresses Cupid with the words Dante puts on the lips of Saint Bernard: "Benigne Love, thow holy bond of thynges." He declares that he has learned through the experience of love the divine truth "that mercy passeth right," and expresses to Criseyde the hope that he will continue to advance along the way of perfection "through the vertu of [her] heigh servyse." Criseyde is, he says, the God-appointed "steere" for his life (III.1254–91).

The religious imagery in Book III encourages us to read the consummation scene as a self-revelation of the God Who is Love and Who manifests Himself in the created order.[38] Criseyde becomes, as it were, a vessel of grace and a transparency of Eternal Love, coming from Him and leading Troilus back to Him. While Criseyde can hardly be likened to the Beatrice of Revelation in the *Commedia*, she does resemble the earthly Beatrice, who inspired desires in the youthful Dante which led him "to love the Good beyond which there's no thing to draw our longing," and whose beauty offered him a remote preparation for the vision of God.[39]

---

38. See Alfred David, "The Hero of the *Troilus*," *Speculum* 37 (1962): 566–81; T. P. Dunning, "God and Man in *Troilus and Criseyde*," in *English and Medieval Studies Presented to J. R. R. Tolkien*, ed. Norman Davis and C. L. Wrenn (London: Allen and Unwin, 1962), pp. 164–82; Lonnie J. Durham, "Love and Death in *Troilus and Criseyde*," *Chaucer Review* 3 (1968): 1–11; Peter Dronke, "The Conclusion of *Troilus and Criseyde*," *Medium Aevum* 33 (1964): 47–52; Peter Heidtmann, "Sex and Salvation in *Troilus and Criseyde*," *Chaucer Review* 2 (1968): 246–63.

39. Dante Alighieri, *Purgatorio*, trans. Allen Mandelbaum (Berkeley: University of California Press, 1982), 31: 22–24. The *Commedia* as a whole, of course, illuminates the *descensus* pattern. The success of Dante's virtuous descent *ad inferos* depends, paradoxically, on his having made a vicious descent there. Because Dante sees his own sins, real and potential, punished vicariously in the damned and atoned for by the souls in purgatory, he becomes capable of an ascent to the Empyrean. Similarly, Troilus must see his own lower passions mirrored in Diomede's before his love for Criseyde is perfected in love for God. See Steve Ellis, "Chaucer, Dante, and Damnation," *Chaucer Review* 22.4 (1988): 282–94; Winthrop Wetherbee, *Chaucer and the Poets: An Essay on "Troilus and Criseyde"* (Ithaca: Cornell University Press, 1984), pp. 109–10, 177–78; Elizabeth D. Kirk, " 'Paradis Stood Formed in Hire Yën': Courtly Love and Chaucer's Re-Vision of Dante," in *Acts of Interpretation: Essays on Medieval and Renaissance Literature in Honor of E. Talbot Donaldson*, ed. Mary J. Carruthers and Elizabeth D. Kirk (Norman, Okla.: Pilgrim Books, 1982), pp. 257–77. For a contrasting view, see Karla Taylor, *Chaucer Reads "The Divine Comedy"* (Stanford, Calif.: Stanford University Press, 1989).

Although the narrator tells us that Troilus and Criseyde spent "many a nyght" (III.1713) together through the machinations of Pandarus, only the first, memorable night is described in detail. The other trysts are, we are told, simply repetitions of the first, differing from one another only in a steady intensification of the lovers' mutual joy until it surpasses the power of expression and "passeth al that herte may bythynke" (III.1694). The effect of this kind of narrative treatment is that the many nights the lovers spent together all merge into the one that is fully described. The *aube*-lyrics, in which Criseyde complains about the shortness of the night, and Troilus about the coming of "cruel day" (III.1450), bring the poem's dramatic action to a point "at the termes of the nyght," somewhere near the boundary line between heaven and earth where matter straining upward touches upon the purely spiritual. Similarly, in the Boethian myth, Orpheus leads his beloved Eurydice upward to the "laste boundes of helle" (*Boece* III.m12:56–58).

It is there, at the utmost limit of man's unaided ability to integrate his being toward Above and direct his desires toward the Supreme Good, that Orpheus falters. He looks upon Eurydice and loses her. In the myth that loss hinges upon a mysterious and seemingly arbitrary "lawe . . . and covenaunt" that Pluto imposes upon Orpheus when he gives him the gift of his wife: "til he be out of helle, yif he loke byhynde hym, . . . his wyf schal comen ageyn unto us." The Neoplatonic poetry of the metrum suggests that Orpheus' heroic effort is bound to fail—first of all, because man cannot ever really be "out of helle" while he remains in the flesh, his soul joined to the body and subject to its drives; secondly, because "love is a grettere lawe and a strengere to hymself (*thanne any lawe that men mai yyven*")" (*Boece* III.m12:49–55). The same love that wondrously suspends the powers of suffering, death, and decay makes the lover especially vulnerable to those same powers.

The very arbitrariness of the condition Pluto attaches to the "yifte" of Eurydice suggests that there *is* no explanation for Orpheus' failure except that it simply belongs to the nature of loving in a fallen world. Because love urges the lover on *"into cleernesse of soveryn good,"* it necessarily brings him into an encounter with his own creaturely limitation and sinfulness "at the laste boundes of helle" (*Boece* III.m12:63, 57–58). At the last the lover *must* be disappointed in one way or another if he is to learn that the temporal good that reflects the "sovereyn good" so beautifully is only a reflection after all. Indeed, as Bernardus says, the meditative or virtuous descent ("per considerationem") to creatures must finally include a recognition of their frailty ("eorum cognita fragilitate") and a painful detachment from them ("eis abiectis").[40]

Orpheus' backward look at Eurydice becomes, in the commentary tradition on the myth, a symbol for man's inordinate attachment to earthly goods, his distorted sense of their worth. Turning away from the light, looking "abakward on Eurdyce his wif," Orpheus fixes "his eien into the put of helle" and beholds the "lowe thinges of the erthe" (*Boece* III.m12:58–59, 65, 70). Bernardus, in his Virgilian commentary, and Guillaume de Conches in his twelfth-century interpretation of metrum 12, both identify Eurydice with "naturalis concupiscentia"—that is, with natural concupiscence, with the appetite for the good and pleasurable.[41] When that drive, rooted in man's sensual nature, is directed by man's higher nature toward the "sovereyn good," then Eurydice herself becomes identified with "the noble good celestial." Conversely, when "naturalis concupiscentia" becomes entangled "in erthly thinges," then Eurydice becomes associated with the "lowe thinges of the erthe" (*Boece* III.m12:66–70). Eurydice, in short, has two faces, depending on whether Orpheus associates her with light or darkness, *aeternitas* or *temporalia*, heaven or hell.

The dramatic action of the myth presents that either-or proposition in terms of two descents that occur in sequence—the virtuous *descensus* of Orpheus that becomes an ascent, and the vicious descent of Eurydice, who is lost as she falls back into the underworld. Lady Philosophy's final interpretation of the myth as a virtuous descent that fails to achieve its goal, however, suggests that the either-or proposition is grounded upon a reality that is both-and. The beauties of creation are good, both as a sign pointing beyond themselves to the Creator and in themselves as his "yifte." Fallen human beings, their nature flawed and broken, are unable to sustain this bifocal vision of created goods, and striving to do so necessarily involves them in an ongoing redemptive process of attachment and detachment, taking in and letting go, receiving and sacrificing.

Like Eurydice in the myth, Criseyde has two faces. In the ascend-

40. *Commentary*, p. 30.
41. See Jane Chance Nitzsche, *The Genius Figure in Antiquity and the Middle Ages* (New York: Columbia University Press, 1972, 1975), pp. 48–49.

ing action "fro wo to wele" in the first three books, her countenance is "lik of Paradys the ymage"; beginning in Book IV her face is "al ychaunged in another kynde," and so marked with the "tokenyng of hire peyne, / That to biholde it was a dedly thyng" (IV.864–71). She is alternately hot and cold, bright and cloudy, like a day "in March, that chaungeth ofte tyme his face" (II.765). Indeed, the imagery of the poem associates her again and again with nature, with seasonality, with "chaungynge," with promises made and broken. As Charles Muscatine says, "Her ambiguity is her meaning."[42] Criseyde's double potentiality for good and evil, life and death, becomes a symbol for all the things of this world as they awaken our love, inspire our attachment, and necessitate our detachment. As Criseyde goes, so "goth the world" (V.1434).

In Boethius' version of the myth, Orpheus loses Eurydice in the single moment when he looks upon her. The narrative action reaches a certain high point and then plunges abruptly downward in a *descensus* that leaves Orpheus disconsolate (or dead, according to the way Chaucer translates the word "occidit"), and Eurydice back in Hades. Similarly, in Chaucer's *Troilus* there is a definite break or *caesura* in the action at the beginning of Book IV, which opens with the image of Fortune's turning wheel, the invocation of the Furies and "cruel Mars," and the narrator's announcement that "hennesforth" the "matere of [his] book" will be "how Criseyde Troilus forsook" (IV.15–25). In rapid succession the narration recounts the Trojan defeat, the taking of Antenor, the Greek assembly where Calkas requests the exchange of Antenor for Criseyde, and the Trojan parliament where the proposal is ratified. With the decision of the Trojans "to forgon Criseyde" (IV.195), Troilus finds himself bereft of the "wight that most is to hym deere" (IV.285) and effectually confronted with her irrevocable loss.

The last two books of the *Troilus* are filled with images of death and allusions to the underworld appropriate to the *descensus vitii* of the narrative action. "The chaungynge of Criseyde" (IV.231) defines the second of Troilus' "double sorwes," even as the downfall of Eurydice illustrates the vicious descent in Bernardus' commentary: "Taliter Euridicem legimus descendisse."[43]

42. Charles Muscatine, *Chaucer and the French Tradition* (Berkeley: University of California Press, 1957), p. 164.
43. *Commentary*, p. 30.

When Criseyde learns of the parliament's decision to offer her in exchange for Antenor, she considers "fro heven into which helle" she is fallen since she must forego "the syghte / Of Troilus" (IV.712–14). Like Proserpina, she resolves to bring about her own death by taking "no mete or drynke." She promises Troilus that her clothes "shul blake ben in tokenyng" that she is "out of this world agon." She bequeaths her "herte and ek the woful goost therinne" to Troilus, holding out the hope that they will be reunited in the afterlife "in the feld of pite" (IV.789) like "Orpheus with Erudice, his feere" (IV.775–91). Finally, in answer to Troilus' fear that she will fail to keep her promise to return to Troy, Criseyde calls upon Juno to cast her down to dwell "eternalich in Stix, the put of helle" if ever she "be fals" (IV.1534–40). Her capitulation to Diomede in the Greek camp, then, represents the last step in her *descensus vitii*. In her broken troth, in her association with a frankly carnal and opportunistic lover, Criseyde, like Eurydice, finds herself existentially in "the put of helle" among the "lowe thinges of the erthe" (*Boece* III.m12:65, 70).

Troilus, too, is incorporated into the *descensus* pattern through his love for Criseyde. His immediate response to the parliament's decision is to withdraw, almost insane with grief, to his chamber where he strikes "his hed to the wal, his body to the grounde" and prays for death: "O deth, allas! why nyltow do me deye?" (IV.224,250). He commands his soul to "unneste," depart from his body, and "folowe alwey Criseyde" (IV.305–307). At the same time he declares that Criseyde's soul will never be separated from his, even though he must feel and lament the pain of separation from her forever "down with Proserpyne" (IV.473). When Troilus bids his private farewell to Criseyde, he leaves her chamber like a soul "rente" from the body; and, we are told, his pains are such that they "passen every torment down in helle" (IV.1698, 1700). After her departure Troilus spends many a restless night tossing and turning "in furie, as doth he Ixion in helle" (V.212). His dreams portend his death, as does the screeching owl "which that hette Escaphilo" (V.319). He experiences the sensation of falling "depe / From heighe o-lofte" (V.258–59) without being able to break that fall. Finally, tormented with jealousy, he writes to Criseyde, "to me youre absence is an helle" (V.1396).

Troilus' "helle," is different from Criseyde's, however. She seeks to escape from her loneliness by a deeper descent into *temporalia*, by clinging to whatever immediate security Diomede (or whoever) can offer her. Troilus, on the other hand, gradually withdraws from passing things into a mental universe, into memory, into a history that partakes of *aeternitas*. Living in Troy, he lives in the past, for wherever he goes things "com hym to remembraunce" (V.562). He keeps "the proces" of past events "in memorie," and reconstructs it as a narrative, observing that "men myght a book make of it, lik a storie" (V.583–85). When Cassandra correctly interprets the dream of the boar to betoken Diomede's winning of Criseyde, Troilus defends his lady by making her legendary, by comparing her to Alceste, who sacrificed herself for her husband "as us the bokes telle" (V.1533). The present, bitter disappointment cannot rob Troilus of the Criseyde who once was, and who continues her existence in his mind. As Winthrop Wetherbee observes, "This wholly private perception of her meaning for him will endure to the end, unaffected by the historical realities that are soon to be forced upon him."[44] Thus, even when Troilus knows "oute of doute" (V.1644) that Criseyde has taken a new lover, he finds himself unable to "unloven [her] a quarter of a day" (V.1698). In his refusal to embrace a "newe love" (IV.415), Troilus resembles the legendary Orpheus, whose decision never to remarry enraged the Thracian women.[45] Like the mystic soul deprived of consolation, Troilus holds fast to the revelation granted him and continues to orient his being toward the "steere" (V.638) he once saw and can no longer see.

The poet-narrator of Chaucer's *Troilus* grounds his art in the poetry of Troilus, in his *inventio*, in his *memoria*, even as Lady Philosophy's poetry in Boethius' metrum depends upon and continues Orpheus' song. Chaucer's narrator "helpeth loveres . . . to pleyne" (I.11) by providing a narrative frame for lyric utterance. Troilus, we are told, begins to seek Criseyde's love by singing a song, and the narrator endeavors to reproduce that *canticus* with "every word right" (I.397). The narrator carefully sets off two of Troilus' songs (I.400–20; V.638–44) and one of his letters (V.1317–1421) with appropriate headings; the rest of Troilus' lyricism is embedded in the narrator's own in the form of reported direct discourse. Muscatine counts "thirty-odd lyric monologues" assigned to Troilus in

44. Wetherbee, *Chaucer and the Poets*, p. 178.

45. See John Block Friedman, *Orpheus in the Middle Ages* (Cambridge: Harvard University Press, 1970), pp. 169–70, for a fifteenth-century treatise celebrating Orpheus as a faithful lover.

the poem—monologues that Rowe likens to the "song of the soul."[46] Like Orpheus, who sings a "newe song" in the "houses of helle" (*Boece* III.m12.33,19), Troilus sings his love songs in a city beseiged and doomed to be destroyed. Orpheus moves the deities of the underworld to release Eurydice by making use of "al that evere he hadde resceyved and lavyd out of the noble wells of his modir (Callyope) the goddesse" (*Boece* III.m12.21–24); similarly, the narrator invokes Calliope (III.45) when he attempts to tell how Troilus succeeds in winning Criseyde. Like Orpheus, whom the later Middle Ages considered an eloquent exemplar for the courtly lover, Troilus can "wel speke of love" (II.503), and that enables him to move not only Criseyde but also the readers of his history.[47]

Lady Philosophy reports that Orpheus, who is able to "overcomen alle thinges"—inanimate nature, beasts, men, and even the gods— with his songs, cannot "asswagen" (*Boece* III.m12.15–6) his own grief. This, too, would seem to be Troilus' fate. Book V, the last book of the *Troilus*, is marked by the breaking of his music. During his visit at Sarpedoun he can hardly bear to hear anyone "maken melodie" (V.462) in Criseyde's absence. He composes a single "song of wordes but a fewe" in honor of his "steere," and then promptly falls again "into his sikes olde" (V.633–46). His long letter to Criseyde is as fruitless as a piping into "an ivy lef" (V.1433). After a final complaint addressed to Criseyde, Troilus resolves "withouten moore speche" (V.1716) to seek his own death on the battlefield. Pandarus, too, falls silent—"I kan namore seye" (V.1743)—and the poem's action comes quickly to a close.

The reader is likely to respond to the first part of Chaucer's epilogue in the same way the prisoner does to Lady Philosophy's moralization of the Orpheus-Eurydice myth. Having listened to her as she sings "softly and delitably the forseide thinges," the prisoner is reminded by the woes of Orpheus of his own sufferings and the pain he has "nat al outrely foryeten." He stops Lady Philosophy with a question about the problem of evil, forestalling "the entencioun of hir that entendede yit to seyn some othere thinges" (*Boece* IV.p1.1– 8). As Wetherbee observes, the myth of the metrum has an "undertone of suppressed feeling which is at odds with [its] ostensible

46. Muscatine, *Chaucer and the French Tradition*, p. 135; Rowe, *O Love!*, p. 78.
47. See Friedman, *Orpheus in the Middle Ages*, chap. 5, for a discussion of Orpheus and Eurydice as archetypal courtly lovers.

exemplary purpose"; its images give "eloquent expression to the very impulse it is intended to curb, the attachment to earthly things," and awaken in the prisoner an emotional response that makes him resistant to the lesson he is supposed to learn: "Blisful is he that mai unbynden hym fro the boondes of the hevy erthe!" (*Boece* III.m12.2–3).[48]

Similarly, the reader of Chaucer's *Troilus* is told that Troilus' "lighte goost ful blisfully is went / Up to the holughnesse of the eighthe spere" (V.1808–09) where, freed from the prison of the body, he suddenly looks down upon the earth from a new perspective and begins to despise his own mortal existence and "this wrecched world" (V.1817). The lesson that Troilus learns is apparently the same one the reader is expected to learn, for the narrator launches into a summary comment on "false worldes brotelnesse" and "wrecched worldes appetites," urging "yonge, fresshe folkes" to turn away "fro worldly vanyte" (V.1832, 1851, 1835, 1837).

Here, as in Boethius' *Consolation*, there is a tension between philosophy and poetry, moralitee and myth. Chaucer himself draws attention to that problem when the narrator describes Troilus laughing at the "wo / Of hem that wepten for his deth" (V.1821–22)— Troilus' amusement being directed, of course, not only at his historical mourners (Priam and the Trojan populace), but also at his narrator and those readers who are moved by his tragedy and reminded of their own "sorwes in lovynge." The narrator, after all, pictures himself as a "sorwful instrument" who weeps as he writes, matching a "sorwful tale" with a "sory chere" (I.10,14). At the same time, the narrator has invited his readers to respond to his "matere" in a similar sympathetic way: "If any drope of pyte in yow be, / Remembreth yow on passed hevynesse" (I.23–24).

If, as the narrator states explicitly, the work as a whole assumes "the form of olde clerkis speche / In poetrie" (V.1854–55), then the "poetical Muses" (*Boece* I.p1.43) would seem to have a subtle way of undermining the process of philosophical consolation in both the Orpheus-Eurydice metrum and Chaucer's *Troilus*. It is one thing, after all, to despise "this wrecched world," and quite another thing to detach one's heart from "this litel spot of erthe that with the se /

---

48. Winthrop Wetherbee, *Platonism and Poetry in the Twelfth Century: The Literary Influence of the School of Chartres* (Princeton: Princeton University Press, 1972), pp. 78–79.

Embraced is" (V.1815–17). Philosophy, its language abstract and general, enforces the necessity of dialectic, distance, and detachment, while poetry, its most powerful images rooted in the concrete and sensory, continues to affirm the beauty of "this world, that passeth soone as floures faire" (V.1841), and the sacramentality of a Criseyde. Nicholas Trevet, whose commentary on the Boethian myth was certainly known by Chaucer, hints at this same polarity when he asserts that one ascends to heaven through the power of philosophical poetry ("per suavem eloquentiam coniunctam sapientiae"), and then observes that the sweetness of such an ascent means passing through many delights that impede virtue and make a successful ascent almost impossible: "sed quia ascensus ad caelestia difficultatem habet et ideo subtractionem multarum delectationum / quae impediunt virtutem per quam sit ascensus."[49]

Boethius deals with the tension between the poetry of the Orpheus myth and its philosophical import by having the prisoner articulate his emotional response and pose the question that occasions Lady Philosophy's continued discourse. Chaucer, on the other hand, having told a story that insists on the necessity of both attachment to and detachment from earthly goods, resolves the problem inherent in the contradictory movement of love by establishing a parallel between Troilus and Christ that allows the unsuccessful human *descensus* to be incorporated into the perfect pattern of the *descensus Dei* Who made humankind "after his ymage" (V.1839), became a man himself in Mary's womb, redeemed humanity through his passion and death, and victoriously harrowed hell.

Troilus in the epilogue, like Orpheus in the commentary tradition, becomes a type of Christ.[50] Shortly after having described Troilus' suffering, death, and ascension among the fixed stars, the narrator refers his readers to Christ Who "right for love / Upon a crois, oure

49. Quoted in Friedman, *Orpheus in the Middle Ages*, pp. 111–12. In his *Mythologies*, Fulgentius treats the Orpheus myth as an allegory of the art of music. His interpretation, incorporated into the well-known early tenth-century Boethian commentary of Remigius of Auxerre, explicitly links the story of Orpheus and Eurydice to the problematic relationship between art and inspiration, abstract theory and actual practice, in the educational process. See *Fulgentius the Mythographer*, trans. Leslie George Whitbread (Columbus: Ohio State University Press, 1971), pp. 96–97; Rossi, p. 88.

50. See Friedman, chap. 3, for a discussion of Orpheus as a type of Christ. See George H. Brown, "The Descent-Ascent Motif in *Christ II* of Cynewulf," *JEGP* 73 (1974): 1–12, for a useful survey of scriptural and patristic writings emphasizing Christ's victorious Incarnational descent and ascent.

soules for to beye, / First starf, and roos, and sit in hevene above."
After having spent the whole poem describing Troilus' fidelity in
love, the narrator points to "sothefast Crist," Who "nyl falsen no
wight" (V.1842–60).

These parallels between Troilus and Christ establish the frame
within which the poet-narrator asks, and the reader answers, the
question: "And syn [Christ] best to love is, and most meke, / What
nedeth feynede love for to seke?" (V.1847–48). The question succinctly poses the problem of the poem and brings us back to the
purpose of the meditative descent to creatures. Ultimately a person
"nedeth feynede loves for to seke"—including the "feynede loves" of
fictive romance—in órder to come to know the meaning of divine
love with an affective knowledge. Bernardus, in his discussion of the
descensus virtutis, speaks about the soul's final conversion "ad invisi-
bilia penitus"—that is, toward invisible realities from deep within,
from the depths of the heart.[51] This kind of conversion is rooted
in one's personal experiences of pain and joy, in one's sensual nature,
in poetry as well as philosophy. Having suffered Troilus' "double
sorwes" together with him, the reader has made a meditative descent
that turns into an ascent, leading him back to the Triune Source of all
love that reigns "ay in thre, and two, and oon" (V.1864).

Even as the love story of Orpheus and Eurydice in Boethius' *Consolation* encapsulates the whole journey of the soul from and to the
Eternal Fatherland, so too in the High Middle Ages the psychological stages in the unfolding of love from self-centered cupidity to
charity define the heroism of suffering lovers who first descend to the
love of creatures and then, from and through that attachment, ascend to the love of God. The suffering of these Boethian lovers—like
the suffering of Job—incorporates them into the pattern of Christ's
heroic descent and victorious ascension and thus disposes them to
receive grace and salvation. The sufferings of Abelard, the tearful
wandering of Dante, and the "double sorwe" of Troilus lead them in
the end to a consolation that is more than philosophical, to God
Himself who is the Comforter.

51. *Commentary*, p. 30. In connection with the notion of affective knowledge, one
is reminded of Saint Bernard's treatment of carnal love in *De diligendo Deo* as a
primitive, but good and necessary, form of love of God, rooted in human nature as a
composite of body and soul.

6   Ghostly Chivalry

Love itself constitutes heroism for the Boethian lover who endures its pains and who is purified and redeemed through love in the process of spiritual ascent. As a correlative to the lover's *iter mentis*, chivalric romance emphasizes the deeds of valor that are inspired by divine and human love and that give it outward expression. In the world of the quest, as we shall see, armed combat becomes the close analogue, not the opposite of Joban spiritual contest, even as the knight assumes the different faces of Job as (1) opponent of Satan, (2) crusader against malefactors, (3) penitent self-conqueror, and (4) victor over despair. Indeed, these four faces of Job enable a typological approach to the general subject of knightliness, which, as Andrea Hopkins rightly insists, "is central to any literary concept of medieval romance" within the framework of heroic tradition.[1]

Charting the complex historical process which converts the Gregorian allegorical warfare of the late sixth century into the literal "ghostly chivalry" of the High Middle Ages entails an archeology of medieval chivalry in its successive periods of development.[2] We can distinguish four different periods, each with a different representation of Job. In the early Christian period, soldiers like Saints Martin

---

1. Andrea Hopkins, *The Sinful Knights: A Study of Middle English Penitential Romance* (Oxford: Clarendon Press, 1990), p. 31.

2. The phrase is taken from Christine de Pizan's *Epistle of Othea to Hector* (1400; translated into English by Stephen Scrope, 1440). For a discussion of the work, see Beverly Kennedy, *Knighthood in the Morte Darthur* (Cambridge: D. S. Brewer, 1985), pp. 17–18.

and Sebastian freely lay down their arms, even as Job was stripped of his possessions, in order to enter as God's athletes into a new arena of testing. Radically countercultural, they reject the false pagan letter of physical combat for the veiled truth of spiritual heroism, even as Saint Gregory's *Moralia* uses martial allegory to explicate the otherness of Job's heroic virtue.

In the immediate aftermath of the eleventh-century Investiture Controversy, the first and second crusades inaugurated a new era in which Job becomes a model for the Christian layman who braves the physical and spiritual dangers of this world and whose pure intention affirms and redeems secular military action. Signed with the cross, Job stands as the Bernardine patron not only of the historical Knights Templar and the crusaders, but also of Grail knights like Galahad. Rather than rejecting arms, they take them up as the outward sign of their inward devotion, reliteralizing the Joban allegory of weapons as they use them against God's enemies.

Faced with the repeated failures of the crusades and the painfully apparent gap between chivalric ideals and actual knightly practice, the late Middle Ages tended to reconceive the relationship between earthly and heavenly chivalry, representing their otherness as horizontal and moral, rather than simply vertical and sacramental. Thus in *Sir Gawain and the Green Knight* (late fourteenth century) and Malory's *Tale of the Sankgreall* (1469) the synchronic otherness of earthly arms and spiritual virtues, which defines their mutual relationship in the essentially static, exegetical, and hierarchical terms of allegory, modulates into a diachronic, Boethian otherness of "before" and "after," involvement and detachment, time and eternity. In this Boethian framework Job becomes a model for penitent knights like Lancelot and Gawain, whose ultimate success depends on their humility, and whose sanctity derives providentially from the *felix culpa* of their sin.[3]

Finally, in the Protestant poetics of sixteenth-century England the near-despair of Spenser's Redcrosse knight defines him as a new Job

---

3. As Hopkins notes, *Sir Ysumbras*, a popular Middle English romance (14th century), varies the Joban pattern of the Eustace legend so that "instead of the hero's virtue being tested, found true, and rewarded, his sin is repented of, atoned for, and forgiven" (p. 20). Among other romances with similar penitential plots, Hopkins cites *Guy of Warwick*, *Sir Gowther*, *Roberd of Cisyle*, and *Sir Gawain and the Green Knight*.

whose patience must endure his own mutability and whose constancy consists paradoxically in change—so much so that the very distinction between literal and allegorical meaning is lost as each translates into the other in a continual, paranomastic other-speaking.[4] Spenser thus begins where Malory ends, converting the instability and penitence of Lancelot into the shapeshifting world of Redcrosse who, unlike Lancelot, cannot rely on any of his own works, but only on God's grace. At the end of a long chivalric tradition, the "old dints of deepe wounds" (*The Fairie Queene* I.1.i) in Redcrosse's armor recall the historical succession of Christian knights who, taken together, define both who Redcrosse is and who he is not.[5]

Opponent of Satan

As we have seen, Saint Gregory the Great's *Moralia in Job*, building upon an earlier Stoic and Christian tradition, ascribes spiritual weaponry to Job and treats him as the champion of God in the cosmic contest between God and the Adversary. That reading led Bede and Rabanus Maurus to classify the Book of Job as a biblical epic in contradistinction to the heroic poems of classical antiquity, whose heroes stand as shadowy types of the true heroism embodied in Job and Christ.

In this generic context, the central icon of the Job story—the divestment of the hero—assumes a twofold importance. When Job, confronted with the loss of his goods and the death of his children, tears his garments in submission to God's will, declaring, "Naked came I out of my mother's womb, and naked shall I return thither" (Job 1:21), his self-divestment looks backward to the ornate shields and protective accoutrements of Homer's protagonists and forward to the nakedness of Christ who stripped himself of heavenly glory, became a man, suffered and died in order to enter again into his

4. For studies linking literary metamorphoses to paranomasia, see Frederick M. Ahl, *Metaformations: Soundplay and Wordplay in Ovid and Other Classical Poets* (Ithaca: Cornell University Press, 1985), and Maureen Quilligan, *The Language of Allegory: Defining the Genre* (Ithaca: Cornell University Press, 1979).

5. I use throughout *The Works of Edmund Spenser: A Variorum Edition*, ed. Edwin Greenlaw, Charles G. Osgood, Frederich M. Padelford (Baltimore: Johns Hopkins University Press, 1932).

glory (cf. Phil. 2:6–11). This double perspective on Job in the exegetical tradition provided Christian writers, in turn, with a biblical model for a new heroic substance and style: the subject of spiritual, not physical, warfare, related appropriately in the unadorned *sermo humilis*.[6]

The early saints' lives, as exemplifications of this new heroic mode, call attention to the physical and rhetorical divestment practiced respectively by the saints and the narrators of their stories. In this category Sulpicius Severus' Life of Saint Martin (fourth century) has a special importance as a literary exemplar that defined many of the conventions of medieval hagiography. Sulpicius prefaces his *Vita Sancti Martini* with a rejection of "that foolish ideal of valor" celebrated in Homer: "Not only is it folly to imitate" men like Hector; "it is madness not to oppose them with all eagerness."[7] Sulpicius' own *Vita* purports to provide a rival, Christian variety of heroic literature, featuring a saint who seeks "eternal life" rather than pagan *fama*, who leaves Caesar's army to become a soldier of God, who strips himself of his military cloak to clothe the naked, and who willfully disarms himself in order to enter into a life of spiritual combat.[8]

When Ælfric, following Sulpicius, retells the story of Martin, it assumes the contours of the *historia* of Job, the Old Testament saint who prefigures him as "godes cempa" (2.226).[9] In his Homily on Job,

6. The classic essay on the Christian plainstyle is, of course, Erich Auerbach's "*Sermo Humilis*," in *Literary Language and Its Public in Late Latin Antiquity and in the Middle Ages*, trans. Ralph Manheim (London: Routledge and Kegan Paul, 1965), pp. 27–66.

7. Sulpicius Severus, *Writings*, trans. Bernard M. Peebles, The Fathers of the Church 7 (Washington, D.C.: Catholic University of America Press, 1949, repr. 1970), p. 103.

8. Sulpicius' work inspired imitation by Christian writers, many of whom appropriated some of the formal conventions of heroic poetry in saints' *legenda* and biblical paraphrases. Paulinus of Périgueux, for instance, versified Sulpicius' *Martiniana* in six books of hexameters to present a Christian hero "Non arma arripiens hominis, sed signa salutis, / Tegmine nec fidens clypei, sed nomine Christi" (PL 61, c1013). For studies of this tradition, see A. H. Chase, "The Metrical Lives of St. Martin of Tours," *Harvard Studies in Classical Philology* 43 (1932): 51–76; Sherry L. Reames, "Saint Martin of Tours in the 'Legenda Aurea' and Before," *Viator* 12 (1981): 131–64; Raymond Van Dam, "Images of St. Martin," *Viator* 19 (1988): 1–27.

9. *Ælfric's Lives of the Saints*, ed. Walter W. Skeat, vol. 1, EETS o.s. 76 and 82 (London: Oxford University Press, 1881 and 1885, repr. 1966) and vol. 2, EETS o.s. 94 and 114 (London: N. Trübner, 1890; Kegan Paul, 1900). Parenthetical citations are by volume and page. For a discussion of Ælfric's marked emphasis on Martin as a

Ælfric has Job boast of his works of charity. Clothed with righteousness ("ymbscryd mid rihtwisnysse"), Job has covered the poor with
the fleece of his sheep.[10] Martin's own practice of charity also emphasizes the clothing of the naked (2.222: "he . . . nacode scrydde").
Indeed, Christ Himself appears to Martin in the form of a poor,
naked man ("ænne þearfan nacodne") to whom Martin gives half of
his own cloak, exposing himself in the process to the bitter cold. This
miracle at the start of Martin's career becomes a sort of leitmotif
throughout the *Vita* as Martin continues to clothe the naked (see
especially 2.276–77), while the devil apes and inverts the Christological epiphany, appearing to Martin and Martin's monks on more
than one occasion, dressed in royal raimant (2.266: "mid purpuran
gescryd and mid cynelicum gyrlum") and claiming to be Christ (see
also 2.270–71). Martin and his monks, however, seek to see only the
naked and suffering Savior in this world and dress themselves poorly
in hairshifts, judging soft clothing (2.240: "hnesce gewæda") to be
sinful.

   Nakedness as a sign of heroic charity is directly wedded to military
divestment in Martin's *Vita*. The story of Martin clothing the beggar
immediately precedes the extended account of Martin's refusal to
serve in Julian's army. Eager to fight for God ("þæt ic gode campige
heononforð"), Martin insists that he can no longer fight for the
emperor: "ic eom godes cempa ne mot ic na feohtan" (2.226). Accused of cowardice, Martin offers to march at the head of the troops,
armed only with the sign of the cross, through the enemy lines: "and
ic fare orsorh / mid rode-tacne gescyld, na mid readum scylde / oðð
mid helme þurh þæs heres werod."

   As Anne Middleton observes, "Martin rejects a hero's gear for the
whole armor of God, another world of values, and another language."[11] The references to helmut and shield in the context of

---

soldier, see Marcia A. Dalbey, "The Good Shepherd and the Soldier of God: Old
English Homilies on St. Martin of Tours," *NM* 85.4 (1984): 422–34.

   10. *Ælfric's Catholic Homilies, The Second Series*, ed. Malcolm Godden, EETS
supplementary series no. 5 (London: Oxford University Press, 1979), p. 261. Parenthetical citations are by title (CH 2) and page.

   11. Anne Middleton, "Ælfric's Answerable Style: The Rhetoric of the Alliterative
Prose," *Studies in Medieval Culture* 4.1 (1973): 86. Middleton refers to the rendering
of this scene in Ælfric's Homily 34 (CH 2.289), but her observation also generally
applies to the longer version in the *Lives*.

rhythmic, alliterative lines recall the native tradition of heroic vernacular poetry that remains as a mere trace under erasure in Ælfric's prose, stripped bare of its characteristic diction and variation. Precisely that difference, the departure from heroic convention, defines a new kind of heroism and a rival form of epic.

Ælfric, however, goes beyond his *auctor* Sulpicius in wedding content and form. Ælfric's stylistic nakedness, his rejection in theory and practice of prolixity and *ornamentatio*, matches the iconographic action of his saints who strip themselves of glory.[12] "Brevity," as Ælfric observes in the Latin preface to his *Lives of Saints*, "does not always deprave speech, but oftentimes makes it more charming" (1.4–5: "non semper brevitas sermonem deturpat sed multotiens honestiorem reddit"). Similarly, in Ælfric's preface to the second homily series, he rejects artificiality, verbosity, and obscure terms ("non garrula verbositate aut ignotis sermonibus") in order to edify his auditors with simple speech: "simplici locutione" (CH 2.1).

Ælfric's rejection of rhetorical adornment complements the actions of the saints in his *Vitae* who, like Martin, either strip themselves of clothing or weapons or both, or are stripped by their pagan torturers. The Emperor Constantine, for instance, mindful of Christ's humility, dismounts from his horse at the gate of Jerusalem, takes off his purple vestments, and walks barefoot (2.150: "mid nacodum fotum") toward the cross. The kings Abdon and Sennes also renounce their kingdoms to face, naked, their martyrdom as Christians (2.56–59). Edmund, king and martyr, recalls Christ's command to Peter to sheath his sword (Matt. 26:52) and throws away his weapons to face Hingwar unarmed (2.320–322). The Christian soldiers in the company of Maurice, recalling the same words of Christ—"he het petrum behydan his swurd"—fearlessly cast aside their weapons and hasten to their execution at the hands of men who subsequently divide their weapons and garments as spoils (2.162).

The specific reference in these martyrologies to Matthew 26:52 and Saint Martin's insistence that the law of Christ forbids him to fight suggest the radical countercultural pacifism advocated by Ter-

12. Ælfric actually used the adjective "naked" as a synonym for "literal" when discussing biblical narrative ("nacedan gerecednisse"). See *The Old English Heptateuch: Ælfric's Treatise on the Old and New Testament and his Preface to Genesis*, ed. S. J. Crawford, EETS 160 (London: Oxford University Press, 1922), p. 77.

tullian in the early Christian debate about military service. While Saint Augustine's early formulation of a theory of just war generally sanctioned a defensive Christian soldiery, the refusal to bear arms remained a clear option of conscience for individual Christians and an expression of high calling. Thus even in a Christendom largely committed to the crusades, pacifist views were heard. A broadside nailed to the door of St. Paul's cathedral in 1395 quoted Matthew 26:52 ("Qui gladio percutit gladio peribit") to oppose the granting of indulgences to crusaders.[13] Middle English sermons recall David's refusal of armor in his encounter with Goliath and insist that a person "ouer-charched with armour, or with clothes" is impeded in his spiritual fight with the devil.[14] Christ himself, we are told repeatedly, entered the lists against Satan and Death as an unarmed knight.[15] Indeed, Christ's refusal of earthly weapons in order to wield naked, spiriutal power, to be strong in weakness, continued to define Christian heroism in the essentially passive terms of martyrdom. Thus, as Irving Zupnick reminds us, "the nude Sebastian balances out the nude figure of Job" in Giovanni Bellini's famous San Giobbe altar (late 1480s), a martyr pierced with arrows, but rapturously serene.[16]

Crusader against Malefactors

Unlike the pacifist ideal, according to which the Opponent of Satan unconditionally renounces earthly arms and military service in order to wage spiritual warfare, the ideal of the Crusader dictates the combined employ of physical and spiritual force, perceives their analogy, and insists upon their sacramental relatedness. After Constantine's celebrated, visionary victory "in hoc signo," in the sign of

13. See Terry Jones, *Chaucer's Knight: The Portrait of a Medieval Mercenary* (Baton Rouge: Louisiana State University Press, 1980), n. 10, p. 245.

14. *Middle English Sermons*, ed. Woodburn O. Ross, EETS 209 (London: Oxford University Press, 1940, repr. 1960), p. 104.

15. Ibid., p. 38. Among the many instances of this image, recall the Christ-Knight in *Piers Plowman* (B Version, Passus XVIII; C Version, Passus XXI).

16. Irving L. Zupnick, "Saint Sebastian: The Vicissitudes of the Hero as Martyr," in *Concepts of the Hero in the Middle Ages and the Renaissance*, ed. Norman T. Burns and Christopher J. Reagan (Albany: State University of New York Press, 1975), p. 251.

the cross, and Augustine's formulation of a Just War theory, kings like Oswald of England envisioned a new Christian social order in which well-intended, defensive military service could be reconciled with the Gospel, even with problematic texts such as Matthew 26:52.[17] In the eleventh century the Investiture Controversy and the Peace and Truce of God Movements combined to sanction defensive war against pagans and heretics and the use of arms to maintain public order. As Jean Leclercq explains, papal policy during the Gregorian reform consistently extended "the domain of legitimate violence" and eventually found its doctrinal justification in the writings of the canon lawyer Anselm of Baggio who, at the request of Gregory VII, clarified the Church's power to wage war (1083–86).[18] Anselm's attempt "to conciliate war and peace" by insisting on "the goal of charity" then prepared the way for Pope Urban II's declaration of the First Crusade in 1095 and set the stage for all subsequent crusades.[19]

The ideal of Christian warfare articulated by Anselm distinguishes the Christian from the pagan warrior not so much by his outward action as by his inward intention. In the popular formulation of this characteristically medieval ideal, we may distinguish three different stages: the founding of the Knights Templar (1119), the Bernardine call to the crusades (1145), and the social establishment of knighthood in general as a High Order.

The Knights Templar

Sometime between 1128 and 1136 Saint Bernard addressed a letter of encouragement to Hugh of Payns, founder of the Knights Templar. The chivalry that Bernard praises as "new" (*nova militia*) marks the beginning of the medieval idea of knighthood. As we shall see, Bernard essentially reliteralizes the Joban allegory of spiritual warfare, incarnating its spirit in a historical form, joining together

17. For a recent treatment of this topic in Anglo-Saxon poetry, see my "Holofernes' Head: *Tacen* and Teaching in the Old English *Judith*," *Anglo-Saxon England* 18 (1989): 117–33.

18. Jean Leclercq, "Saint Bernard's Attitude toward War," *Studies in Medieval Cistercian History* 2, ed. John R. Sommerfeldt, Cistercian Studies Series, No. 24 (Kalamazoo, Mich.: Cistercian Publications, 1976), p. 7.

19. Ibid., p. 9.

the physical and spiritual combat that earlier exegesis had separated as antitypes.[20]

The opening sentences of "De laude novae militiae" firmly establish that incarnational and allegorical emphasis. Bernard observes that a "new sort of chivalry has appeared on earth" (p. 289) in precisely that region "where once He Who came from on high visited in the flesh."[21] Even as Christ once "cast out the princes of darkness," now He "exterminates their satellites" through "the arm of His valiant men." Even as Christ redeemed humankind through His cross, "now also He works the redemption of His people" through the Templars.

The novelty of this chivalry, as Bernard observes, consists precisely in its two-tiered, analogical structure, "because it tirelessly wages an equal and double war, both against flesh and blood and against the spiritual forces of evil in the other world" (p. 289). The Knight of the Temple "clothes his body with the armor of iron and his soul with the armor of faith" (p. 290): "ut corpus ferri, sic animum fidei lorica induitur" (p. 214). Thus he is "a man of both types" ("uterque homo"), resisting both bodily enemies and vice or demons.

Aware that his reliteralization of allegory could be misinterpreted, his close analogy of physical and spiritual warfare reduced to an identification of the two, Bernard warns that his literal interpretation of scriptural texts, especially from Jeremiah and Isaiah, ought not to supplant their spiritual meaning. The historical conquest of Jerusalem by the Templars should not substitute in their minds for the gaining of Heaven in the afterlife, nor may "that which is seen . . . erase that which is believed" (p. 294). The Holy City must remain a "figure of our mother who is in heaven": "figuram, quae in caelis est mater nostrae" (p. 219).

Bernard's argument that it is permissible, even laudable, for a

20. For a treatment of this tendency toward reification, see John P. Hermann, *Allegories of War: Language and Violence in Old English Poetry* (Ann Arbor: University of Michigan Press, 1989).

21. For the English text I use "In Praise of the New Chivalry," trans. David Herlihy, in *The History of Feudalism*, ed. David Herlihy (New York, Evanston, and London: Harper and Row, 1970), pp. 288–98; for the Latin text, "De laude novae militiae," in *Tractatus et opuscula*, vol. 3 of *S. Bernardi Opera*, eds. J. Leclercq and H. M. Rochais (Rome: Editiones Cistercienses, 1963), pp. 207–39. Subsequent citations are parenthetical by page.

Christian to fight—an outward action common to both the "new chivalry" and the old—forces him, like Anselm of Baggio, to empha-size the inward difference in attitude and intention. Worldly chivalry endangers a man in both body and soul because it entails violence out of wrong motives: anger, the appetite for empty glory, the desire for worldly possession. "For these reasons," Bernard insists, "it is safe neither to kill nor to succumb" (p.292): "Talibus certe ex causis neque occidere, necque occumbere tutum est" (p. 216). On the other hand, if Christ is the cause of soldiering (p. 215: "Christus . . . causa militandi"), one can be fearless in life and death, in victory and defeat. "The battle," Bernard says, "cannot end badly" (p. 291) (p. 215: "pugnae exitus malus esse non poterit"), if one acts out of a pure intention. Therefore, "the soldier of Christ kills in safety and dies in greater safety" (p. 292) (p. 217: "Miles, inquam, Christi securus interimit, interit securior"). If he kills, "he commits not homicide but . . . malicide" ("non homicida sed . . . malicida") as a defender of Christians and protector of peace. If he dies, his death is a martyrdom meriting eternal life.

As Leclercq observes, the radical purity of intention enjoined by Bernard on the Templars united and subordinated military service "to a life of prayer," so much so that the Templar ideal combined not only the literal and allegorical dimensions of warfare but also the responsibilities of two distinct social states.[22] The Templar should possess both the strength of the knight ("militis fortitudo") and the gentleness of the monk ("monachi mansuetudo") and discipline soul and body accordingly.

The Bernardine Call to the Crusades

When, after the fall of Edessa in 1145, Pope Eugenius commis-sioned him to preach the Second Crusade, Bernard issued a series of encyclicals that were, as Leclercq notes, basically "an extension of what he had previously written with regard to the Templars."[23] He continues to emphasize that a noble intention can sanctify combat. In his Letter to the English People, for instance, Bernard urges them to

22. Leclercq, "St. Bernard's Attitude," p. 25.
23. Ibid., p. 30.

stop fighting among themselves and embrace instead "a cause for which [they] can fight without danger to [their] souls; a cause in which to conquer is glorious and for which to die is gain."[24] In so doing Bernard effectively creates what Leclercq has called "a kind of Crusader mystique" in which the crusader takes up the cross and risks death as a "voluntary penitent."[25]

Bernard also continues to draw a parallel between spiritual and physical warfare, interpreting Luke 22:38 (in preference to its synoptic parallel, Matt. 26:52) not as a pacifist injunction but as a scriptural support for the doctrine of the Church's two swords. In his letter to the Templars, Bernard writes, "Let both swords held by the faithful be drawn against the necks of their enemies" (p. 293). Later, in both Letter 399 to Pope Eugenius and *De consideratione*, Bernard speaks of the crusades as a second passion of Christ in which the clergy should wield a spiritual sword; the knight, at their call, a material one: "Both of Peter's swords must be drawn whenever necessary; the one by his command, the other by his hand."[26]

When Bernard reserves spiritual combat (in an exclusive sense) to priests and religious and assigns to the laity the double work of spiritual and physical warfare, he places Templar and crusader alike under the explicit patronage of Job. As John R. Sommerfeldt has shown, Bernard's social theory distinguishes three different social orders—prelates, consecrated virgins and celibates, and married people—according to the respective biblical types of Noah, Daniel, and Job (see Ezechiel 14:14): "Porro tres homines, tres ordines Ecclesiae signant."[27] Job, according to Bernard, typifies the *conjugati* and, more generally, the *plebs Domini*, the laity, who by vocation are engaged in secular pursuits, dispensing temporal goods: "substantiam hujus mundi bene dispensans." Of the three social orders, the laity represented by Job face the greatest dangers, surrounded, as

24. "Letter 391," in *The Letters of St. Bernard of Clairvaux*, trans. Bruno Scott James (Chicago: Henry Regnery, 1953), p. 462.
25. Leclercq, "St. Bernard's Attitude," pp. 31–32.
26. "Letter 399," in *The Letters*, p. 471. See also "De consideratione," in *S. Bernardi Opera*, vol. 3, IV.iii.7, p. 454.
27. See John R. Sommerfeldt, "The Social Theory of Bernard of Clairvaux," in *Studies in Medieval Cistercian History*, Cistercian Studies, No. 13 (Spencer, Mass.: Cistercian Publications, 1971), pp. 35–48; St. Bernard, "Sermo XXXV," in *Sermones de diversis*, PL 183, c634.

they are, by the most difficult trials and temptations. Indeed, the difficulty of their long, laborious, and dangerous passage through life ("laboriosum et periculosum etiam et longum iter") proves the heroism of the few who successfully transverse it: "tam paucos . . . pertransire."[28] Even as Job could call life a warfare, the lay person in Bernard's division of social orders and responsibilities can literally term it a crusade and a pilgrimage.[29]

The High Order of Knighthood

Saint Bernard's support of the Templars and the crusades established a religious view of knighthood that came to be codified in Ramón Lull's *Libro del orden de caballeria* (late thirteenth century). Soon translated into French, it became the standard treatment of chivalry for the next two hundred and fifty years, finally reaching Sir Thomas Malory's contemporaries in the English translation of William Caxton (1484). Elaborating on Bernardine social theory and the notion of two Petrine swords, *The Book of the Ordre of Chyvalry* sets the order of knighthood side by side with the clerical order and insists that the former "is moche necessary as touchyng the gouernement of the world."[30]

Lull first distinguishes, in Caxton's translation, between the complementary duties of "the knyght espyrytuel, that is the preest, and the knyght terryen" (p. 74). In a world where "Charyte, Loyaulte, Trouthe, Iustyce, and Veryte" (p. 14) have declined, "cruelte, Iniurye, desloyalte and falsenes" must be opposed by analogous orders along two different fronts: "For by the clerkes they shold haue deuocion and loue to god, and by the knyghtes they shold doubte to doo wronge, trayson, and barate the one to another" (p. 23). In this scheme God commissions the *oratores* to wield the weapons of "good ensample and scyence" (p. 20) and teach the faith, even as he chooses the

28. St. Bernard, *De diversis*, PL 183, c634–35. See also "Sermo IX," in *De diversis*, PL 183, c566; "In nativitate Domini, Sermo I," PL 183, c118–19.

29. As Sommerfeldt notes, despite the monastic asceticism of the Templars, "it is safe to include them in the general classification of the laity" (p. 45) and, therefore, under the type and patronage of Job.

30. *The Book of the Ordre of Chyvalry*, trans. William Caxton, ed. Alfred T. P. Byles, EETS o.s. 168 (London: Oxford University Press, 1926), p. 115. Citations hereafter are parenthetical.

bellatores "to mayntene and deffende the holy feyth catholyque" (p. 24) by "force of armes" (p. 21). Furthermore, since both orders represent divine vocations and serve the same ultimate ends, "the grettest amytye" (p. 26) should exist between knights and clerks.

Christian knights should not only complement those who pray through martial action but also couple spiritual and physical warfare within their own calling. The knight should, as Lull advises, exercise his body in jousts, his soul through the practice of virtue. His "custome and usage" ought to include the hearing of Mass and sermon, prayer, and adoration as a means to recall "the deth and fylthe of this world," "the paynes of helle," and "celestyal glory" (p. 109). His fortitude, moreover, most properly "remayneth and dwelleth in noble courage ageynst the seven dedely synnes" (p. 97)—so much so that his physical warfare is a public, sacramental expression of *psychomachia*.

Like Saint Bernard, Lull envisions a Christian knighthood in which pure motives and pacifist aims justify violence as a defensive action. Thus God's chosen knights "vaynquysshe the mescreaunts whiche daily laboure for to destroye holy chirche" (p. 25) and "mayntene and deffende wymmen, wydowes and orphanes and men dyseased and not puyssaunt ne stronge" (p. 38).

Properly motivated, the knight's outward action mirrors his inward disposition, even as his martial accoutrements take on sacramental "sygnefyaunce" (p. 76). The knight carries a spear "to sygnefye trouthe," a helmet "to sygnefye shamefastnes" (p. 77), a hauberk to represent "a castel and fortresse ageynst vyces and deffaultes" (p. 78), and a shield to signify the protective "offyce of a knyght" (p. 82). Most important, perhaps, the warrior carries "a swerd, whiche is made in semblaunce of the crosse" as an outward sign that even as Christ vanquished Death through crucifixion, "al in lyke wyse a knyght oweth to vaynquysshe and destroye the enemyes of the crosse by the swerd" (pp. 76–77).

Lull's "lytyl booke" (p. 13) thus extends Bernard's argument and places the whole order of chivalry under the sign of the cross, the special mark of the Knights Templar and the crusaders. As Beverly Kennedy notes, it advances the belief "that God himself ordained knighthood to undertake the task of temporal governance," even as He selected Job to be His champion in the conflict with Satan, and that True Knighthood therefore consists in following an essentially religious vocation addressed to laymen and exercised in the dangerous moral and corporeal circumstances of a warfaring world.[31]

Penitent Self-Conqueror

Given a mirror like Lull's *The Book of the Ordre of Chyvalry*, it was, as Andrea Hopkins insists, culturally "impossible for an individual knight to see himself and his function in entirely secular terms."[32] The religious ideal of knighthood was, however, so high that, confronted with the scandalous misconduct of the crusades and what Larry Benson has termed the "considerable discrepancy between ideals and actualities in the late Middle Ages,"[33] it found its principal exemplar, as R. R. Bolgar puts it, "not in a real, but in a purely fictional character . . . the unblemished Galahad" of the Grail quest.[34] Caxton, therefore, appends to his translation of Lull's *Book* an exhortation to contemporary "knyghtes of Englond" to "rede the noble volumes of saynt graal, of lancelot, of galaad" (p. 122) and follow the example of English nobles and kings, like Edward I, Edward III, and Henry V, who took the "noble ordre of chyualrye" (p. 125) seriously as a measure for their deeds.

As we have seen, the Bernardine ideal of the warrior saint, which came to be embodied in Galahad, presupposes the knight's pure intention and a sacramental commingling of secular and spiritual combat. In this conceptual framework, there are only two kinds of knights: the true, heavenly knights, who kill and die only for the sake of Christ and His Church, and the false, earthly knights, whose violent actions have other motives and who thereby put themselves at serious risk. In either case, determining the truth or falsity of the knight requires allegoresis, penetrating the veil of appearances and outward signs to discover his actual intent. Thus the Cistercian *La*

---

31. Kennedy, *Knighthood in the Morte Darthur*, p. 13.
32. Hopkins, *The Sinful Knights*, p. 19.
33. Larry D. Benson, *Malory's Morte Darthur* (Cambridge: Harvard University Press, 1976), p. 147.
34. R. R. Bolgar, "Hero or Anti-Hero? The Genesis and Development of the *Miles Christianus*," pp. 120–46, in *Concepts of the Hero*, p. 123.

Queste de Saint Graal (circa 1225) narrates a quest that puts the Round Table severely to the test; separates heavenly knights (like Galahad, Percival, and Bors) from earthly ones (like Gawain); and employs a markedly typological method that alternates between accounts of chivalric adventures and their exegesis by hermits, who disclose the "high meaning" of what has occurred.

In the Grail quest, moreover, armor and weapons frequently test the inner disposition of the warriors who wear and wield them. The quest demands the sacramentality of the sign, its outward pointing to a correspondent, inward reality. Therefore only Galahad, "the very paragon of knighthood," can hang the wondrous shield "bearing a red cross on a white ground" around his neck without injury to himself, whereas sinful knights like King Baudemagus who presume to bear the shield inevitably incur dishonor, suffer wounding, and risk death.[35] Gawain commits a similar sacrilege when he, disregarding Lancelot's warning, attempts to draw the sword reserved for Galahad and thus exposes himself to wounding by the same weapon. Nascien, King Varlan, and Parlan, the Maimed King, all dare, despite their unworthiness, to unsheathe the mysterious sword in the ship and are killed or crippled as a result, whereas Galahad takes it into his hand with impunity.

The two-edged sword in the French *Queste*, which distinguishes in a radical way between the practitioners of heavenly and earthly chivalry, leaves little space for a middle ground, for striving but imperfect knights whose motives are mixed and in need of purification. That space in both the *Queste* and in Malory's *Tale of the Sankgreal* is occupied, albeit in different ways, by the humbled, penitential figure of Lancelot.

In Galahad and Lancelot, Galahad's father and potential alter ego, the Grail quest represents two different faces of Job. Galahad, like the Job of allegory, is a sinless type of Christ, a warrior of God, and a victor over the devil. As the hermit in the *Queste* tells him, "Your coming must be compared to the coming of Jesus Christ" (*Q*, p. 64). Lancelot, on the other hand, resembles the tropological Job,

35. *The Quest of the Holy Grail*, trans. P. M. Matarasso (Baltimore: Penguin Books, 1969–70), p. 54. Hereafter citations are parenthetical. For the standard edition of the French text, see Albert Pauphilet, ed., *La Queste del Saint Graal* (Paris: H. Champion, 1921, 1967).

the moral exemplar who, humbled by his sins and temporal losses, performs penance. As Hugh of St. Victor explains it, the historical Job who sits upon the dunghill and whose name is interpreted *dolens*, allegorically signifies Christ who, renouncing coequal glory with the Father, embraced our miserable human condition. At the same time he represents, at the level of moral application, "the just man or penitent soul who composes a dunghill in his memory out of all the sins he has committed and, by sitting and meditating upon it not just for an hour but perseveringly, ceases not to weep over it" ("Job quemlibet justum vel animam poenitentem potest significare, quae componit in memoria sua sterquilinium ex omnibus peccatis quae fecit, et non ad horam, sed perseveranter super hoc sedendo et meditando flere non cessat").[36]

In both the French *Queste* and Malory's *Tale of the Sankgreal* Lancelot begins his penance by taking upon his lips the words of Job, "cursing the day that he was born" (*Q*, p. 85), when, shortly after leaving Camelot, he realizes how his sins impede his progress in the greatest quest of all. Alone in the forest at night, Lancelot dismounts at a crossroads near an abandoned chapel, disarms himself, and lies down to sleep. Stupefied, Lancelot witnesses the approach of a sick knight in a litter who prays aloud and then communes with the healing Grail. Paralyzed, unable to speak or move in response, Lancelot hears himself denounced as a great sinner and sees the stranger knight seize his horse and arms and bear them off. Dispossessed and dishonored, Lancelot spends the night in lamentation, bewailing his sin and the wickedness of his life.

The French *Queste*, taking its cue from the initial echo of Job 3:1, proceeds to explicate Lancelot's past in the tradition of Joban exegesis. Under moral pressure, Lancelot confesses to a hermit his adulterous love for Guinevere and renounces it, resolving to live chastely. Five days later a humbled Lancelot encounters another hermit who reminds him of the virtues that were his own when he first became a knight: virginity, humility, long-suffering, rectitude, and charity (*Q*, pp. 141–42). The list of virtues recalls the initial description of Job as a "vir simplex et rectus ac timens Deum et recedens a malo" (Job 1:1). The hermit goes on to explain that the Old Enemy, seeing Lancelot "so armed and girt on every side" (*Q*, p. 142) with

36. Hugh of St. Victor, *De scripturis et scriptoribus sacris*, PL 175, c12; translation mine.

Joban perfection, decided to use Guinevere as another Eve, an explanation that parallels Gregory the Great's description in the *Moralia* (3.8,12–14) of Satan's employ of Job's wife and her blandishments against Job. Finally, through Guinevere's glance, Satan "let fly a dart which caught [Lancelot] undefended" (*Q*, p. 143) and, blinded by lust, Lancelot lost all the virtues he once possessed.

Whereas Lancelot's sin makes him, in his spiritual deprivation, the antitype of Job, his penitence likens him to the Job of tropology. On the quest for the Grail, as yet another hermit tells Sir Gawain and Hector, Jesus Christ has "humbled Lancelot to the point where He [has] stripped him bare" (*Q*, p. 172). Seeing himself "naked of all the virtues that should clothe a Christian," a penitent Lancelot pleads for forgiveness, and Christ responds by stripping him of his sins and arraying him in the patience and humility symbolized by his hair shirt.

Malory's Lancelot, like the Lancelot of the *Queste*, enters his Joban penitential path after cursing "the time that he was bore" (M, p. 895) and calling himself "a verry wrecch and most unhappy of all knyghtes."[37] Malory, however, tells Lancelot's story in a way that systematically eliminates the allegorical level that is so prominent in the French *Queste* in the form of lengthy eremetical interpretations. Malory omits, for instance, the entire speech that catalogs Lancelot's initial virtues and depicts him as a fallen Job, replacing it with what Sandra Ness Ihle has termed "an extremely terse rendering of the major theme of a long sermon in the *Queste*."[38] Malory's hermit simply tells Lancelot that he would be "more abeler than ony man lyvynge" (M, p. 927) to see the Grail, were it not for his "synne."

Malory's abridgement of doctrinal exegesis and his general lack of sympathy with the typological method of the *Queste* marks a turning away from a primarily sacramental understanding of Christian knighthood, grounded in a static, vertical relationship between outward action and inward intent, material and spiritual combat. As Beverly Kennedy observes, "Malory could not accept the Cistercian author's view that there are only two types of knights."[39] Indeed, as

37. I quote from *The Works of Sir Thomas Malory*, ed. Eugène Vinaver, rev. P. J. C. Field, 3d ed., 3 vols. (Oxford: Clarendon Press, 1990), giving citations parenthetically by page.

38. Sandra Ness Ihle, *Malory's Grail Quest: Invention and Adaptation in Medieval Prose Romance* (Madison: University of Wisconsin Press, 1983), p. 124.

39. Kennedy, *Knighthood in the Morte Darthur*, p. 216.

Dhira B. Mahoney phrases it, whereas Malory "faithfully transmits the central dichotomy of the *Queste* between worldly and spiritual chivalry," he expresses the message of his thirteenth-century source "in language and thought that is characteristic of the religious temper of fifteenth-century England."[40] In that idiom the allegorical, vertical distance between sign and signified is displaced into the temporal, horizontal distance between what was and will be—an essentially providential and Boethian displacement that opens up the middle ground of process, conversion, and becoming.

Mahoney rightly emphasizes "Malory's introduction of the concept of stability in connection with the evaluation of Lancelot's achievement."[41] Departing from his source, Malory adds to the hermit's speech to Gawain and Hector the following comment about Lancelot and his quest for the Grail: "And ne were that he ys nat stable, but by hys thoughte he ys lyckly to turne agayne, he sholde be nexte to enchev[e] hit sauff sir Galahad, hys sonne; but God knowith hys thought and hys unstablenes. And yett shall he dye right an holy man" (M, p. 948). Continuing the same theme, Malory's Galahad, unlike the Galahad of the *Queste*, entrusts to Sir Bors the following last message for his father: "and as sone as ye se hym bydde hym remembir of this worlde unstable" (M, p. 1035)—a message Bors delivers: "Also, sir Lancelot, sir Galahad prayde you to remembir of thys unsyker worlde, as ye behyght hym whan ye were togydirs more than halffe a yere" (M, p. 1036).

Lancelot, however, promptly forgets "the promyse and the perfeccion that he made in the queste" (M, p. 1045) and relapses into adultery, his mind "sette inwardly to the quene." Unstable in his direct striving for holiness, Lancelot is nonetheless fixed in his attachment to his lady, a secondary cause who both obstructs and mediates Lancelot's relationship to God, as he struggles to combine his courtly service to her with his devotion to his earthly king and heavenly Lord. Committed to a fundamentally religious view of knighthood, Lancelot cannot, even in the face of his own divided loyalties and the terrible divisions that destroy the Round Table, abandon the attempt to live up to the oath of Camelot that pre-

40. Dhira B. Mahoney, "The Truest and Holiest Tale: Malory's Transformation of *La Queste del Saint Graal*," pp. 109–28 in *Studies in Malory*, ed. James W. Spisak (Kalamazoo, Mich.: Medieval Institute Publications, 1985), p. 110.

41. Ibid., p. 121.

scribed, as Larry Benson notes, the "basic virtues of knighthood, not very much different from those proclaimed at the Council of Clermont as a guide for the first Crusaders."[42] He wants to serve Guinevere, Arthur, and God, even as he fails to do so.

In Malory's providential, Boethian view of things, the element of eternity in the steadfast love between Lancelot and Guinevere makes them in the end receptive to, and deserving of, grace; their long-term adultery, a *felix culpa*. As Malory affirms, Guinevere "had a good ende," because "whyle she lyved she was a trew lover" (M, p. 1120). Her love for Lancelot, and his for her, had "stabylyté" over a period of many years, retaining its Maylike freshness and flourishing, unlike the "unstable love in man and woman" (M, p. 1119) that is all too common "nowadayes," marked by seasonal change, wintry erasure of "grene summer," "fyeblenes of nature," lack of endurance, and hasty fluctuation from "hote" to "colde."

Thus, when Arthur has died and Camelot itself has passed away, a penitent Lancelot and Guinevere continue to love each other, but with a selfless love that finally supports, rather than rivals, their love of God. As Benson asserts, "Lancelot enters the religious life not because he forsakes his earthly love but because he remains true to it."[43] When Guinevere, a nun at Amesbury, enjoins Lancelot "for all the love that ever was betwyxt [them]" (M, p. 1252) to forsake her company and pray for her that she "may amende [her] mysselyvyng," Lancelot responds by embracing "the selff desteny" (M, p. 1253) Guinevere has chosen for herself and promises, "Ever for you I caste me specially to pray." Earlier, after the quest for the Grail, Guinevere's love led Lancelot to "turne to the worlde agayne." Now that same bond between them urges Lancelot to share Guinevere's life of penance: "And therfore, lady, sythen ye haue taken you to perfeccion, I must nedys take me to perfection, of ryght" (M, p. 1253). Thus, as Stephen C. B. Atkinson phrases it, when Lancelot "turns away from Guinevere at the nunnery, he turns toward the Grail world," but this time he does so at Guinevere's urging and in moral union with her.[44]

The "stabylyté" of Lancelot's love for Guinevere enables him to persevere in the religious life, to withdraw from earthly pursuits, and finally to enter heaven with laughter and smiles, in the "swettest

---

42. Benson, *Malory's Morte Darthur*, p. 148.
43. Ibid., p. 244.
44. Stephen C. B. Atkinson, "Malory's Lancelot and the Quest of the Grail," in *Studies in Malory*, p. 149.

savour" (M, p. 1258) of sanctity. Unlike his son Galahad, however, who leaves "this wrecched worlde" (M, p. 1034) after beholding "spirituall thynges" with his bodily eyes, Lancelot must first renounce his secular knighthood in order to achieve spiritual chivalry as a priest, practicing in temporal succession what Galahad, the pure knight, is able to combine at once. Formerly unstable in his pursuit of holiness, Lancelot attains a Joban steadfastness through a conversion process marked by what Mahoney terms "that particularly Boethian contrast between this fickle, unreliable, 'corrumpable' world with the perfection and 'perdurability' of the next."[45]

Whereas, as Benson demonstrates, "the retirement of a knight to a hermitage is almost a convention of romance," beginning with Ramón Lull's knight-hermit, the withdrawal of Malory's Lancelot does not simply seal and complete his chivalric career; it also marks a definite break with it, a penitential turning away from its mixed motives.[46] As Lancelot confesses while on the Grail quest, he performed most of his "grete dedis of armys" (M, p. 897) for the queen's sake, and he "never dud . . . batayle all only [for] Goddis sake, but for to wynne worship and to cause [himself] the bettir to be beloved." Unlike the "wyse knyght" of Lull and Caxton, who betakes himself to a hermitage "for nature faylled in hym by age and hadde no power ne vertu to vse armes as he was woned to do," and because he was afraid to dishonor his former achievements through "the feblenesse of his body" (p. 4), Lancelot, "the nobleste knyght of the world" (M, p. 1255), withdraws to atone by prayer and fasting for his "pryde" (M, p. 1256) and "unkyndenes." In so doing he makes up what was lacking in his earthly knighthood, perfecting its imperfection through a complementary, and radically other, "ghostly chivalry."[47]

Victor over Despair

As a penitent knight whose humility affirms the chivalric ideal that he has failed to realize, the Lancelot of the *Queste* prefigures many

45. Mahoney, "The Truest and Holiest Tale," p. 123.
46. Benson, *Malory's Morte Darthur*, p. 194.
47. Mahoney compares the laughter of Lancelot to the laughter of Troilus at his ascension and remarks that the Boethian ending of Malory's *Morte*, like that of Chaucer's *Troilus*, "does not negate the passionate, earthly drama that precedes it, but puts it in perspective" (p. 124).

penitent knights of the later Middle Ages—among them, Guy of Warwick, Sir Isumbras, Roberd of Cisyle, Sir Gowther, Gawain of *Sir Gawain and the Green Knight*, and Malory's Lancelot. Indeed, as Andrea Hopkins has shown, the narrative pattern of an initial sin repented of, atoned for, and finally forgiven, belongs to what Derek Pearsall has termed "the central tradition" of Middle English romance, embodied "from 1340 onwards in a series of romances with a marked unity of plot-material."[48] John Barbour places even the hero of the *Bruce* (1375) firmly in this same generic tradition when he remarks that Robert Bruce "mysdyd thar gretly" when he killed John Comyn in a church, and "Tharfor sa hard myscheiff him fell / That Ik herd neuir in Romanys tell / Off man sa hard sted as wes he, / That eftirwart com to sic bounte."[49]

The idea of heroism evident in this definition of romance derives, as we have suggested, from both the step-by-step unblinding of Boethius and the tropological reading of Job as a model for the repentant sinner who recognizes his sinfulness and atones for it through the patient endurance of multiple trials. A similar heroic image and pattern, explicitly informed by Job as an Everyman, appears in late medieval drama. As Lawrence Besserman has shown, morality plays like *The Castle of Perseverance* (c. 1400) and *Mankind* (c. 1465) invoke Job as a *miles Christi* who can serve as a model for every human being.[50] Humanum Genus, like Job, comes naked into the world, and Mercy reminds Mankynde, "[Job] was of your nature and of your fragylyte."[51] Mankynde's final victory as "Chrystys own Knight" in the "batell betwyx þe soull and þe body" depends, moreover, on both his "grett pacyence . . . in tribulacyon" and the firmness of his Boethian and Joban resolve "to haue remo[r]s and memory of [hym]sylff."[52]

48. Derek Pearsall, "The Development of Middle English Romance," *Medieval Studies* 27 (1965): 91–116; Hopkins, *The Sinful Knights*. For a different view, see John Finlayson, "Definitions of Middle English Romance," *Chaucer Review* 15 (1980–81): 44–62, 168–81.

49. John Barbour, *The Bruce*, ed. Walter W. Skeat, EETS extra series 11, 21, 29, 55 (London: N. Trübner, 1870–79), book 2, p. 27.

50. See Lawrence L. Besserman, *The Legend of Job in the Middle Ages* (Cambridge: Harvard University Press, 1979), pp. 107–11.

51. See *The Castle of Perseverance*, in *The Macro Plays*, ed. Mark Eccles, EETS o.s. 262 (London: Oxford University Press, 1969), lines 16–17, 275–91; *Mankind*, line 289.

52. *Mankind*, in *The Macro Plays*, lines 229, 227, 286, 319.

This popular, exemplary reading of Job gradually tended to undermine the allegory of Job as a sinless *alter Christus*, reopen the
theological issue of divine justice, and call into question the meaning
of Job's literal blasphemies and despairing complaints. Two questions in particular fascinated the Protestant exegetes of the sixteenth
century: Was Job, in fact, guilty and deserving of punishment? And
did Job sin, more or less grievously, by falling into despair?

In answer to the first question, Protestant theologians affirmed the
scriptural description of Job as a virtuous man and not a hypocrite.
On the other hand, their emphasis on the universal depravity of
human nature led them to insist, in Robert Burton's words, that God
"may punish all, if he will, and that justly for sin" and that His choice
to punish some like Job "is to make a way for his mercy that they
repent and be saved, to heal them, to try them, exercise their patience, . . . make them call upon him," and cause them "to put
confidence, and have an assured hope in him, as Job had."[53]

In answer to the second question, Protestant exegetes tended to
attribute the sin of despair to Job, a sin for which he ultimately
repents and is forgiven by God. Citing Luther, Calvin, Beza, Bren-
tius, Mercerus, and others, Barbara Kiefer Lewalski calls attention to
their "focus on the Jobean dialogues, as revealing Job's human frailty
and the imperfections to which even the saints are subject."[54] Indeed,
as Lewalski notes, "The Geneva Bible depicts Job as one who finds in
himself Paul's 'battel betweene ye spirit and the flesh, Rom. 7:18,
and after a maner yeeldeth, yet in the end he getteth victorie, though
he was in the meane time greatly wounded.' "[55]

The "greatly wounded," despairing, Protestant Job—so unlike the
happily singing Job who appears as God's minstrel in Langland's
Piers Plowman—figures prominently in Robert Burton's *The Anatomy of Melancholy* (1621).[56] Burton concludes his encyclopedia with

53. Robert Burton, *The Anatomy of Melancholy*, ed. Floyd Dell and Paul Jordan-
Smith (New York: Tudor, 1927, 1955), p. 964. Subsequent citations are parenthetical.
54. Barbara K. Lewalski, *Milton's Brief Epic: The Genre, Meaning, and Art of
Paradise Regained* (Providence, R.I.: Brown University Press, 1966), p. 18.
55. Ibid., p. 24.
56. Langland depicts Job as a man who sang in his sorrow, and "Alle his sorwe to
solace thorw that song turnede" (*Piers Plowman: An Edition of the C-Text*, ed. Derek
Pearsall [Berkeley and Los Angeles: University of California Press, 1979], Passus
XVIII.18). Job, of course, stands as the chief biblical model and counterpart for
Langland's allegorical character, Patience.

a long treatment of Religious Melancholy as a variety of Love-Melancholy. Under that heading Burton subsumes all the diseases of excess and defect to which religious persons are prone, paying particular attention to despair, which constitutes "an Epitome of hell, an extract, a quintessence, a compound, a mixture of all feral maladies, tyrranical tortures, plagues and perplexities" (p. 946).

According to Burton, there are two kinds of despair: "the final, incurable despair of reprobates and the temporal despair that is "a rejection of hope and comfort for a time, which may befall the best of God's children" (p. 937). Both Job and David, Burton says, fell victim to temporal despair, which "ebbs and flows with hope and fear," but is "a grievous sin howsoever" and can lead to suicide. By God's permission, the Devil "lays hold on" the person "whom God forsakes" (p. 938), and he is then possessed by "a fearful passion, wherein the party oppressed thinks he can get no ease but by death, and is fully resolved to offer violence unto himself, so sensible of his burthen, and impatient of his cross, that he hopes by death alone to be freed of his calamity . . . and chooseth with Job 'rather to be strangled and die than to be in his bonds' " (pp. 937–38). In this state the whole soul is affected, the heart "grieved, the conscience wounded, and the mind eclipsed with black fumes arising from those perpetual terrors" (p. 938).

Christians in despair, unlike the early martyrs who were "most cheerful and merry in the midst of their persecutions," frequently complain against God "as David did . . . . as Job did" (p. 947). Citing the expression of David's "temporary passion" in Psalms 88 and 102, Burton remarks, "Job doth often complain in this kind" (p. 938). Anguished, Job calls God his enemy, and David complains against Him; "yet neither Job nor David did finally despair. Job would not leave his hold, but still trusted in him, acknowledging him to be his good God" (p. 966). Unlike the many who "die obstinate and wilful in this malady," Job is one of those who "are able to resist and overcome, seek for help, and find comfort, are taken from the chops of Hell, and out of the Devil's paws . . . out of their own strength and God's assistance" (pp. 949–950).

The Joban victory over despair is, in Burton's understanding, primarily a victory over the devil, but also a triumph over "the melancholy humour itself, which is the Devil's bath" (p. 938). Certain people, Burton insists, are especially susceptible to despair "by reason of their ill-disposed temper" and by their very make-up inclined "to distrust, fear, grieve, mistake, and amplify whatsoever they pre-posterously conceive." Such people are, moreover, especially vulner-able in a religious climate where "thundering Ministers . . . speak of judgment without mercy" (p. 941) and where a dogmatic predestina-tion encourages vigilant introspection, leading them to "doubt of their Election, how they shall know it, by what signs."

As a biblical hero who temporarily despairs, Job thus becomes a powerful model for the Protestant Christian whose religious experi-ence and personal salvation necessarily include the polaric, subjec-tive recognition of one's own total depravity, utter helplessness, and just damnation, on the one hand, and the completely unmerited gift of God's grace and mercy, on the other. Indeed, as Burton's *Anatomy* shows, Job's story stands as a paradigmatic, biblical test-case for the various Tudor theories of melancholy that were, in Donald Beecher's words, "called upon to explain despair—that persistent condition of the religious life, and a condition central to the Protestant religious experience."[57] Their clinical analysis of the so-called Elizabethan malady conditioned and reflected, as it were, their diagnosis of Job's spiritual ailment.

In his two encounters with despair, Spenser's Redcrosse knight embodies this new Joban image of the Christian knight. Like Gala-had and the Gawain of the *Pearl*-poet, he appears in the sacramental signs of Christian knighthood, bearing "Vpon his shield" and "on his brest a bloudie Crosse" in "deare remembrance of his dying Lord" (*FQ* I.1.2). Like Lancelot and Gawain, however, his motives are mixed. He enters his quest not purely for God's sake but "To winne him worship" and Gloriana's "grace to haue" (I.1.3). He is, moreover, a melancholic by temperament: "Right faithfull true he was in deede and word, / But of his cheere did seeme too solemne sad" (I.1.2).

Deceived again and again, misled instead of instructed by the hermit Archimago, Redcrosse unwittingly falls deeper and deeper into sin the more he struggles against its personifications. After his nearly fatal battle against Sans Joy, a much weakened Redcrosse en-counters Despair in a climactic episode that proves to be, as Beecher

---

57. Donald Beecher, "Spenser's Redcrosse Knight: Despair and the Elizabethan Malady," *Renaissance and Reformation* 11.1 (1987): 114.

puts it, "the trial not only of a diseased conscience but of an unsteady and pessimistic complexion."[58]

Despair mirrors Redcrosse's own mental and physical condition, even as he anticipates Burton's anatomy of the diseased imagination. "Musing full sadly in his sullein mind" (I.9.35), a Despair with hollow cheeks and sunken eyes sits "low . . . on the ground," not unlike Job on the dunghill or ashheap. He inhabits a nightmarish landscape of caves and crags and carcass-strewn cliffs, haunted by the shrieks of owls and the wailing of ghosts. His temptation of Redcrosse, moreover, concludes on a specifically Joban note. Upholding the justice of the all-seeing God, Despair confronts Redcrosse with his sin and with death as the divinely decreed, universal sentence for sinners: "Is not his law, Let euery sinner die: / Die shall all flesh?" (I.9.47; Job 34:15). He implores Redcrosse, "die soone, O faeries sonne," and places in his suicidal hand a dagger.

Una's active intervention to save Redcrosse, her recall of God's mercy and Redcrosse's election, looks forward to the knight's second encounter with and victory over despair in the House of Holiness. Instructed by Fidelia, Redcrosse is so sensible of God's perfection and his own "sinfull guilt" (I.10.21) that he again despairs and desires "to end his wretched dayes." In this Joban condition he requires the help of a Joban leech, "the which had great insight / In that disease of grieued conscience, / And well could cure the same; His name was *Patience*" (I.10.23).

Unlike Malory's Lancelot, who curses the day of his birth (cf. Job 3:1) and performs great penances, but who never despairs or contemplates suicide, Redcrosse is brought again and again to the brink of self-destruction in the ongoing, iterative process of his conversion. Also unlike Lancelot, whose story ends in his eremitic departure from the world and a saintly, visionary death, Redcrosse withdraws briefly to the "litle Hermitage" (I.10.46) where Contemplation abides and sees the New Jerusalem, only to return again to resume his secular career. Redcrosse's chivalric destiny requires him to live daily with the "guilt of bloudy field: / For bloud can nought but sin, and wars but sorrowes yield" (I.10.60), until he, a sinner (by justice) and a saint (by mercy), hangs up his shield.

58. Ibid., p. 118.

Indeed, his very existence demands that he live with not only the ingrained guilt of his human nature, but also the guilt of a fallen world that manifests itself in constant inconstancy. The shape-shifting world of Redcrosse, which mingles inner and outer realities and conflates literal and allegorical meanings in a continual, para-nomastic metamorphosis, prefigures the Boethian world of the Mutability Cantos. Unlike the unstable Lancelot of the Grail quest, who finally attains stability by Guinevere's example, God's grace, and his own striving, Spenser's Redcrosse triumphs over his own mutability only by embracing and enduring it as God's will. In this respect, he is like the narrator of the "Two Cantos of Mutabilitie" who loathes "this state of life so tickle" (VII.8.1) and longs for eternal rest: "O! that great Sabbaoth God, grant me that Sabbaoths sight" (VII.8.2). Rejecting the self-willed closure and apparent stability attainable through suicide, Redcrosse awaits his homeward call to the "blessed end" (I.10.61) of a celestial eternity, a call deferred until his achievement of "famous victorie" (I.10.60) and issued outside the temporal frame of Spenser's ever-mutable, continuous allegory.

The "cruell markes" and "old dints" (I.1.1) in Redcrosse's newly inherited armor proclaim him the heir and continuer of a long heroic tradition that looks back to the heroes of Homer and Virgil (especially in Duessa's Canto 5 descent to Hades), Saint Paul's soldier of Christ, Prudentius' *Psychomachia*, Boethius' *Consolatio*, Gregory the Great's *Moralia in Job*, Saint Bernard's Crusader-knight, and Malory's *Morte Darthur*. A composite, mixed, and mutable figure, Redcrosse is stable in his instability, a Joban Lancelot and a sinner-saint, whose repeated victories over despair enable his continued existence in a Protean world.

7 The Miltonic Trilogy

If Spenser's Redcrosse Knight stands at the apogee of a continuous tradition of heroic poetry mediated from classical times to the Middle Ages through Boethius and Job, Milton's heroes—Adam, Christ, and Samson—represent a climactic return to the disjunctive origins of that tradition. Milton separates and consciously polarizes the classical and Christian elements that Spenser mixes together, thus emphasizing their mutual antagonism and putting it to creative use. Even as Isidore, Rabanus, and Bede singled out the Book of Job as an example of heroic poetry in the Christian canon ("apud nos") that answered and surpassed the poems of Homer and Virgil in its expression of epic truth, Milton, like many of his Protestant contemporaries, discovered in Job both a personal exemplar of "the better fortitude / Of Patience and Heroic Martyrdom / Unsung" (*Paradise Lost* 9.31–33) and a poetic model for "argument / Not less but more Heroic than the wrath / Of stern Achilles" conveyed in an "answerable style" (*PL* 9.13–15, 20).[1]

Milton's definition of Christian heroism in contrastive and comparative terms ("better," "not less but more") requires him simultaneously to use the familiar terms and images of pagan heroism and to demonize them, lest they be misread and reified by his generally war-approving auditors. In *Paradise Lost*, therefore, Milton uses Satan

---

1. Throughout this chapter I use Merritt Y. Hughes, ed., *John Milton: Complete Poems and Major Prose* (New York: Odyssey Press, 1957), giving citations parenthetically by line.

himself to show the dangers of reading the classical epics literally and imitating their superficial heroism. As James A. Freeman and Francis C. Blessington have shown, Satan consistently casts himself in the part of an epic or chivalric hero, parodies epic conventions, and assigns a similar role to his divine Opponent, whereas Christ and God resist that set of literal generic expectations. In the process, as Freeman notes, "Milton's unprecedented way of conflating demon with soldier . . . demonstrates that only a fallen creature idolizes war" and thus allows his readers to "free [themselves] from its unwarranted fascination and concentrate upon some 'better fortitude' (*PL* IX.31)."[2]

Similarly, in *Paradise Regained*, Satan judges Christ by his own standards and tempts Him with the "manlier objects" (*PR* 2.225) associated with both conventional military heroism—"high designs, / High actions" (*PR* 2.410–11), "Great acts" (*PR* 2.412), the "fame and glory" (*PR* 3.25) of martial conquest, the command of thousands "in warlike muster" (*PR* 3.308), imperial rule—and its eloquent celebration in pagan oratory, epic, and tragedy. Satan expects Christ to want to be either Achilles or Homer, even as he does. In both *Paradise Lost* and *Paradise Regained*, however, Christ adheres to a completely different set of values and frustrates Satan's expectations in fulfillment of angelic prophecy: "hee all unarm'd / Shall chase thee with the terror of his voice" (*PR* 4.626–27).

Using both Satan as a parody of Achilles, Ulysses, and Aeneas and the Philistine warrior, Harapha, as a figure of the *miles gloriosus* enables Milton to achieve a negative definition of Christian heroism by specifying what it is not. The more difficult task of presenting a positive definition, illustrated by "deeds / Above Heroic" and "long unsung" (*PR* 1.14–15, 17), requires Milton, as Blessington says, "to show how the classics lead back to the Bible" from which Greece first derived and "Ill imitated" (*PR* 4.339) the arts of eloquence.[3] As we shall see, that Miltonic "leading back" from the classics to the

2. James A. Freeman, *Milton and the Martial Muse: "Paradise Lost" and European Traditions of War* (Princeton: Princeton University Press, 1980), pp. 222–23. See also John M. Steadman, *Milton's Epic Characters: Image and Idol* (Chapel Hill: University of North Carolina Press, 1959, 1968).

3. Francis C. Blessington, *"Paradise Lost" and the Classical Epic* (Boston and London: Routledge and Kegan Paul, 1979), p. 103.

Bible proceeds through Boethius' *Consolation*, as a vital classical and Christian link, to the Book of Job. Depending on whether Milton is reflecting Job as a repentant sinner (*Paradise Lost*), a sinless Christ-figure (*Paradise Regained*), or a despairing sufferer (*Samson Agonistes*), he uses Boethius' *Consolation* in various ways to connect his biblical heroes—Adam, Christ, and Samson—to the pagan heroes from which they radically differentiate themselves, thus laying bare the epic truth that heroic literary convention, as a poor imitation of a scriptural original, has obscured. Boethius, in short, reads the classics figuratively, whereas Satan reads them literally. His *Consolation* thus provides the necessary means for Milton to make incomparables comparable, cross the synapse between pagan and Christian, and assert and maintain a paradoxically discontinuous epic continuity.

In his quest for a biblical exemplar of true heroism, Milton, like many of his contemporaries, found in Job an outstanding model of what Burton O. Kurth has termed "heroic faith, patience, and fortitude in the face of trial and suffering."[4] Indeed, Milton's indebtedness to the Book of Job is a critical commonplace. As Mary Ann Radzinowicz asserts, Milton's prose writings during the post-Restoration period indicate that he "was thinking profoundly about the meaning of the Book of Job," a theological and philosophical consideration that "issued into the double ethical insights of *Paradise Regained* and *Samson Agonistes*" and contributed essentially to his understanding of heroism.[5] In addition, as Barbara Kiefer Lewalski has demonstrated, "a tissue of references and allusions to Job" points to it as "the chief model" for "the over-all structure of *Paradise Regained*" as a "brief epic"[6]; whereas, as Kurth and Radzinowicz suggest, *Samson Agonistes* derives its structural principles, at least in part, from the Renaissance reading of Job as a drama and tragedy.[7]

The Book of Job is, in fact, a subtext common to all three of

4. Burton O. Kurth, *Milton and Christian Heroism: Biblical Epic Themes and Forms in Seventeenth-Century England* (Hamden, Conn.: Archon Books, 1959, 1966), p. 134.

5. Mary Ann Radzinowicz, *Toward "Samson Agonistes": The Growth of Milton's Mind* (Princeton: Princeton University Press, 1978), p. 260.

6. Barbara K. Lewalski, *Milton's Brief Epic: The Genre, Meaning, and Art of "Paradise Regained"* (Providence: Brown University Press, 1966), p. 110.

7. See Kurth, *Milton and Christian Heroism*, p. 69; Radzinowicz, *Toward "Samson Agonistes*," p. 232; Lewalski, *Milton's Brief Epic*, pp. 18–20.

Milton's major poems, each of which, however, reads and imitates Job in a radically different way. Taken together, *Paradise Lost, Paradise Regained*, and *Samson Agonistes* thus form a trilogy that provides what Georgia Christopher, in another context, has termed "a consummate example of Reformation biblical exegesis."[8] Their respective and divergent encounters with Job, their juxtaposition as related poems, and the "ensuing dialogue between them" suggest, in Joseph Wittreich's words, "that they are not autonomous but dependent upon one another for their meaning" as parts of a single whole.[9]

Arnold Stein's important, early observation that "Milton's whole poetic vision is to be found in the three major poems" takes on new meaning when we explore their related but separate exegetical engagements with the Book of Job.[10] The marked thematic and structural differences among the three poems, with their respective temporal perspectives on the past (*Paradise Lost*), the future (*Paradise Regained*), and what Stein calls "the full present" (*Samson Agonistes*) derive from the different exegetical levels at which they approach Job as a common subtext. *Paradise Regained* imitates the Book of Job according to its Christological allegory, focusing on the frame narrative; *Samson Agonistes*, on the other hand, imitates Job according to its historical letter, focusing on the problematic Dialogue of Consolation between the despairing Job and his well-intended friends; finally, *Paradise Lost* imitates Job according to its tropological and moral meaning. The later works, *Paradise Regained* and *Samson Agonistes*, published together in 1671, stand (to use Radzinowicz's phrase) as "a double sequel" to *Paradise Lost*.[11] They separate, in relation to Job, the literal and allegorical levels that *Paradise Lost*, as an overtly instructive work, combines in its biblical and Boethian rhetoric.[12]

As the centerpiece in Milton's exegetical trilogy, *Paradise Regained*

8. Georgia B. Christopher, *Milton and the Science of the Saints* (Princeton: Princeton University Press, 1982), p. 253. Christopher uses the phrase to describe the inclusion of autobiographical elements in *Samson Agonistes*.

9. Joseph Wittreich, *Interpreting "Samson Agonistes"* (Princeton: Princeton University Press, 1986), p. 330. Wittreich sees the three major works "joined in strife, engaged in contention" (p. 332), with Apocalypse as "their subtext" (p. 338).

10. Arnold Stein, *Heroic Knowledge: An Interpretation of "Paradise Regained" and "Samson Agonistes"* (Hamden, Conn.: Archon Books, 1965), p. 205.

11. Radzinowicz, *Toward "Samson Agonistes,"* p. 230.

12. I have argued elsewhere that the tropology of biblical texts is, by definition, rhetorical and that it typically combines the *pathos* of the literal text with the *logos* of its

insists overtly on the typological relationship between the sinless Job and Christ and on the parallel between their temptations by Satan. As Lewalski notes, "the character Job is named on six occasions (I.147,369,425; III.64,67,95), the Book is quoted twice (I.33,368), and either the Book itself or the tradition of commentary explaining it is alluded to on at least ten other occasions."[13] In Milton's epic narrative of Christ's temptation in the desert (Luke 4:1–13), Satan, who "fail'd in *Job* / Whose constant perseverance overcame / Whate'er his cruel malice could invent" (1.147–49), fails once more in his multiple temptation of the "patient Son of God" (4.420). Christ, who stands "Proof against all temptation as a rock / Of Adamant, and as a Center, firm" (4.533–34), thus mirrors "righteous Job" whose "patience won" (1.425–26) and affirms the allegorical relationship, long established by Gregorian exegesis, between the Old Testament hero and Himself.

Samson Agonistes, in contrast, joins together the biblical figures of Samson (Judges 13–16) and Job according to the contemporary Protestant interpretation of Job 3:1–42:6. "In this reading," Lewalski observes, "the Job story records a fall from material prosperity and moral righteousness, and the dialogues exhibit much dramatic tension and the agonizing questioning of the universal order."[14] We have seen that, unlike Gregory the Great, who read Job's utterances of literal despair as a deliberate allegory, Protestant theologians saw in Job's outcry actual impatience toward God and sinful, albeit temporary, despair. As Radzinowicz has shown, Milton himself adopts this literal reading in *De doctrina christiana*, where he attributes sin even to saints like Job, and it clearly colors his portrait of Samson as an example "of moral perplexity, the sufferer brought to the verge of despair, followed by moral recovery."[15] This impatient, despairing, Joban Samson is, as Lynn Veach Sadler insists, "vitally different" from the unmoved, constant Job of the allegorical tradition.[16]

---

dogmatic allegory in appealing for the practical, moral application of scripture by its auditors. See *The Song of Songs in the Middle Ages* (Ithaca: Cornell University Press, 1990).

13. Lewalski, *Milton's Brief Epic*, p. 110.

14. Ibid., p. 19.

15. Radzinowicz, *Toward "Samson Agonistes,"* p. 248. She cites the relevant passages from *De doctrina* on pp. 237 and 247.

16. Lynn Veach Sadler, *Consolation in "Samson Agonistes": Regeneration and Typology*, Elizabethan and Renaissance Studies (Salzburg: Institut für Anglistik und Amerikanistik, 1979), p. 126.

Paradise Lost provides yet a third imitation of Job, based on tropo-logical exegesis, in the virtuous figure of Adam, who falls, despairs, repents, and finally puts his visionary faith, as Job does, in Christ: "I know that my Redeemer liveth" (Job 19:25). This version of the Job story emphasizes the moral lesson to be derived from it and essen-tially combines the unfallen Job of Christological allegory with the fallen Job of literal despair to create an imitable narrative of personal redemption.

Milton, moreover, structures *Paradise Lost, Paradise Regained,* and *Samson Agonistes* according to the exegetical modes of reading that delineate their respective representations of Job. *Paradise Lost,* as we shall see, achieves its educational ends by adopting the generic form of a Boethian instruction poem. *Paradise Regained,* itself based on an allegorical reading of Job as a sinless type of Christ, is made up of a series of allegories as Satan tempts Christ and Christ answers him, exposing the falseness of his carnal promises point by point through a truthful "other speaking." Christ answers Satan's "dark, / Ambiguous and with double sense deluding" (*PR* 1.434–35) oracles with God's "living Oracle" (1.460); accounts his "specious gifts no gifts but guiles" (2.391); renames Satan's proffered riches "the toil of Fools" (2.453); calls his glory "false glory" (3.69), his martial display "ostentation vain of fleshly arm" (3.387), his pagan wisdom "little else but dreams, / Conjectures, fancies" (4.291–292); until Satan, "discover'd in his fraud" (4.3), falls from the pinnacle of the temple. Vanquishing "by wisdom hellish wiles" (1.175), the Son systemati-cally exposes the ingrained *ironia* of Satan's speeches, "compos'd of lies" (1.407).

Samson Agonistes, on the other hand, valorizes what is said *ad litteram* to affirm what Kurth has termed "the literal sufficiency of the Bible as the divinely appointed manual of instruction for the individ-ual soul."[17] Samson hears his own sentiments expressed in the sloth-ful despair of Manoa, the self-indulgent excuses of Dalila, and the presumptuous swaggering of Harapha. In a homeopathic process of "like cures like," Samson gradually ceases to speak as he has heard others speaking, until the only word that remains to him is God's.[18]

---

17. Kurth, *Milton and Christian Heroism,* p. 4.
18. See Raymond B. Waddington, "Melancholy against Melancholy: *Samson Ago-nistes* as Renaissance Tragedy," in *Calm of Mind: Tercentenary Essays on "Paradise Regained" and "Samson Agonistes,"* ed. Joseph Anthony Wittreich, Jr. (Cleveland: Case Western Reserve University Press, 1971), pp. 259–87.

As Christopher rightly observes, "*Samson Agonistes* is a logomachy between God's promise and human ones."[19]

At the beginning of the tragedy, Samson doubts "Divine Prediction" (line 44): "Promise was that I / Should *Israel* from *Philistian* yoke deliver" (lines 38–39). He makes his "own default" (line 45) responsible for the unfulfilled divine promise, even as he implicates God in his downfall—the God who "motion'd" (line 222) him to marry infidel wives as a means of accomplishing "*Israel*'s Deliverance, / The work to which [he] was divinely call'd" (lines 225–26). While he affirms God's justice and power, Samson lacks faith in God's election of him as an instrument: "the strife / With mee hath end; all the contest is now / 'Twixt God and *Dagon*" (lines 460–62).

His step-by-step rejection of the comforts offered to him by Manoa and Dalila as reasons to go on living gradually leads him back to a radical, unconditional belief in God's literal word and his "part from Heav'n assign'd" (line 1217). The "rousing motions" (line 1382) that impel him to the unexpected fulfillment of divine prophecy in Dagon's temple reflect back on the "intimate impulse" that "motion'd" (lines 222–23) him earlier to marry the woman of Timna and Dalila and thus make everything that has happened part of a powerful, providential order in which God's word finds historical fulfillment in spite of, and indeed through, human error and sin. In that mysterious order God's oracle ultimately means Samson's death—a death not unambiguously equated in its literal terms with suicide and revenge.

This reading of *Samson Agonistes* as an affirmation of the Bible's literal truth finds corroboration in its pattern of Joban allusions. Samson, guilt-stricken, blinded, and reduced to slave labor by his Philistine captors, opens the drama with a soliloquy in which he laments his terrible losses "As one past hope, abandon'd, / And by himself given over" (lines 120–21). Like Job he curses the day of his birth: "Why was my breeding order'd and prescrib'd" (line 30). The chorus of friends who come "To visit or bewail" (line 182) him, bringing "Counsel or Consolation" (line 183), recall Job's comforters. Close echoes of Job, especially at lines 203–4 and 667, strengthen the analogy between the dramatic situations, even as all the characters— including Samson himself—initially repeat the error of Job's friends in finding only one meaning in Samson's suffering: God's just pun-

19. Christopher, *Science of the Saints*, pp. 233–34.

ishment of sin. Only gradually does Samson find another meaning in it through meditation on and belief in God's prophetic word. As he waits for and cooperates with its fulfillment, he displays "Heroic magnitude of mind" (line 1279) and "patience . . . the exercise / Of saints" (lines 1287–88), *sapientia et fortitudo.*[20]

The Joban pattern in the drama finds a telling gloss in Milton's "Of True Religion" (March or April, 1673), where he reflects on the difference between heresy and error. Whereas heresy involves a willful rejection of the Scriptures, error results from "misunderstanding the Scripture after all sincere endeavours to understand it rightly."[21] Milton prefaces his survey of the various theological errors rampant in the contemporary Protestant denominations with the remark that "it is a humane frailty to err" (p. 423) and that "God will assuredly pardon" all his fellow Protestants "as he did the friends of Job, good and pious men, though much mistaken, as there it appears, in some Points of Doctrin" (p. 424). Salvation will result, despite all error and variance in understanding, simply as a result of firmly believing in the literal Word: "But so long as all these profess to set the Word of God only before them as the Rule of faith and obedience; and use all diligence and sincerity of heart, by reading, by learning, by study, by prayers for Illumination of the holy Spirit, to understand the Rule and obey it, they have done what man can do" (pp. 423–24).

Milton's Samson, like his Protestant readers, does "what man can do" in believing, against all appearances and ordinary expectations and apart from his own desert, that "Divine Prediction" (line 44) will be achieved in and through him "with a power resistless" (line 1404). His blind faith in God's Word leads him, in a way that is profoundly unreasonable, to consolation in its fulfillment. As the chorus expresses it, "Living or dying thou hast fulfill'd / The work for which thou wast foretold / To *Israel*" (lines 1661–63), the exact coincidence between divine prophecy and human history inspiring belief in a

20. For studies dealing with this general ethical theme, see Paul R. Baumgartner, "Milton and Patience," *Studies in Philology* 60 (1963): 203–13; Ann Grossman, "Samson, Job, and 'The Exercise of Saints,' " *English Studies* 45 (1964): 212–24; A. B. Chambers, "Wisdom and Fortitude in *Samson Agonistes*," *PMLA* 78 (1963): 315–20; William O. Harris, "Despair and 'Patience as the Truest Fortitude' in *Samson Agonistes*," *ELH* 30 (1963): 107–20.

21. John Milton, "Of True Religion, Haeresie, Schism, Toleration," in *Complete Prose Works*, vol. 8 (New Haven: Yale University Press, 1982), p. 423. Subsequent citations are parenthetical.

providential, albeit inscrutable and apparently cruel, design: "All is best, though we oft doubt" (line 1745).

At the end of *Samson Agonistes* the chorus affirms God's providential governance of the world, even as they earlier declared His existence and justice (lines 293–94). These tenets, on which Lady Philosophy bases her whole instruction of Boethius, console Samson, who discovers them, not in "Consolatories writ / With studied argument" (lines 657–58), but through grace and divine revelation: "Some source of consolation from above" (line 664). A prisoner like Boethius, "Betray'd, Captiv'd" (line 33), Samson languishes in cavelike "dark, dark, dark, amid the blaze of noon" (line 80). A patient in need of remedies, he suffers "The tumors of a troubl'd mind" (line 185). Submerged in misfortune, he presents a "mirror of our fickle state" (line 164). Like Boethius, who remembers who and what he is by seeing himself reflected in the mythic figures of Orpheus, Odysseus, Agamemnon, and Hercules, Samson grows in self-knowledge as he encounters aspects of himself in Manoa, Dalila, and Harapha. When he finally stands, moreover, "With both his arms on those two massy Pillars / That to the arched roof gave main support" (lines 1633–34) and "head erect" (line 1639), he recalls the Boethian Hercules, detached from earthly things and inwardly prepared to return to the eternal "Father's house" (lines 1717, 1733).

As Sadler argues, "The question is not so much that Boethian situations and echoes are present, but the use Milton makes of them."[22] When Milton uses both Job and Boethius to configure his Samson and represent Samson's growth in self-knowledge, he discovers in the biblical letter the revealed epic truth that Boethius had found veiled in classical mythology. The Boethian lens corrects, as it were, the Philistine (and Satanic) tendency to read and imitate the Greek and Roman epics literally as heroic poems, even as it establishes a common ground between them and the tales of biblical heroism they have "ill imitated." Samson is, as it were, a truer Hercules than Hercules.[23] He knows himself to be morally and physically weak; and in that acknowledged, abyssmal, Pauline weak-

22. Sadler, *Consolation*, p. 93. She provides a useful survey of Boethian influences in the Renaissance on pp. 94–104.

23. For the commonplace association of Samson with Hercules, see F. Michael Krouse, *Milton's Samson and the Christian Tradition* (1949; New York: Farrar, Straus, and Giroux, 1974), pp. 44–45.

ness, he is strong (compare 2 Corinth. 12:9–10). Rising like Hercules at Etna, Phoenix-like, from the flames and ashes, Samson professes "his faith in God as the source of strength and power" and acts out of what Michael Lieb has called a "theology of strength."[24] Echoing Job 19:25, he declares, "My trust is in the living God" (line 1139), and surrenders himself blindly to the power of a God he cannot see or understand.

Unlike the Boethian Samson, who only gradually acquires inner freedom and self-knowledge, the Boethian Christ of *Paradise Regained* knows himself from the very beginning to be the Son of God. A second, sinless Job, Christ is also a true philosopher, "unmov'd" (4.109) by Satan's offers of false goods—pleasure, wealth, power, fame—and able to answer him "sagely" (4.285), knowing all that the "Wisest of men" (4.276) have known, and more. Like Boethius' Lady Philosophy (*Consolation* I.p3), Christ points out that the Stoics, the Epicureans, and the Skeptics have all fallen short of true wisdom, lacking, as He says, the fundamental self-knowledge that stems from divine revelation: "Ignorant of themselves, of God much more, / And how the world began, and how man fell, / Degraded by himself, on grace depending" (4.310–12). Attached to the Father as the Supreme Good and absolutely obedient to His will, Christ patiently leaves the work of redemption "To his due time and providence" (3.440), whereas Satan urges Christ repeatedly to take immediate action: "Thou yet art not too late" (3.42). The Boethian echoes in the juxtaposition of true and false goods and temporal and eternal perspectives, as well as in the providential themes, contextualize Christ's startling association of Job with Socrates as examples of true heroism akin to His own:

Who names not now with honor patient *Job*?
Poor *Socrates* (who next more memorable?)
By what he taught and suffer'd for so doing,
For truth's sake suffering death unjust, lives now
Equal in fame to proudest Conquerors.

(3.95–99)

24. Michael Lieb, *The Sinews of Ulysses: Form and Convention in Milton's Works* (Pittsburgh: Duquesne University Press, 1989), p. 130. For the "Theology of Strength," see pp. 98–138.

The greatness of Christ, as a second, unfallen Job and a preredeemed Boethius, consists precisely in stasis; remaining unchanged, unmoved; adhering in a mutable world to what is eternal: "[H]e said and stood" (4.561).

Whereas *Samson Agonistes* and *Paradise Regained* stress respectively the mortality and the divinity of human nature, and thus separate as much as possible the weeping Boethius from the serene Philosophia, the sinner from the saint, the letter from the allegory, *Paradise Lost* combines the two foci in its Boethian rewriting of the Book of Job, interpreted tropologically. As we have seen, according to the moral interpretation of Job, the protagonist is neither a sinless saint nor a despairing sinner, but a humble penitent who meditates perseveringly on his sinfulness and its consequences and thus comes to both a heartfelt knowledge of himself and hopeful longing for the heavenly *patria*. This ethical reading of Job as the story of Adam and Everyman implies a developmental narrative and appeals rhetorically to its audience for imitation in a way that easily assimilates the formal structure of the *Consolation of Philosophy*. As we shall see, Milton represents the tropological Job in the last two books of *Paradise Lost*, using the conventions of the *consolatio* to frame all of salvation history, personal and collective, in an epic poem of instruction.

Milton never names Job in *Paradise Lost*, but he portrays Adam in a way that clearly prefigures the Old Testament saint. Initially rich in material and spiritual goods, virtuous, and enjoying God's favor, Adam is tested by Satan and loses everything. Like Job he curses the day of his birth and wishes for death: "How gladly would I meet / Mortality my sentence" (10.775–76). Like Job he confronts his own nakedness. Like Job he is tempted to suicide by his wife: "Let us seek Death" (10.1001). The hill where he sees the visions of history resembles the mound where Job sits, contemplative, and laments. Beholding the Flood, Adam mourns in Joban fashion, "as when a Father mourns / His children, all in view destroy'd at once" (11.761–62). Like Job Adam affirms God's justice ("Him after all Disputes / Forc't I absolve" [10:828–29]) and "patiently" detaches himself from the Eden he has "justly . . . lost" (11.287–88).

These initial analogies between Adam and Job determine the direction of angelic instruction in the last two books. At God's bid-

ding, Michael the Archangel gives Adam prophetic insight into future events "thereby to learn / True patience" (11.360–61). Adam
should become, like Gregory the Great's philosophical Job, a keeper
of the Golden Mean: "by pious sorrow, equally inur'd / By modera-
tion either state to bear, / Prosperous or adverse" (11.362–64). With
Joban faith in the promised redeemer, Adam is to see the whole
course of history governed by a salvific plan, take "Providence" as his
"guide" (12.647) in everyday life, "live well" (11.554), and leave the
length of his days to Heaven.

Adam's education by Michael, moreover, prefigures the Joban
formation of the saints by the Holy Spirit Who comes "To guide them
in all truth, and also arm / With spiritual Armor, able to resist /
Satan's assaults, and quench his fiery darts" (12.490–92). Milton's
description of the saints' "spiritual Armor" clearly recalls the patristic
and medieval image of Job as God's athlete, whose contest with
Satan radically revised the definition of "Valor and Heroic Virtue"
(11.690), making it synonymous with martyrdom. "Suffering for
Truth's sake," Michael explains, "Is fortitude to highest victory"
(12.569–70) in the new redemptive order where "things deem'd
weak" subvert the "worldly strong" (12.567–68).

The marked parallels between Michael's instruction of Adam, the
Holy Spirit's guidance of the saints, and Milton's explicit rhetorical
aim with the audience of his poem help to explain Milton's use of
Boethius' *Consolation* in the last two books of *Paradise Lost*. Here
Milton does not only pair the books of Job and Boethius allusively on
the implicit grounds that they tell comparable stories, approve the
same kind of spiritual heroism, and teach similar moral and providential lessons. Rather, he finds in the actual literary structure of the
Consolation an effective generic means to convey biblical tropology,
to teach what Job teaches.

The Medieval *Consolatio* and the Conclusion of *Paradise Lost*

The didactic strategies of the dialogue in Books 11 and 12 of *Paradise
Lost* conform in all essentials to the pattern of the Boethian consolation. Michael H. Means has defined the medieval *consolationes* as
"instruction poems in which learning brings about a psychological

or spiritual change" in the main character, usually the narrator.[25] Among these "instruction poems" Means lists William Langland's *Piers Plowman, Pearl,* John Gower's *Confessio Amantis,* Guillaume de Lorris' *Roman de la Rose,* and Dante's *Commedia*—all of them inspired by Boethius' *Consolation of Philosophy.* In each of these poems a didactic dialogue between the human sufferer and some superior guide occasions the psychological action of the consolation. The urgent need for instruction frequently necessitates the use of visions which give rise to questions and commentary and dispose the patient to accept the authority of the guide. In didactic dialogues of this kind the consolation of the sufferer depends upon his ability to learn the lesson the guide teaches him. This learning typically takes place in discernible stages as the auditor grows in self-knowledge. The process, moreover, is a painful one as the suffering person moves from his initial complaints to his final cure. The remedy of revelation, in the end, leaves the patient prepared to face the demands of the situation in which he finds himself with a certain inner detachment, peace, and strength.

The *consolatio* genre, according to Means, is a creative synthesis of two other kinds: the ancient apocalypse and the classical *consolatio mortis.*[26] As the critics of *Lycidas* have long recognized, Milton was familiar with the Ciceronian consolation and its Augustinian adaptation.[27] It is equally certain that Milton knew the medieval *consolatio* as that genre came to be defined by its great *exempla.* I do not, however, want to argue that Boethius' *Consolation,* or any other *consolatio* for that matter, is Milton's "source." My contention is simply this: that Milton employed the conventions of that genre in Books 11 and 12 of *Paradise Lost* so as to make the pedagogical purpose of the whole unmistakable and achievable.

The issue of reader response cannot be considered apart from the question of genre for the simple reason that the reader's recognition of kind informs his expectations of the work, prepares him for what is predictable in the text, and disposes him to cooperate with the conventions, to co-act with the artifact. The generic conventions that

25. Michael H. Means, *The Consolatio Genre in Medieval English Literature* (Gainesville: University of Florida Press, 1972), p. 104.
26. Ibid., pp. 10–11.
27. See Don Cameron Allen, *The Harmonious Vision* (Baltimore: Johns Hopkins University Press, 1954), pp. 41–70.

inform the pattern of exchange between Adam and Michael also govern the appropriate reader response to the concluding books and give us a standard by which we can measure the pedagogical effectiveness of *Paradise Lost* as a whole. The reader's learning belongs to the instruction poem even as the *catharsis* of pity and fear belongs to tragedy. Because the medieval *consolatio* weds divine revelation with conversion, with the healing of the human heart, it is a mode eminently suited to further Milton's twofold educational aim: to "assert Eternal Providence" (1.25) and bring his audience to the inward conviction that God is just in all His dealings with humankind—that is, to achieve a justification of God that simultaneously justifies his readers by increasing their faith.

Textual evidence suggests that Milton deliberately chose to structure the last two books of *Paradise Lost* in the *consolatio* style. As Joseph H. Summers points out, both the Trinity manuscript and the notes for "Adam Unparadiz'd" reveal that Milton originally planned a mechanical separation of sorrow and comfort in the conclusion, Adam first being reduced to despair by the facts of the future and then comforted by the allegorical figures of Faith, Hope, and Charity who appear to him and who are seemingly detached from the horrors of history.[28] Milton abandoned that scheme in favor of a didactic dialogue between Adam and Michael in which "good with bad" (11.358) is intermingled throughout, "supernal Grace contending / With sinfulness of Men" (11.359–60) in each of the revelations. The latter form, of course, is better suited for the progressive, subtle refinement of feeling in Adam and, therefore, in Milton's audience.

At the outset of the revelations Milton explicitly defines their purpose in terms of Adam's and our affective response. The revelations are meant to be consolatory:

> Dismiss them not disconsolate; reveal
> To *Adam* what shall come in future days,
> As I shall thee enlighten, intermix
> My Cov'nant in the woman's seed renew'd;
> So send them forth, though sorrowing, yet in peace.
>
> (11.113–17)

---

28. Joseph H. Summers, *The Muse's Method: An Introduction to "Paradise Lost"* (Cambridge: Harvard University Press, 1962), p. 197.

Later Michael ascribes a second pedagogical purpose to the disclosures. Adam and we are

> thereby to learn
> True patience, and to temper joy with fear
> And pious sorrow, equally inur'd
> By moderation either state to bear,
> Prosperous or adverse.
>
> (11.360–64)

Adam's knowledge of the future, then, is a secondary, instrumental kind of learning. The poet's principal aim is the affective education of the audience in the person of Adam. That Adam "may'st believe, and be confirm'd" (11.355) in his understanding of God's providential care, His encompassing and ever-present "goodness and paternal Love" (11.353), he is granted a revelation of "what shall come in future days" (11.357). Adam's foreknowledge of those events precipitates an inward "learning" of Joban patience. At the end of the revelations Adam is ready, not only to depart from the Garden, but also to die, to leave "this transient World" (12.554): "Greatly instructed I shall hence depart, / Greatly in peace of thought" (12.557–58). The parallel construction is a telling one. In the usual meaning of the *consolatio*, instruction and consolation are nearly synonymous. The heart comes to feel what the mind, enlightened by faith, perceives.

Milton announces his educational objective very clearly in Book 1, and he accomplishes it in the *consolatio* of Books 11 and 12. He is ultimately interested, not in the reader's self-knowledge, but in the reader's appreciative, personal knowledge of God. Stanley Fish is patently wrong in his contention that the reader arrives at "the terminal point" of his education in Book 9 when he falls with Adam and, in this way, comes to recognize his own fallenness.[29] Certainly the experiential knowledge of one's own sinfulness is an essential precondition for the affective learning of divine love, but it is the lesser of the two learnings. In Book 9 neither Adam nor the reader has learned the ultimate lesson that Milton wants him to learn. Only

---

29. Stanley Fish, *Surprised by Sin: The Reader in "Paradise Lost"* (New York: St. Martin's Press, 1967), p. 271.

in Book 12 does Adam come to see all of life, all of history, as a providential unfolding. Only then does he incorporate himself into the New Adam, Christ.

If the reader is to learn what Adam learns and do what Adam does, he must identify himself with Adam as the epic comes to its close. Such an identification is not only the means for Milton to achieve the reader's education; it is also, in a certain sense, synonymous with the goal of education. As Milton himself writes, "The end . . . of learning is to repair the ruins of our first parents by regaining to know God aright."[30] We are, in short, to become Adam anew even as he is renewed in the knowledge and the love of God.

If the reader comes to a deeper self-knowledge through the first ten books of the epic—as Fish assures us he does—that self-knowledge, that new-found humility, should enable him to lose himself in the last two books. Detachment from self is certainly required of the reader if he is to identify with Adam and occupy the ego of the text. The reader might balk at such a demand. He might prefer to take the part Fish assigns to him: that of an emotionally uninvolved spectator who watches while Adam struggles to adjust to the all-too-familiar post-lapsarian conditions. He might wish (as Fish does) to withdraw from the immediate reading experience and quietly reconstruct the preceding events of the epic while Adam is being "chastened and instructed."[31] Milton admittedly takes a risk. The reader who has not sufficiently experienced his own fallenness might cling to his own, albeit accidental, superiority and yield to the temptation to stand apart from Adam "as an advanced pupil to a novice."[32] Indeed, many readers do so, and they are the ones who complain that Milton's conclusion is boring and aesthetically unsatisfactory. They mistakenly assume that the poem teaches them nothing and asks nothing more of them than this: "to provide traditional interpretations for a succession of biblio-historical tableaux."[33] They miss the invitation for identification and its attendant affective challenge.

On the other hand, those readers, "fit . . . though few" (7.31), who respond to Milton's conclusion as a *consolatio* recognize that the

---

30. "Of Education," in *Complete Poems and Major Prose*, p. 631.
31. Fish, *Surprised by Sin*, p. 300.
32. Ibid., p. 288.
33. Ibid., p. 286.

poem invites them, even expects them, to identify themselves with Adam. Such readers feel the whole insistent force of convention encouraging them to abandon their individual particularity, to displace themselves into the "I" of the poem and appropriate the words of the speaker. Adam, like all the suffering speakers of the *consolationes*, is Everyman. Theology, typology, and generic convention all define him as a corporate personality inclusive of his audience. In framing his conclusion as a *consolatio*, Milton continues a poetic tradition which, as Judson Boyce Allen has demonstrated, tends toward the achievement of an occupiable ego, of a human discourse that is generic rather than particular.[34] The audience of such a poem is expected to impersonate what is said, even as young lovers appropriate the lyrics of pop songs and pious Christians occupy the "I" of the psalms. Adam's situation is typical, his speeches almost proverbial. There are no surprises; indeed, there cannot be. When Adam speaks, he speaks for all of us.

Milton asks his readers to feel the emotion that Adam expresses— the earthly grieving as well as the ecstatic, religious joy. The challenge of Books 11 and 12, like that of all the *consolationes*, is an affective challenge. The learning of God's justice, like the learning of patience, is an education of the heart. Milton wants his readers to see death and sickness, war and sin, as if they had never seen them before; to feel the guilt of Adam, to weep as he weeps, to rejoice as he rejoices. As a *consolatio* the conclusion of *Paradise Lost* does what earlier religious poetry did in enacting (to borrow a phrase from Allen) "the appropriate emotional attitude toward the fact that some relatively simple Christian event or doctrine is true."[35] To the degree that readers succeed in identifying with Adam, they succeed in making that "appropriate emotional attitude" their own.

If Milton blatantly employs all the conventions of the Boethian *consolatio* in Books 11 and 12, he does so in order to free his readers into making a conventional response, the right one. He wants his readers to be able, finally, to respond in a typical—and therefore,

34. See Judson Boyce Allen, "Grammar, Poetic Form, and the Lyric Ego: A Medieval *A Priori*," in *Vernacular Poetics in the Middle Ages*, ed. Lois Ebin, Studies in Medieval Culture (Kalamazoo, Mich.: Medieval Institute Publications, 1984), pp. 199–226.
35. Ibid., p. 211.

ideal—Christian way to the workings of God in life, in history. He wants his readers to feel what they should feel about sin, about suffering, about salvation. We are seldom as contrite as we should be, seldom as compassionate, seldom as grateful and joyful. Because our emotional responses to events, both actual and imaginary, usually do not correspond to the dictates of faith and reason, the poet must first make his audience aware of that discrepancy and then gradually apply correctives until the affections are purified, and the heart knows truth. The conventions of the *consolatio* allow Milton to do just that. The human sufferer freely vents his emotions and expresses himself while the healer helps him, step by step, to learn from his mistakes. At the end of the exchange the exterior situation in which the patient finds himself remains the same; inwardly, however, the patient is peaceful, purged of misdirected passions, and newly fortified to face whatever challenges he must face.

In all of the medieval *consolationes* the sufferer is enlightened, and thereby comforted, by a guide or guides, allegorical or typological, who somehow partake of the divine *numen*. Boethius' Lady Philosophy is such a figure, as is the God of Love in the *Roman de la Rose*. The Pearl-maiden, Dante's Virgil, Beatrice, and Bernard function similarly. In this company of characters, Milton's Michael is a guide par excellence, being God's messenger and having been ordered by Him to "reveal / To *Adam* what shall come in future days, / As I shall thee enlighten" (11.113–15). Adam calls Michael his "safe Guide" (11.371), his "Teacher" (11.450), the "True opener" (11.598) of his eyes, a "Celestial Guide" (11.785), a "Heav'nly instructor" (11.871), the "Enlight'ner of my darkness" (12.271), the "Prophet of glad tidings" (12.375), and finally, a "Seer blest" (12.553). In entrusting Adam's education and consolation to a single guide, rather than to several, Milton duplicates the pattern in what Means has termed the "pure" *consolationes*.[36]

Fish complains that Michael's official position as teacher "defines and limits" him in such a way that he is actually less effective pedagogically than the epic narrator in the preceding ten books.[37] I would argue, on the other hand, that Milton consciously emphasizes the

36. Means distinguishes between the "pure" *consolatio*, in which there is a single guide, and the "fragmented" *consolatio*, in which there are several.
37. Fish, *Surprised by Sin*, p. 288.

conventionality of Michael's position in order to urge his readers to take their correspondent, conventionally defined part in the *consolatio*: that of the learner. Everything depends on the reader's identification with Adam.

Like the first-person narrators of the earlier *consolatio* poems, Adam is in sore distress prior to the revelations. He is "To sorrow abandoned, . . . / And in a troubl'd Sea of passion tost" (10.717–18). In his attempt to unburden himself he complains aloud in the great soliloquy of Book 10 (720–844). Conscience-stricken, full of fear and horror at the gravity of his sin, Adam finds himself "from deep to deeper plung'd" (10.844) into despair. When he finally relents at Eve's confession of guilt and forgives her, he becomes capable of believing in God's forgiveness of them both, and the two retire, humbly weeping and praying, to the place of judgment. Adam anticipates a twofold gift from God, enlightenment and consolation:

> And what may else be remedy or cure
> To evils which our own misdeeds have wrought,
> Hee will instruct us praying, and of Grace
> Beseeching him, so as we need not fear
> To pass commodiously this life, sustain'd
> By him with many comforts, till we end
> In dust, our final rest and native home.
>
> (10.1079–85)

Adam proves himself worthy of consolation, first by his prayer of repentance, and then by his submission to the edict of exile from Eden. The Father grants the revelations conditionally: "If patiently thy bidding they obey, / Dismiss them not disconsolate" (11.112–13). This kind of initial testing is also characteristic of the medieval *consolatio*. Lady Philosophy, for instance, first scolds the prisoner; then she allows him to "shewe [his] greife" in a loud lament; finally she asks "certayne questyons for to knowe the state of [his] mynd" before applying any of her remedies.[38] The prisoner's profession of

---

38. Boethius' *Consolation of Philosophy, Translated from the Latin by George Colville, 1556*, ed. Ernest Belfort Bax, Tudor Library (London: David Nutt, 1897), pp. 18, 26. Other Renaissance translations include those of Queen Elizabeth (1593) and I. T. (1609).

belief in Providence convinces Lady Philosophy that her patient can indeed be cured and is, therefore, deserving of her consolation. Adam passes a similar test when he humbly submits to God's "great bidding" (11.314) that Eve and he leave the Garden. Michael immediately responds to Adam's acquiescence by offering him the gift of foreknowledge: "Ascend / This Hill" (11.366–67).

Milton emphasizes that Michael must prepare Adam's eyes to behold the visions, removing the film produced by "that false Fruit that promis'd clearer sight" (11.413) and purging the visual nerve. This action, too, has its counterpart in the *Consolation of Philosophy* when Lady Philosophy wipes the narrator's eyes with her mantle. The weeping prisoner's drowsiness in Boethius' *Consolation*, the tears and sleep of the *Pearl* narrator, the dream visions of the seeker in *Piers Plowman*—all provide a generic context for Adam's seeming slumber on the mountain: he "Sunk down and all his Spirits became intranst" (11.420).

When Adam first opens his eyes on the mountain, he is not a saint, not a prophet, not Daniel, not John on Patmos. He sees visions because he needs to become holy, not because he is holy. Apocalypse *per se* does not account for the instructive force of the last visions and the psychological conversion precipitated by them as Adam learns to interpret typologically.[39] There is a creative tension in the relationship between Adam and his instructor, between the patient and his physician, that is absent in the relationship between John and Jesus in the Book of Revelation. The didactic dialogue in Milton's epic differs distinctly from the biblical discipleship that humbly receives and records what is revealed: "Write down what you see, and send the book to the seven churches" (Revelation 1:11).

When Adam opens his eyes at Michael's command, he sees a series of six visions that dramatize "Th' effects which [his] original crime hath wrought" (11.424) upon himself and his descendants. In the murder of Abel he beholds Death for the first time. In the Lazar-house he encounters "many shapes / Of Death" (4.467–8). He sees the sons of Gods in the tents of wickedness, ensnared by lust. He

---

39. For treatments of the apocalyptic nature of the final visions, and of *Paradise Lost* as a whole, see Leland Ryken, *The Apocalyptic Vision in "Paradise Lost"* (Ithaca: Cornell University Press, 1970), and Joseph Anthony Wittreich, Jr., *Visionary Poetics: Milton's Tradition and His Legacy* (San Marino, Calif.: Huntington Library, 1979).

witnesses the bloody wars on the plains. Then he watches the flood waters rise, depopulating the earth, drowning his sinful offspring. Finally, Adam is granted a vision of Noah and the rainbow "Betok'ning peace from God, and Cov'nant new" (11.867).

Because Milton's primary concern is the affective education of his audience, he purposely emphasizes what is known, what is familiar to his readers. Milton's poetic apocalypse does not restrict itself to a communication of transcendental and ideal realities outside of time; rather, it assimilates the harsh realities of everyday experience into revelation. Adam sees in vision things familiar to Milton's readers—sickness, death, war, and sin—so that they might see them anew as part of a providential pattern.

During the visions at the beginning of the *consolatio* Milton confronts his readers with their own lack of integrity, with their need for affective education. Each disclosure repeats the pattern: the readers know what Michael knows; at the same time, they feel what Adam feels. The reader knows that he should not judge "what is best / By pleasure, though to Nature seeming meet" (11.603–4) and yet he, like Adam, is "soon inclin'd to admit delight" (11.596) in sensual pleasure. The reader knows that he should have a certain holy indifference toward life and death, and yet he too has revolted against suffering; he has wished to die; in dark hours he has, like Job and Adam, imagined it better to "end here unborn" (11.502). Adam expresses emotions common to all of us. This is the shocking thing. Milton forces the audience into the realization that, in spite of their knowledge of the scriptures, in spite of their knowledge of the faith, they have all felt, and often feel, like unregenerate, uninstructed Adam.

Adam responds to the visions with bitter tears, with questions, with occasional complaints, with misunderstanding, and with horror. Michael is strict with him, withholding neither the consequences of the Fall nor Adam's responsibility for them. The revelations bring Adam to understand the seriousness of his sin by unveiling its effects. He sees generation after generation perpetuating his original disobedience, idolatry, ambition, and lust, and in this way he reexperiences his own Fall. At the end of the fifth vision Adam is "comfortless" (11.760), overwhelmed with weeping, scarcely able to speak to the angel. He complains that the visions have brought him no consolation at all; rather, that they have made his fate more unbearable. He finds "the ways of God" (1.26) hard to accept, and in his emotional response to the events of history Adam articulates the typical reaction of a fallen man to the painful realities of his condition. Indeed, Adam voices *our* reaction. As Summers notes, "fewer readers . . . have been disturbed by the comfort at the end of the poem than by the feeling that there is not enough comfort."[40] Through Adam's complaints Milton takes the rhetorical risk of a self-critical *consolatio*, a *consolatio* that first complains about its own lack of consolation and only then supplies what is lacking. In this way Milton makes it clear that the only lasting foundation for peace and joy is humility and the recognition of our misery as sinful creatures.

Adam's learning in Book 11 of *Paradise Lost* corresponds to the kind of initial instruction in the medieval *consolationes*. Like the "weaker remedy" of Lady Philosophy, the visions and Michael's commentary on them serve to detach Adam from his perception of things. Like the narrator of *Pearl*, Adam fails to comprehend what he sees. Again and again he finds himself mistaking the appearance for the reality, his passions clouding his understanding. When he finally learns to distrust himself and to trust his guide instead, Adam is ready to be initiated into the community of faith through an acceptance of divinely revealed truth.

At the sight of Noah and the sign of the Covenant, Adam revives and rejoices:

> Far less I now lament for one whole World
> Of wicked Sons destroy'd, than I rejoice
> For one Man found so perfet and so just
> That God voutsafes to raise another World
> From him, and all his anger to forget.
>
> (11.874–8)

Adam's emotional response at this point coincides with his faith. He grasps the significance of the rainbow intuitively, and Michael praises him for his new understanding.

Adam's joy at seeing Noah represents a new affective challenge for the reader. Milton wants his reader to break out of his habitual lack

---

40. Summers, *The Muse's Method*, p. 188.

of feeling and share Adam's joy, appropriate his sentiment at the sign of the Covenant. As Milton himself notes in *Areopagitica,* "passions . . . rightly tempered are the very ingredients of virtue."[41] Accordingly, the Miltonic *consolatio* serves to direct the force of feeling toward the goods of salvation.

After Michael's explanation of the rainbow, Adam falls silent. The archangel pauses, waits for him to speak, and recognizes in Adam's contemplative mood a sign that he is ready to enter a new stage in the educational process. Similarly, the narrator in Boethius' *Consolation* falls silent in his longing to hear Lady Philosophy's discourse, and she recognizes in that attitude a readiness for the "stronger remedy": "I well perceyued the same, when thou being styll, makynge no noyse and herkenyng, receyuydest my words. And that I had expected or reuocate the habite of thy mynde, that thou hast now, (or that is more true) that I had perfyted the habite or maner of thy mynde."[42]

At this point in the poem the prophecies become verbal rather than visual, a change perfectly in keeping with the psychological action of a *consolatio.*[43] Since any inner healing presupposes that the patient first be humbled, the "gentler remedy" typically reduces him to weakness, dependence, and receptivity. At the end of Book 11 Adam is emotionally and physically exhausted, barely able to see. As Michael says, "objects divine / Must needs impair and weary human sense" (12.9–10). Moreover, Adam is ready to listen to his guide, to "give due audience, and attend" (12.12), having discovered that the archangel perceives a providential pattern in events that his unaided senses cannot discern. Adam rarely interrupts Michael's narrative in Book 12, and this pattern of increased silence is also characteristic of

41. Milton, *Areopagitica,* in *Complete Poems and Major Prose,* p. 733.

42. *Boethius' Consolation,* p. 53. I. T.'s 1609 translation renders the same passage (III.p1) as follows: "I perceived as much, as thou sayest, when I sawe thee hearken to my speeches with so great silence and attention, and I expected this disposition of thy mind, or rather more truely caused it my selfe" (*The Consolation of Philosophy in the Translation of I. T.,* ed. William Anderson [Arundel: Centaur Press, 1963], p. 61).

43. Although most critics have seconded Joseph Addison's complaint that the shift is aesthetically unsatisfactory (see *Spectator* No. 369), a few have argued that it is appropriate and even effective for various symbolic reasons. See Raymond Waddington, "The Death of Adam: Vision and Voice in Books XI and XII of *Paradise Lost,*" *MP* 70 (1972): 9–21; Barbara K. Lewalski, "Structure and Symbolism of Vision in Michael's Prophecy," *Paradise Lost,* Books XI and XII," *PQ* 42 (1963): 25–35.

a *consolatio.* As Means notes, in the third section of Boethius' *Consolation* the once vocal prisoner "becomes a fairly docile student, for the most part silently following his teacher's arguments or humbly assenting to them."[44]

When Adam does interpose a comment it is, with one exception, joyful and exclamatory.[45] After Michael's long account of God's Covenant with Abraham and his descendants, including the story of Moses and the exodus from Egypt into the Promised Land, Adam indicates that he has gained new peace and understanding:

> now first I find
> Mine eyes true op'ning, and my heart much eas'd,
> Erewhile perplext with thoughts what would become
> Of mee and all Mankind; but now I see
> His day, in whom all Nations shall be blest.
>
> (12.273–7)

When Adam hears of the Nativity, he is "with such joy / Surcharg'd" (12.372–5) that he speaks impetuously, anticipating a martial solution to the conflict between Christ and the Anti-Christ. Similarly, when Adam learns of the Resurrection and the ultimate redemption of the world, he is "replete with joy and wonder" (12.468) and bursts into an *exultet*: "O goodness infinite, goodness immense!" (12.469). Again and again the poet focuses on Adam's feelings as he enacts the appropriate emotional response to the tenets of faith. In doing so, Milton invites his audience to occupy the Adamic ego.

Even as Michael permitted Adam the emotional release of tears, he allows him to express enthusiasm, but he takes care to temper Adam's joy with a vivid account of Christ's Passion, and a prediction that the Church will undergo struggle, schism, corruption from within, and persecution from without, until the end of time. Nevertheless, Michael describes the apocalyptic new Paradise twice (12.463–5, 545–51) and also promises a "paradise within" (12.587) the virtuous and faithful man, so that Adam may be "cheer'd / With meditation

44. Means, *The Consolatio Genre*, p. 31.

45. Adam's first remark in Book 12, a judgment against Nimrod and the builders of Babel, may be considered transitional, since it refers to the time between the Covenant God made with Noah and the one He made with Abraham, "our Father in faith."

on the happy end" (12.604–5). Michael, in short, is a "Comforter" (12.486) not unlike the Holy Spirit Himself, Who arms God's chosen ones with "spiritual Armor" (12.491) and rewards the martyrs with "inward consolations" (12.495) that support and sustain them in their suffering.

At the end of the revelations, Adam declares himself to be "Greatly instructed . . . , / Greatly in peace of thought" (12.557–8). The twofold aim of the *consolatio* has thus been achieved. Adam has learned "that to obey is best, / And love with fear the only God, to walk / As in his presence, ever to observe / His providence, and on him sole depend" (12.561–4). Michael approves Adam's formulation, telling him, "This having learnt, thou hast attain'd the sum / Of wisdom" (12.575–6). In his commentary on this passage, Fish notes that the reader must admire Adam for his readiness to actualize the words: "Thy will be done."[46] Surely Milton wants his audience to do more than that. He wants his readers to make Adam's response their own, and he has structured the concluding books as a *consolatio* in order to facilitate that appropriation. Milton's Adam is not merely a model, worthy of the reader's admiration and imitation; he is the reader's own potential self. Adam as Everyman includes the reader to the extent that the reader has cooperated with the poem and occupied Adam's "I." The *consolatio* offers the reader no alternative: to stand outside of Adam is to stand outside of the poem.

Michael's final words to Adam and Eve are also addressed to us. He tells them that although they will be sad in the days to come as a necessary result of "evils past" (12.604), they will yet be "much more cheer'd" by God's sure promise of redemption, the foreknowledge they have of a "happy end" (12.605). If the consolation Adam receives is not the bliss of Paradise, it is nonetheless the promise of that bliss and the comfort that comes from believing in a promise— human openness and faith being a necessary precondition and even a kind of guarantee for all divine fulfillment.

In structuring the last books as a *consolatio*, Milton has allowed us to experience our own redemption, the redemption of all human-kind, through the psychological and spiritual conversion of a single representative sinner and sufferer: Adam. Even as Adam learns to

46. Fish, *Surprised by Sin*, p. 291.

accept himself, his need of redemption, and finally his Redeemer, so too we participate in that same process of reconciliation. If the aim of the poem as a whole is to "assert Eternal Providence, / And justify the ways of God to men" (1.25–6), the final revelations serve to teach Adam that same lesson: to submit to God's just will and "ever to observe / His providence" (12.563–4) in the events of history. The visions, together with Michael's narrative, help Adam to make the connection between Eden and the exile, the curse and the promise, the past and the future, himself and his descendants, the memory of an earthly Paradise, the reality of Paradise lost, and the hope of one to be regained. Most important, the last books serve to universalize Adam's experience, making him Everyman, making us Adam, enabling us to leave the imaginative realm of Milton's epic in a manner not unlike that of Adam and Eve as they take "thir solitary way" (12.649) out of the Garden. Michael's success with his pupil, Adam, enables Milton, in turn, to be successful with us. If we can accept the ending of Milton's poem, we can also accept life with all of its vicissitudes more courageously than before, having been inwardly fortified by the "strong remedy" of his *consolatio.*

Taken together, then, Milton's three major poems form a trilogy that provides an extended commentary on the Book of Job. Milton's exploration of heroism leads him to read and imitate the Book of Job at various exegetical levels—literal, allegorical, and moral—each taking a different point of reference and assuming a different literary form. Diffuse, brief, and dramatic, Milton's respective reworkings of Job in *Paradise Lost, Paradise Regained,* and *Samson Agonistes* not only emphasize heroic truth over epic form; by their common, albeit diverse engagement with Boethius' *Consolation,* they point to a truth hidden under many veils, both scriptural and pagan, to know which is to be able to answer the question "which before us lies in daily life" (*PL* 8.193), to know ourselves and God. Balancing Adam's visions at the beginning of his trilogy with Samson's blindness at the end, Milton insists that there is no single answer, not even in Scripture, and that the Joban question will remain even after we, falling silent, have ceased to ask it: "God of our Fathers, what is man!" (*SA,* line 667).

CONCLUSION

Under the heading of "epic truth" this book has dealt with a range of medieval and Renaissance works that are normally subsumed under the generic label "romance"— exotic saints' legends; the love stories of Orpheus and Eurydice, Abelard and Heloise, Dante and Beatrice, Troilus and Criseyde; the tales of penitent knights like Lancelot and Redcrosse; the paradisal temptations of Milton's heroes. In so doing it has indicated an inner relationship and historical continuum between two "orders of literature" whose formal difference, William Paton Ker remarks, "is as plain as the difference in the art of war between the two sides of the battle of Hastings."[1]

The differences between medieval epic and romance have been cataloged by literary historians in now-familiar ways. Epic, they say, belongs to the Heroic Age; to closed, centripetal, clannish societies. Romance belongs to the Age of Chivalry; to open, centrifugal, mobile societies. Epic celebrates the great leader on whom a whole people depends for its survival. Romance isolates the lonely individual whose spiritual and military adventures, undertaken for personal motives of love and honor, take place in an unbounded, beautiful, and dangerous world. Epic impersonates its characters, endowing them with mimetic, dramatic quality; romance, on the other hand, personifies ideas within an imaginative, otherworldly universe. Epic offers a concrete—romance, an abstract, ideational—description of things. In sum, as Ker insists, "Whatever Epic may mean, it implies some weight and solidity," whereas "Romance means nothing, if it does not convey some sense of mystery and fantasy."[2]

1. William Paton Ker, *Epic and Romance* (New York and London: Macmillan, 1908, 1931), p. 4.
2. Ibid.

Ker's descriptive terms, which oppose epic "matter" to romantic "spirit," broadly parallel traditional, exegetical ones, which set the carnal "letter" apart from the allegorical "spirit" of a text. The parallel is not merely accidental. This book argues that the formal disjuncture that we typically associate with generic revolution, with the sudden rise of romance and the virtual disappearance of epic in the Middle Ages, conceals a historical continuity between the two genres that derives from the inseparability of modes of reading and writing. The Middle Ages interpreted classical epic in a way that entailed its subsequent imitation as romance. There is, in short, a direct relationship between the two "allegories" of epic—its interpreted "other speaking," represented in the commentary tradition, and its imitated "other speaking" in the form of its generic twin, romance.

Ker is right when he says that romance is somehow "included in epic"—not so much as a constitutive, episodic subgenre, however, but rather as a level of meaning veiled and hidden behind the epic letter, revealed through allegorical interpretation (*poetarum enarratio*), and then creatively reinscribed as romance.[3] Romance concerns itself openly with what epic is truly (albeit covertly) about. Whereas interpreting classical epic provided a means to know oneself (in keeping with the Delphic oracle), romance imitates the very process of coming to self-knowledge through figural interpretation. As Eugène Vinaver has phrased it, "The marriage of matter and meaning, of narrative and commentary, was the key to the new kind of narrative poetry—the poetry that assumed in the reader both the ability and the desire to think of an event in terms of what one's mind could build upon it, or descry behind it."[4] The medieval writer was expected not only to tell a tale, but also "to reveal the *meaning* of the story" as he or she told it.[5]

Critics writing about medieval romance—from Ker to Vinaver to Fredric Jameson—often comment on the motif of combat between two knights who blindly join arms against one another, only to discover in the end, when the visors are raised, that they are brothers.[6] If we imagine the relationship between epic and romance as

---

3. Ibid., p. 31. See also pp. 32–33.
4. Eugène Vinaver, *The Rise of Romance* (New York and Oxford: Oxford University Press, 1971), p. 23.
5. Ibid., p. 17.
6. See Ker, *Epic and Romance*, pp. 5–6; Vinaver, *Rise of Romance*, pp. 101–5;

such a combat, then a helmeted Romance, as the ascendant genre of the Chivalric Age, discovers its own face in that of its defeated brother when Epic is unmasked; when its hidden truth, its meaning, is revealed.

As a historical genre, the "heroic poetry" of the Middle Ages characteristically joins together the literatures we separate as "epic" and "romance." It insists on both a figural continuity with the epics of antiquity and a formal departure from their literary conventions. It finds its critical authorization for both demands, moreover, in its chief exemplars, the paired works of Job and Boethius. Ker is right in his impressionistic association of the end of epic invention with scriptural exegesis and "the spell of the preacher," on one hand, and the "paradox" of King Alfred's Anglo-Saxon translation of Boethius, on the other.[7] As textual analogues, the Book of Job and Boethius' *Consolation of Philosophy* both record the trials of an innocent sufferer, dramatize his questioning response, and articulate belief in Divine Providence. They both ask and answer the explicit question, "What is a human being?" In them, therefore, the threefold "epic truth" of human nature appears, no longer as something deliberately veiled in order to be explicated in a marginal commentary or interlinear gloss, but as a direct poetic expression in its own right.

The two works present that "epic truth," however, from complementary perspectives of stasis and kinesis. Job's typological relationship to Christ, and therefore, his heroism, depend on his sinless steadfastness, on his remaining firm and unchanged when everything around him changes. Boethius' heroism, on the other hand, requires him to convert, grow in self-knowledge, and progress in his attachment from earthly to eternal things. These differences help to distinguish, and establish a relationship of creative tension between, two opposed poles in medieval romance, whose narratives indicate both stability and movement, and typically juxtapose the temporal perspectives of time and eternity.

When Boethius imitates the epics of Homer and Virgil, as they

---

Fredric Jameson, "Magical Narratives: Romance as Genre," *NHL* 7 (1975): 135–63. For a recent collection of essays on romance as a genre, see *Romance: Generic Transformation from Chrétien de Troyes to Cervantes*, ed. Kevin Brownlee and Marina Scordilis Brownlee (Hanover: University Press of New England, 1985).

7. Ker, *Epic and Romance*, pp. 46–47.

had been interpreted, by making their moral allegory literal in the plot of a philosophical quest for self-knowledge, he prepares the way for romance as a genre whose typical hero is a questioning interpreter and whose story unfolds in a providential series of adventures, each of which challenges him to understand figuratively the signs and marvels he sees, the stories he hears, the sufferings he endures.

The road to self-knowledge, however, which tests the human limits of a person's mortal, rational, and divine being, requires the fortitude of a Job and a patience commensurate with the endurance of process, suspension, amplification, mystery, and repeated trial. As a model for romance, the Book of Job lays bare the "epic truth" of human nature by placing its naked hero in the contested middle ground between time and eternity, fortune and providence, earth and heaven, Satan and God. Thus, as Patricia A. Parker has observed, a Joban " 'patience' . . . continues to inhabit that liminal or preliminary space of 'trial' which is the romance's traditional place of testing"— even in the works of Milton, who rejects the "externals of romance" along with those of epic.[8]

As we have seen, the intertextual pairing of the Book of Job with Boethius' *Consolation* expresses itself differently in the separate varieties of medieval romance, depending on which of the two is foregrounded as an exemplar. Saints' *legenda*, modeled strongly on the Job of Gregorian interpretation, tend to present static heroes and heroines in opposition to Boethian and Satanic forces of destruction and change. Amatory romance, on the other hand, foregrounds the *Consolation* according to the pattern of the myth of Orpheus and Eurydice, and then extends its progressive stages of spiritual growth into a history of personal salvation by assimilating the lover's sufferings to those of Job and Christ. Chivalric romance, in its early expressions, focuses on the static image of Job as the perfect *miles Christi*, whereas in the later Middle Ages it likens first the repentant Job of tropological interpretation and then the despairing Job of literal exegesis to the dynamic Boethius, who laments, learns, and finally rejoices. In Renaissance literature the image of Job conforms more and more to that of the weeping Boethius. While Milton preserves

Joban stasis in his portrayal of Christ in *Paradise Regained*, the Joban images in *Paradise Lost* and *Samson Agonistes* lose their stability and assume the characteristic movement and mutability of the Boethian model.

As the elliptic poles of stasis and kinesis gradually converge into one, the medieval tradition of heroic poetry comes to an end, and even its exemplars are displaced into different genres. Boethius' *Consolation* ceases to be considered an epic imitation of Martianus, Virgil, and Homer; and the Book of Job appears, no longer as a biblical heroic poem to rival the *Iliad*, but rather as a drama and a tragedy. In both cases the literal "matter" that remains when the "spirit" that governed its interpretation vanishes can no longer support an epic classification on purely formal grounds.

Thus, at the end of a long literary history, the virtues that the Middle Ages attributed to Job, especially wisdom and fortitude, belong no longer to man but to God, even as eternity belongs not to the things of this world, but to the next. Isidore of Seville derives the word "hero" from the heavenly realm (*aer*) proper to godlike men. Similarly, John of Salisbury derives the Latin adjective "true" (*verum*) from the Greek word meaning "heroic" (*heron*).[9] The earthly heroes and heroines who greet the dawn of a new, novelistic order of literature, however, characteristically share in the mutability and unreliability of the universe that surrounds them, rather than in the heavenly "truth," which is, as John of Salisbury describes it, "secure, stable, certain, and clear."

9. Isidore of Seville, *Etymologiae* VIII.ii.98, PL 82, c325; John of Salisbury, *The Metalogicon: A Twelfth-Century Defense of the Verbal and Logical Arts of the Trivium*, trans. Daniel D. McGarry (Berkeley: University of California Press, 1955), p. 255.

BIBLIOGRAPHY

Primary Sources

Ælfric. *Ælfric's Catholic Homilies: The Second Series.* Ed. Malcolm Godden. EETS Supplemental Series, no. 5. London: Oxford University Press, 1979.
———. *Ælfric's Lives of Saints.* 2 vols. Ed. Walter W. Skeat. London: Kegan Paul, Trench, Trübner and Co., 1900.
———. *The Old English Heptateuch: Ælfric's Treatise on the Old and New Testament and His Preface to Genesis.* Ed. S. J. Crawford. EETS 160. London: Oxford University Press, 1922.
Achilles Tatius. *Leucippe and Clitophon.* Trans. John J. Winkler. In *Collected Ancient Greek Novels,* ed. B. P. Reardon, 170–284. Berkeley: University of California Press, 1989.
Alain de Lille. "Liber in distinctionibus dictionum theologicalium." PL 210, c687–1012.
Apuleius. *De deo Socratis.* In *De philosophia libri,* ed. Paul Thomas. Stuttgart: B. G. Teubner, 1970.
———. *The Golden Ass.* Trans. Jack Lindsay. Bloomington: University of Indiana Pess, 1932, repr. 1962.
———. *Metamorphoses.* 2 vols. Ed. and trans. J. Arthur Hanson. Loeb Classical Library. Cambridge: Harvard University Press, 1989.
Aquinas, Saint Thomas. *The Literal Exposition on Job: A Scriptural Commentary Concerning Providence.* Trans. Anthony Damico, ed. Martin D. Yaffe. Classics in Religious Studies 7. Atlanta: Scholars Press, 1989.
———. *Treatise on the Virtues.* Trans. John A. Oesterle. Englewood Cliffs, N.J.: Prentice Hall, 1966.
Aristotle. *The Nicomachean Ethics.* Trans. H. Rackham. Loeb Classical Library. London: Heinemann; New York: Putnam, 1926.
Barbour, John. *The Bruce.* Ed. Walter W. Skeat. EETS extra series nos. 11, 21, 29, 55. London: N. Trübner, 1870, repr. 1889.
Bede, Saint. *De arte metrica.* In *Opera didascalica.* Ed. C. B. Kendall. CCSL 123A, 60–143. Turnhout: Brepols, 1975.
Bernard of Clairvaux, Saint. *De laude novae militiae.* In *S. Bernardi Opera,*

vol. 3: *Tractatus et opuscula*, ed. Jean Leclercq and H. M. Rochais, 207–39. Rome: Editiones Cistercienses, 1963.

——. "In Praise of the New Chivalry." Trans. David Herlihy. In *The History of Feudalism*, ed. David Herlihy, 288–98. New York: Harper and Row, 1970.

——. *The Letters of Saint Bernard of Clairvaux*. Trans. Bruno Scott James. Chicago: Henry Regnery, 1953.

Bernard Silvestris. *The Commentary on the First Six Books of the "Aeneid" of Virgil Commonly Attributed to Bernardus Silvestris*. Ed. Julian Ward Jones and Elizabeth Frances Jones. Lincoln: University of Nebraska Press, 1977.

——. *Commentary on the First Six Books of Virgil's "Aeneid."* Trans. Earl G. Schreiber and Thomas E. Maresca. Lincoln: University of Nebraska Press, 1979.

Biblia sacra iuxta Latinam vulgatam versionem. Rome: Vatican, 1951.

Boethius. *Boethius' Consolation of Philosophy, in the 1556 Translation of George Colville*. Ed. Ernest Belfort Bax. Tudor Library. London: David Nutt, 1897.

——. *The Consolation of Philosophy*. Trans. S. J. Tester. Loeb Classical Library. Cambridge: Harvard University Press, 1918, repr. 1978.

——. *The Consolation of Philosophy, in the Translation of I. T.* Ed. William Anderson. London: Arundel, 1963.

——. *De consolatione philosophiae*. Ed. Ludovicus Bieler. CCSL 94. Turnhout: Brepols, 1957.

Burton, Robert. *The Anatomy of Melancholy*. Ed. Floyd Dell and Paul Jordan-Smith. New York: Tudor, 1927, repr. 1955.

Cassiodorus. *Expositio psalmorum*. Ed. M. Adriaen. CCSL 97–98. Turnhout: Brepols, 1958.

The Castle of Perseverance. In *The Macro Plays*, ed. Mark Eccles, 1–111. EETS o.s. 262. London: Oxford University Press, 1969.

Chariton. *Chaereas and Callirhoe*. In *Erotici Scriptores Graeci*, ed. G. A. Hirschig, 415–503. Paris: Didot, 1875.

——. *Chaereas and Callirhoe*. Trans. B. P. Reardon. In *Collected Ancient Greek Novels*, ed. B. P. Reardon, 17–124. Berkeley: University of California Press, 1989.

Chaucer, Geoffrey. *The Riverside Chaucer*. 3d ed. Ed. Larry D. Benson. Boston: Houghton Mifflin, 1987.

——. *The Works of Geoffrey Chaucer*. 2d ed. Ed. F. N. Robinson. Boston: Houghton Mifflin, 1957.

Cicero. *De natura deorum*. Trans. H. Rackham. Loeb Classical Library. Cambridge: Harvard University Press, 1933, repr. 1979.

——. *De oratore*. Trans. E. W. Sutton and H. Rackham. 2 vols. Loeb Classical Library. Cambridge: Harvard University Press, 1942.

——. *Rhetorica ad Herennium*. Trans. Harry Caplan. Loeb Classical Library. Cambridge: Harvard University Press, 1954, repr. 1981.

———. *Tusculan Disputations.* Trans. J. E. King. Loeb Classical Library. Cambridge: Harvard University Press, 1927, repr. 1971.

Dante Alighieri. *The Divine Comedy.* Ed. and trans. Charles S. Singleton. Bollingen Series 80. Princeton: Princeton University Press, 1970–75, repr. 1977.

———. *Purgatorio.* Trans. Allen Mandlebaum. Berkeley: University of California Press, 1982.

———. *La Vita Nuova.* Ed. Tommaso Casini. 3d ed. rev. Luigi Pietrobono. Florence: G. C. Sansoni, 1968.

Epistolae Duorum Amantium: Briefe Abaelards und Heloises? Ed. Ewald Könsgen. Leiden and Cologne: E. J. Brill, 1974.

Fulgentius. *Fulgentius the Mythographer.* Trans. Leslie George Whitbread. Columbus: Ohio State University Press, 1971.

———. *Opera.* Ed. Rudolph Helm. Stuttgart: Teubner, 1898, repr. 1970.

Geoffrey of Vinsauf. *Poetria nova.* Trans. Jane Baltzell Kopp. In *Three Medieval Rhetorical Arts,* ed. James J. Murphy. Berkeley: University of California Press, 1971.

Gregory the Great, Saint. *Moralia in Job.* Ed. M. Adriaen. CCSL 143, 143A, 143B. Turnhout: Brepols, 1979–85.

———. *Morals on the Book of Job.* Trans. anonymous. 3 vols. Oxford: John Henry Parker, 1844–50.

Heliodorus. *An Ethiopian Story.* Trans. J. R. Morgan. In *Collected Ancient Greek Novels,* ed. B. P. Reardon, 349–588. Berkeley: University of California Press, 1989.

———. *Ethiopica.* In *Erotici Scriptores Graeci,* ed. G. A. Hirschig, 225–412. Paris: Didot, 1875.

Hilton, Walter. *Walter Hilton's "Mixed Life," Edited from Lambeth Palace MS 472.* Ed. S. J. Ogilvie-Thomson. Salzburg: Institut für Anglistik und Amerikanistik, 1986.

Historia Apollonii Regis Tyri. Ed. G. A. A. Kortekaas. Groningen: Bouma's Boekhuis, 1984.

Homer. *Iliad.* 3 vols. Ed. Thomas W. Allen. Oxford: Oxford University Press, 1931.

Hugh of St. Victor. "De modo orandi." PL 176, c977–88.

———. *De scripturis et scriptoribus sacris.* PL 175, c9–28.

Isidore of Seville, Saint. *Etymologiae.* PL 82, c73–728.

Jerome, Saint. "De viris illustribus." PL 23, c601–720.

———. "Interpretatio Chronicae Eusibii Pamphili, Praefatio." PL 27, c33–62.

———. "Liber Job." PL 28, c1079–1122.

John Chrysostom, Saint. "Fragmenta in Beatum Job." PG 64, c505–656.

John of Salisbury. *Frivolities of Courtiers and Footprints of Philosophers, Being a Translation of the First, Second, and Third Books . . . of the Polycraticus of John of Salisbury.* Trans. Joseph B. Pike. Minneapolis: University of Minnesota Press, 1938.

———. *The Metalogicon: A Twelfth-Century Defense of the Verbal and Logical*

Arts of the Trivium. Trans. Daniel D. McGarry. Berkeley: University of
    California Press, 1955.
——. *Polycraticus.* PL 199, c379–476.
John the Deacon. *Vita Gregorii.* PL 75, c41–242.
The Letters of Abelard and Heloise. Trans. Betty Radice. New York: Penguin
    Books, 1974.
Lucretius. *De rerum natura.* Trans. W. H. D. Rouse. Rev. Martin Ferguson
    Smith. 2d ed. Loeb Classical Library. Cambridge: Harvard University
    Press, 1924, 1982.
Lull, Ramón. *The Book of the Ordre of Chyvalry.* Trans. William Caxton. Ed.
    Alfred T. P. Byles. EETS o.s. 168. London: Oxford University Press,
    1926.
Macrobius. *Commentarii in Somnium Scipionis.* Ed. Jacob Willis. Leipzig:
    Teubner, 1970.
——. *Commentary on the Dream of Scipio.* Trans. William Harris Stahl.
    Records of Civilization, Sources and Studies 48: New York: Columbia
    University Press, 1952.
Malory, Thomas. *The Works of Sir Thomas Malory.* Ed. Eugène Vinaver.
    Revised by P. J. C. Field. 3d ed. 3 vols. Oxford: Clarendon Press, 1990.
Mankind. In *The Macro Plays,* ed. Mark Eccles, 153–84. EETS o.s. 262.
    London: Oxford University Press, 1969.
Martianus Capella. *De nuptiis Philologiae et Mercurii.* Ed. J. Willis. Leipzig:
    Teubner, 1983.
Middle English Sermons. Ed. Woodburn O. Ross. EETS 209. London: Ox-
    ford University Press, 1940, repr. 1960.
Milton, John. *Complete Poems and Major Prose.* Ed. Merritt Y. Hughes. New
    York: Odyssey Press, 1957.
——. *Complete Prose Works.* 8 vols. New Haven: Yale University Press, 1953–
    82.
Origen. "Selecta in Job." PG 12, c1031–1050.
Ovid. *Heroides and Amores.* Trans. Grant Showerman. 2d ed. Revised by
    G. P. Goold. Loeb Classical Library. Cambridge: Harvard University
    Press, 1914, repr. 1977.
——. *Metamorphoses.* Ed. and trans. Frank Justus Miller. Loeb Classical
    Library, 2 vols. New York: Putnam, 1916.
The Quest of the Holy Grail. Trans. P. M. Matarasso. Baltimore: Penguin
    Books, 1969–70.
La Queste del Saint Graal. Ed. Albert Pauphilet. Paris: H. Champion, 1921;
    repr. 1967.
Piers Plowman: An Edition of the C-Text. Ed. Derek Pearsall. Berkeley and
    Los Angeles: University of California Press, 1979.
"A Pistle of Preier." In *The Cloud of Unknowing and Related Treatises,* ed.
    Phyllis Hodgson. Salzburg: Institut für Anglistik und Amerikanistik,
    1982.
Plato. *Phaedrus.* Trans. Harold N. Fowler. Loeb Classical Library. Cam-
    bridge: Harvard University Press, 1914, repr. 1960.

——. *The Republic.* Vol. 1. Trans. Paul Shorey. Loeb Classical Library. London: W. Heinemann; New York: Putnam, 1930.
Plotinus. *Enneads.* Trans. A. H. Armstrong. 7 vols. Loeb Classical Library. Cambridge: Harvard University Press, 1966.
Porphyry. *On the Cave of the Nymphs.* Trans. Robert Lamberton. Barrytown, N.Y.: Station Hill Press, 1983.
Prudentius. *Psychomachia.* In *Prudentius*, vol. 1, trans. H. J. Thomson. Loeb Classical Library. Cambridge: Harvard University Press, 1949, repr. 1969.
Quintilian. *Institutio Oratoria.* 3 vols. Trans. H. E. Butler. Loeb Classical Library. Cambridge: Harvard University Press, 1921, 1943.
Rabanus Maurus. *De universo.* PL 111, c9–614.
Seneca. *Moral Essays.* 3 vols. Trans. John W. Basore. Loeb Classical Library. Cambridge: Harvard University Press, 1928, 1932, rev. ed. 1958.
——. *Naturales quaestiones.* Vol. 1. Trans. Thomas H. Corcoran. Loeb Classical Library. Cambridge: Harvard University Press, 1971.
——. *Tragedies.* 2 vols. Trans. Frank Justus Miller. Loeb Classical Library. London: Heinemann; New York: Putnam, 1917, repr. 1960.
Servius. *Servii Grammatici qui feruntur in Virgilii Carmina commentarii.* 3 vols. Ed. Georg Thilo and Hermann Hagen. Leipzig, 1881–87.
Severus, Sulpicius. *Writings.* Trans. Barnard M. Peebles. The Fathers of the Church 7. Washington, D.C.: Catholic University of America Press, 1949, repr. 1970.
Sidney, Sir Philip. *An Apology for Poetry; or, The Defence of Poesy.* Ed. Geoffrey Shepherd. London: Thomas Nelson, 1965.
Spenser, Edmund. *The Works of Edmund Spenser: A Variorum Edition.* Ed. Edward Greenlaw, Charles G. Osgood, Frederick M. Padelford. Baltimore: Johns Hopkins University Press, 1932.
Varro. *De lingua latina.* Vol. 1. Trans. Roland G. Kent. Loeb Classical Library. Cambridge: Harvard University Press, 1938, repr. 1977.
Virgil. *The Aeneid.* 2 vols. Ed. R. D. Williams. Basingstroke and London: Macmillan, 1972.
——. *Georgics.* Trans. H. Rushton Fairclough. Loeb Classical Library. Cambridge: Harvard University Press, 1935, rev. ed. 1986.
Wyclif, John. *The English Works of Wyclif.* Ed. F. D. Matthew. EETS 74. London: Trübner, 1880.
Xenophon of Ephesus. *An Ephesian Tale.* Trans. Graham Anderson. In *Collected Ancient Greek Novels,* ed. B. P. Reardon, 125–69. Berkeley: University of California Press, 1989.

Secondary Sources

Ahl, Frederick M. *Metaformations: Soundplay and Wordplay in Ovid and Other Classical Poets.* Ithaca: Cornell University Press, 1985.
Allen, Don Cameron. *The Harmonious Vision: Studies in Milton's Poetry.* Baltimore: Johns Hopkins University Press, 1954.

222   *Bibliography*

Allen, Judson Boyce. *The Ethical Poetic of the Later Middle Ages.* Toronto: University of Toronto Press, 1982.
———. "Grammar, Poetic Form, and the Lyric Ego: A Medieval *A Priori.*" In *Vernacular Poetics in the Middle Ages,* ed. Lois Ebin, 199–226. Kalamazoo, Mich.: Medieval Institute Publications, 1984.
Anderson, Graham. *Eros Sophistes: Ancient Novelists at Play.* Chico, Calif.: Scholars Press, 1982.
Archibald, Elizabeth. "The Flight from Incest: Two Late Classical Precursors of the Constance Theme." *Chaucer Review* 20.4 (1986): 259–72.
Astell, Ann W. "Apostrophe, Prayer, and the Structure of Satire in the Man of Law's Tale." *SAC* 13 (1991): 81–97.
———. "Holofernes' Head: *Tacen* and Teaching in the Old English *Judith.*" *ASE* 18 (1989): 117–33.
———. "Job's Wife, Walter's Wife, and the Wife of Bath." In *Old Testament Women in Western Literature,* ed. Raymond-Jean Frontain and Jan Wojcik, 92–107. Conway: University of Central Arkansas Press, 1991.
———. "The Medieval *Consolatio* and the Conclusion of *Paradise Lost.*" *SP* (1985): 477–92.
———. "Orpheus, Eurydice, and the 'Double Sorwe' of Chaucer's *Troilus.*" *Chaucer Review* 23.4 (1989): 283–99.
———. *The Song of Songs in the Middle Ages.* Ithaca: Cornell University Press, 1990.
Atkinson, Stephen C. B. "Malory's Lancelot and the Quest of the Grail." *Studies in Malory,* ed. James W. Spisak, 129–52. Kalamazoo, Mich.: Medieval Institute Publications, 1985.
Aubertin, C. *Sénèque et Saint Paul.* Paris: Didier, 1872.
Auerbach, Erich. "*Sermo Humilis.*" In *Literary Language and Its Public in Late Latin Antiquity and in the Middle Ages,* 27–66. Trans. Ralph Manheim. London: Routledge and Kegan Paul, 1965.
Austin, Roland Gregory. *Aeneidos liber secundus.* Oxford: Clarendon Press, 1964.
Bakhtin, M. *The Dialogic Imagination.* Ed. Michael Holquist. Trans. Caryl Emerson and Michael Holquist. University of Texas Press Slavic Series, No. 1. Austin: University of Texas Press, 1981.
Baldick, Chris. *The Concise Oxford Dictionary of Literary Terms.* New York: Oxford University Press, 1990.
Baumgartner, Paul R. "Milton and Patience." *SP* 60 (1963): 203–13.
Beecher, Donald. "Spenser's Redcrosse Knight: Despair and the Elizabethan Malady." *Renaissance and Reformation* 11.1 (1987): 103–20.
Benson, C. David. "Their Telling Difference: Chaucer the Pilgrim and His Two Contrasting Tales." *Chaucer Review* 18 (1983): 61–76.
Benson, Larry D. *Malory's Morte Darthur.* Cambridge: Harvard University Press, 1976.
Benton, John F. "Fraud, Fiction, and Borrowing in the Correspondence of Abélard and Héloïse." In *Pierre Abélard, Pierre le vénérable.* Paris: Éditions du Centre National de la Recherche Scientifique, 1975.

Besserman, Lawrence L. *The Legend of Job in the Middle Ages.* Cambridge: Harvard University Press, 1979.

Blessington, Francis C. *Paradise Lost and the Classical Epic.* Boston and London: Routledge and Kegan Paul, 1979.

Block, E. A. "Originality, Controlling Purpose and Craftsmanship in Chaucer's 'Man of Law's Tale.'" *PMLA* 68 (1963): 572–616.

Bolgar, R. R. "Hero or Anti-Hero? The Genesis and Development of the *Miles Christianus.*" In *Concepts of the Hero in the Middle Ages and Renaissance,* ed. Norman T. Burns and Christopher J. Reagan, 120–46. Albany: State University of New York Press, 1975.

Briggs, Ward W. *Narrative and Simile from the Georgics in the Aeneid. Mnemosyne.* Supplement 58. Leiden: E. J. Brill, 1980.

Brown, Emerson, Jr., "Epicurus and Voluptas in Late Antiquity: The Curious Testimony of Martianus Capella." *Traditio* 38 (1982): 75–106.

Brown, George H. "The Descent-Ascent Motif in *Christ II* of Cynewulf." *JEGP* 73 (1974): 1–12.

Brownlee, Kevin, and Marina Scordilis, eds. *Romance: Generic Transformation from Chrétien de Troyes to Cervantes.* Hanover: University Press of New England, 1985.

Buffière, Félix. *Les mythes d'Homère et la pensée grecque.* Paris: Belles Lettres, 1956.

Camargo, Martin. "The Consolation of Pandarus." *Chaucer Review* 25.3 (1991): 214–28.

Carruthers, Mary J. *The Book of Memory: A Study of Memory in Medieval Culture.* Cambridge and New York: Cambridge University Press, 1990.

——. "The Lady, the Swineherd, and Chaucer's Clerk." *Chaucer Review* 17.3 (1983): 221–34.

Cate, Wirt Armistead. "The Problem of the Origin of the Griselda Story." *SP* 29 (1932): 389–405.

Chadwick, Henry. *Boethius: The Consolations of Music, Logic, Theology, and Philosophy.* Oxford: Clarendon Press, 1981, repr. 1983.

Chambers, A. B. "Wisdom and Fortitude in *Samson Agonistes.*" *PMLA* 78 (1963): 315–20.

Chance, Jane. "Chaucerian Irony in the Boethian Short Poems: The Dramatic Tension between Classical and Christian." *Chaucer Review* 20.3 (1986): 235–45.

Chase, A. H . "The Metrical Lives of St. Martin of Tours." *Harvard Studies in Classical Philology* 43 (1932): 51–76.

Childress, Diana T. "Between Romance and Legend: 'Secular Hagiography' in Middle English Literature." *PQ* 57 (1978): 311–22.

Christopher, Georgia B. *Milton and the Science of the Saints.* Princeton: Princeton University Press, 1982.

Cioffari, Vincent. *Fortune and Fate from Democritus to St. Thomas Aquinas.* New York: Columbia University Press, 1935.

Clark, John. *A History of Epic Poetry.* New York: Haskell House, 1900, repr. 1964.

Comparetti, Domenico. *Vergil in the Middle Ages.* 2d ed. Trans. E. F. M. Benecke. London: George Allen & Unwin, 1908, repr. 1966.

Cook, Albert. *The Classical Line.* Bloomington: University of Indiana Press, 1966.

Cooper, Lane. *A Concordance of Boethius.* Cambridge, Mass.: Medieval Academy of America, 1928.

Courcelle, Pierre. *La Consolation de Philosophie dans la tradition littéraire.* Paris: Études Augustiniennes, 1967.

Curtius, Ernst Robert. *European Literature and the Late Middle Ages.* Trans. Willard R. Trask. Bollingen Series 36. London: Routledge and Kegan Paul, 1953, repr. 1963.

Dalbey, Marcia A. "The Good Shepherd and the Soldier of God: Old English Homilies on St. Martin of Tours." *NM* 85.4 (1984): 422–34.

David, Alfred. "The Hero of the *Troilus.*" *Speculum* 37 (1962): 566–81.

——. "The Man of Law Versus Chaucer: A Case in Poetics." *PMLA* 82 (1967): 217–25.

Delasanta, Rodney. *The Epic Voice.* The Hague: Mouton, 1967.

Diehl, Patrick S. *The Medieval European Religious Lyric: An Ars Poetica.* Berkeley: University of California Press, 1985.

Dronke, Peter. "The Conclusion of *Troilus and Criseyde.*" *Medium Aevum* 33 (1964): 47–52.

Dudden, F. Homes. *Gregory the Great: His Place in History and Thought.* Vol. 1. New York: Russell and Russell, 1905, repr. 1967.

Dunning, T. P. "God and Man in *Troilus and Criseyde.*" In *English and Medieval Studies Presented to J. R. R. Tolkien,* ed. Norman Davis and C. L. Wrenn, 164–82. London: G. Allen and Unwin, 1962.

Durham, Lonnie J. "Love and Death in *Troilus and Criseyde.*" *Chaucer Review* 3 (1968): 1–11.

Dwyer, Richard A. *Boethian Fictions: Narratives in the Medieval French Versions of the Consolatio Philosophiae.* Cambridge, Mass.: Medieval Academy of America, 1976.

Elliott, Alison Goddard. "The Power of Discourse: Martyr's Passion and Old French Epic." *Medievalia et Humanistica,* n. s. 11, ed. Paul Maurice Clogan, 39–60. Totowa, N.J.: Rowman and Littlefield, 1982.

Elliott, Robert C. *The Literary Persona.* Chicago: University of Chicago Press, 1982.

Ellis, Roger. *Patterns of Religious Narrative in the "Canterbury Tales."* Totowa, N.J.: Barnes and Noble Books, 1986.

Ellis, Steve. "Chaucer, Dante, and Damnation." *Chaucer Review* 22.4 (1988): 282–94.

Else, Gerald F. *Aristotle's Poetics: The Argument.* Cambridge: Harvard University Press, 1963.

Evans, G. R. *The Thought of Gregory the Great.* Cambridge: Cambridge University Press, 1986.

Finlayson, John. "Definitions of Middle English Romance." *Chaucer Review* 15 (1980–81): 44–62, 168–81.

Fish, Stanley. *Surprised by Sin: The Reader in "Paradise Lost."* New York: St. Martin's Press, 1967.

Forsyth, Neil. *The Old Enemy: Satan and the Combat Myth.* Princeton: Princeton University Press, 1987.

Frakes, Jerold C. *The Fate of Fortune in the Early Middle Ages: The Boethian Tradition.* Leiden and New York: E. J. Brill, 1988.

Frank, Donald K. "Abelard as Imitator of Christ." *Viator* 1 (1970): 107–13.

Freccero, John. *Dante: The Poetics of Conversion.* Ed. Rachel Jacoff. Cambridge: Harvard University Press, 1986.

——. "Dante's Ulysses: From Epic to Novel." In *Concepts of the Hero in the Middle Ages and the Renaissance,* ed. Norman T. Burns and Christopher J. Reagan, 101–19. Albany: State University of New York Press, 1975.

Freeman, James A. *Milton and the Martial Muse: "Paradise Lost" and European Traditions of War.* Princeton: Princeton University Press, 1980.

Friedman, John Block. *Orpheus in the Middle Ages.* Cambridge: Harvard University Press, 1970.

Frye, Northrop. *Anatomy of Criticism: Four Essays.* New York: Atheneum, 1969.

Galinsky, G. Karl. *The Herakles Theme: The Adaptations of the Hero in Literature from Homer to the Twentieth Century.* Oxford: Blackwell, 1972.

Gerould, Gordon Hall. *Saints' Legends.* Boston and New York: Houghton Mifflin, 1916.

Gilson, Étienne Henry. *Dante and Philosophy.* Trans. David Moore. Sheed and Ward, 1949; New York: Harper and Row, 1963.

——. *Heloise and Abelard.* Trans. L. K. Shook. Ann Arbor: University of Michigan Press, 1938, 1960, repr. 1972.

Ginsberg, H. L. "The Legend of King Keret, a Canaanite Epic of the Bronze Age." *BASOR.* Suppl. Studies 2–3, 1946.

Ginsberg, Warren. *The Cast of Character: The Representation of Personality in Ancient and Medieval Literature.* Toronto: University of Toronto Press, 1983.

Glatzer, Nahum H. *The Dimensions of Job: A Study and Selected Readings.* New York: Schocken Books, 1969.

Gleason, Mark J. "Clearing the Fields: Towards a Reassessment of Chaucer's Use of Trevet in the 'Boece.' " In *The Medieval Boethius: Studies in the Vernacular Translations of "De Consolatione Philosophiae,"* ed. Alistair J. Minnis, 89–105. Cambridge: D. S. Brewer, 1987.

Goepp, P. H. "The Narrative Material of *Apollonius of Tyre.*" *ELH* 5 (1938): 150–72.

Gordon, Ida L. *The Double Sorrow of Troilus: A Study of Ambiguities in "Troilus and Criseyde."* Oxford: Clarendon Press, 1970.

Gransden, K. W. *Virgil's Iliad: An Essay on Epic Narrative.* Cambridge and London: Cambridge University Press, 1984.

Greene, Thomas M. *The Descent from Heaven: A Study in Epic Continuity.* New Haven: Yale University Press, 1964.

Griffith, Dudley David. *The Origin of the Griselda Story.* Seattle: University of Washington Press, 1931.

Grossman, Ann. "Samson, Job, and 'The Exercise of the Saints.' " *English Studies* 45 (1964): 212–24.

Gruber, Joachim. *Kommentar zu Boethius De Consolatione Philosophiae.* Berlin: De Gruyter, 1978.

Hägg, Tomas. *The Novel in Antiquity.* Berkeley: University of California Press, 1983.

Hainsworth, J. B. *The Idea of Epic.* Berkeley: University of California Press, 1991.

Hanna, Ralph. "Some Commonplaces of Late Medieval Patience Discussions: An Introduction." In *The Triumph of Patience: Medieval and Renaissance Studies,* ed. Gerald J. Schiffhorst. Orlando: University Press of Florida, 1978.

Hansen, P. A. "ILLE EGO QUI QUONDAM . . . Once Again." *Classical Quarterly,* n.s. 22 (1972): 139–49.

Hardie, Philip R. *Virgil's 'Aeneid': Cosmos and Imperium.* Oxford: Clarendon Press, 1986.

Harris, William O. "Despair and 'Patience as the Truest Fortitude' in *Samson Agonistes.*" *ELH* 30 (1963): 107–20.

Heffernan, Thomas J. "An Analysis of the Narrative Motifs in the Legend of St. Eustace." *Medievalia et Humanistica,* n.s. 6 (1975): 63–89.

Heidtmann, Peter. "Sex and Salvation in *Troilus and Criseyde.*" *Chaucer Review* 2 (1968): 246–53.

Heinrichs, Katherine. " 'Lovers' Consolations of Philosophy' in Boccaccio, Machaut, and Chaucer." *SAC* 11 (1989): 93–116.

Hermann, John P. *Allegories of War: Language and Violence in Old English Poetry.* Ann Arbor: University of Michigan Press, 1989.

Hopkins, Andrea. *The Sinful Knights: A Study of Middle English Penitential Romance.* Oxford: Clarendon Press, 1990.

Huppé, Bernard F. *A Reading of the Canterbury Tales.* Albany: State University of New York Press, 1964.

Ihle, Sandra Ness. *Malory's Grail Quest: Invention and Adaptation in Medieval Prose Romance.* Madison: University of Wisconsin Press, 1983.

Inwood, Brad. *Ethics and Human Action in Early Stoicism.* Oxford: Clarendon Press, 1985.

Jameson, Fredric. "Magical Narratives: Romance as Genre." *NLH* 7 (1975): 135–63.

Jastrow, Morris, Jr. *The Book of Job: Its Origin, Growth, and Interpretation.* Philadelphia: J. B. Lippincott, 1920.

Johnson, William C., Jr. " 'The Man of Law's Tale': Aesthetics and Christianity in Chaucer." *Chaucer Review* 16.3 (1982): 201–21.

Jones, J. W., Jr. "Allegorical Interpretation in Servius." *CJ* 56 (1960–61): 217–26.

———. "The Allegorical Traditions of the *Aeneid.*" In *Vergil at 2000: Com-*

memorative Essays on the Poet and His Influence, ed. John D. Bernard, 107–32. New York: AMS Press, 1986.

Jones, Terry. *Chaucer's Knight: The Portrait of a Medieval Mercenary.* Baton Rouge: Louisiana State University Press, 1980.

Kaske, Robert E. "*Sapientia et Fortitudo* as the Controlling Theme of *Beowulf.*" *SP* 55.3 (1958): 423–56. In *An Anthology of Beowulf Criticism*, ed. Lewis E. Nicolson, 269–311. Notre Dame: University of Notre Dame Press, 1963.

Keen, Maurice. *Chivalry.* New Haven: Yale University Press, 1984.

Kennedy, Beverly. *Knighthood in the Morte Darthur.* Cambridge: D. S. Brewer, 1985.

Ker, William Paton. *Epic and Romance.* New York and London: Macmillan, 1908, repr. 1931.

Kirk, Elizabeth D. " 'Paradis Stood Formed in Hire Yën': Courtly Love and Chaucer's Re-Vision of Dante." In *Acts of Interpretation: Essays on Medieval and Renaissance Literature in Honor of E. Talbot Donaldson*, ed. Mary J. Carruthers and Elizabeth D. Kirk, 257–77. Norman, Okla.: Pilgrim Books, 1982.

Klingner, Friedrich. *Virgil: Bucolica, Georgica, Aeneis.* Zurich and Stuttgart: Artemis, 1967.

Knauer, Georg Nicolaus. *Die Aeneis und Homer: Studien zur poetischen Technik Vergils mit Listen der Homerzitate in der Aeneis.* Göttingen: Vandenhoeck and Ruprecht, 1964.

Kolve, V. A. *The Imagery of Narrative: The First Five Canterbury Tales.* Stanford, Calif.: Stanford University Press, 1984.

Kratins, Ojar. "The Middle English *Amis and Amiloun*: Chivalric Romance or Secular Hagiography?" *PMLA* 81 (1966): 347–54.

Krouse, F. Michael. *Milton's Samson and the Christian Tradition.* 1949; New York: Farrar, Straus, and Giroux, 1974.

Kugel, James L. *The Idea of Biblical Poetry: Parallelism and Its History.* New Haven: Yale University Press, 1981.

Kurth, Burton O. *Milton and Christian Heroism: Biblical Epic Themes and Forms in Seventeenth-Century England.* Hamden: Archon Books, 1959; repr. 1966.

Lamberton, Robert. *Homer the Theologian: Neoplatonist Allegorical Reading and the Growth of the Epic Tradition.* Berkeley: University of California Press, 1986.

——, trans. *Porphyry On the Cave of the Nymphs.* Barrytown, N.Y.: Station Hill Press, 1983.

Laserstein, Käte. *Der Griseldistoff in der Weltliteratur.* Weimar: A. Duncker, 1926.

Lawton, David. *Chaucer's Narrators.* Cambridge: D. S. Brewer, 1985.

Leclercq, Jean. "Saint Bernard's Attitude Toward War." *Studies in Medieval Cistercian History* 2. Ed. John R. Sommerfeldt. Cistercian Studies Series, No. 24. Kalamazoo, Mich.: Cistercian Publications, 1976.

Leicester, H. Marshall, Jr. "The Art of Impersonation: A General Prologue to the *Canterbury Tales*." *PMLA* 95 (1980): 213–34.

LeMoine, Fannie J. *Martianus Capella: A Literary Re-evaluation.* Munich: Salzer, 1972.

Lerer, Seth. *Boethius and Dialogue: Literary Method in "The Consolation of Philosophy."* Princeton: Princeton University Press, 1985.

Lewalski, Barbara K. *Milton's Brief Epic: The Genre, Meaning, and Art of "Paradise Regained."* Providence: Brown University Press, 1966.

———. "Structure and the Symbolism of Vision in Michael's Prophecy, *Paradise Lost*, Books XI and XII." *PQ* 42 (1963): 25–35.

Lewis, C. S. *The Allegory of Love.* New York: Oxford University Press, 1938, repr. 1958.

Lewis, Robert Enzer. "Chaucer's Artistic Use of Pope Innocent III's *De Miseria Humanae Condicionis* in the Man of Law's Prologue and Tale." *PMLA* 81 (1966): 485–92.

Lieb, Michael. *The Sinews of Ulysses: Form and Convention in Milton's Works.* Pittsburgh: Duquesne University Press, 1989.

Mahoney, Dhira B. "The Truest and Holiest Tale: Malory's Transformation of *La Queste del Saint Graal.*" In *Studies in Malory*, ed. James W. Spisak, 109–28. Kalamazoo, Mich.: Medieval Institute Publications, 1985.

Maresca, Thomas E. *Three English Epics.* Lincoln: University of Nebraska Press, 1979.

McAlpine, Monica E. *The Genre of "Troilus and Criseyde."* Ithaca: Cornell University Press, 1978.

McCall, John P. "Five-Book Structure in Chaucer's *Troilus.*" *MLQ* 23 (1962): 297–308.

McInerny, Ralph. *Boethius and Aquinas.* Washington, D.C.: Catholic University of America Press, 1990.

McLaughlin, Mary Martin. "Abelard as Autobiographer: The Motives and Meaning of his *Story of Calamities.*" *Speculum* 42 (1967): 463–88.

Means, Michael H. *The Consolatio Genre in Medieval English Literature.* Gainesville: University of Florida Press, 1972.

Middleton, Ann. "Ælfric's Answerable Style: The Rhetoric of the Alliterative Prose." *Studies in Medieval Culture* 4.1 (1973): 83–91.

Minnis, Alastair J. " 'Glosynge Is a Glorious Thyng': Chaucer at Work on the 'Boece.' " In *The Medieval Boethius*, 106–24.

———, ed. *The Medieval Boethius: Studies in the Vernacular Translations of "De Consolatione Philosophiae."* Cambridge: D. S. Brewer, 1987. *The Medieval Boethius*, 106–24.

——— and A. B. Scott, with the assistance of David Wallace, ed. *Medieval Literary Theory and Criticism c. 1100–1375: The Commentary Tradition.* Oxford: Clarendon Press, 1988.

Monfrin, Jacques. "Le problème de l'authenticité de la correspondance d'Abélard et d'Héloïse." In *Pierre Abélard, Pierre le vénérable*, 409–24. Paris: Éditions du Centre National de la Recherche Scientifique, 1975.

Moore, Edward. *Scripture and Classical Authors in Dante.* Dante Studies. Oxford: Clarendon Press, 1896; New York: Greenwood Press, 1968.

Morse, Charlotte C. "The Exemplary Griselda." *SAC* 7 (1985): 51–86.

Morse, Ruth. *Truth and Convention in the Middle Ages: Rhetoric, Representation, and Reality.* Cambridge: Cambridge University Press, 1991.

Motto, Anna Lydia, and John R. Clark. *Senecan Tragedy.* Amsterdam: Adolf M. Hakkert, 1988.

Muckle, J. T., ed. "Abelard's Letter of Consolation to a Friend (*Historia calamitatum*)." *Mediaeval Studies* 12 (1950): 163–213.

———. "The Personal Letters between Abelard and Heloise: Introduction, Authenticity, and Text." *Mediaeval Studies* 15 (1953): 47–94.

Murphy, James J. *Rhetoric in the Middle Ages: A Study of Rhetorical Theory from Saint Augustine to the Renaissance.* Berkeley: University of California Press, 1974, repr. 1990.

Murrin, Michael. *The Allegorical Epic: Essays in Its Rise and Decline.* Chicago: University of Chicago Press, 1980.

Musa, Mark. *Dante's "Vita Nuova": A Translation and an Essay.* Bloomington: Indiana University Press, 1973.

Muscatine, Charles. *Chaucer and the French Tradition.* Berkeley: University of California Press, 1957.

Mushabac, Jane. "Judith and the Theme of *Sapientia et Fortitudo.*" *Massachusetts Studies in English* 4 (Spring 1973): 3–12.

Neuss, Paula. "Images of Writing and the Book in Chaucer's Poetry." *Review of English Studies* 32 (1981): 385–97.

Newman, John Kevin. *The Classical Epic Tradition.* Madison: University of Wisconsin Press, 1986.

Nichols, Stephen G., Jr. *Romanesque Signs: Early Medieval Narrative and Iconography.* New Haven: Yale University Press, 1983.

———. "The Spirit of Truth: Epic Modes in Medieval Literature." *NLH* 1 (Spring 1970): 365–86.

Nist, John. "Chaucer's Apostrophic Mode in *The Canterbury Tales.*" *TSL* 15 (1970): 85–98.

Nitzsche, Jane Chance. *The Genius Figure in Antiquity and the Middle Ages.* New York: Columbia University Press, 1972, repr. 1975.

O'Daly, Gerard. *The Poetry of Boethius.* Chapel Hill: University of North Carolina Press, 1991.

Otis, Brooks. *Virgil: A Study in Civilized Poetry.* Oxford: Clarendon Press, 1964.

Parker, Patricia A. *Inescapable Romance: Studies in the Poetics of a Mode.* Princeton: Princeton University Press, 1979.

Parry, Adam. "The Idea of Art in Virgil's *Georgics.*" *Arethusa* 5.1 (1972): 35–52. In *Virgil: Modern Critical Views*, ed. Harold Bloom. New York: Chelsea House, 1986.

Payne, F. Anne. *Chaucer and Menippean Satire.* Madison: University of Wisconsin Press, 1981.

Pearsall, Derek. "The Development of Middle English Romance." *Medieval Studies* 27 (1965): 91–116.

Perry, Ben Edwin. *The Ancient Romances: A Literary-Historical Account of Their Origins.* Sather Classical Lectures 1951. Berkeley: University of California Press, 1967.

Petersen, Kate O. "Chaucer and Trivet." *PMLA* 18 (1903): 173–93.

Pope, Marvin, Ed. *Job.* Anchor Bible Series 15. Garden City, N.Y.: Doubleday, 1965.

Pratt, Norman. *Seneca's Drama.* Chapel Hill: University of North Carolina Press, 1983.

Quilligan, Maureen. *The Language of Allegory: Defining the Genre.* Ithaca: Cornell University Press, 1979.

Raby, Frederick J. E. *A History of Christian-Latin Poetry From the Beginning to the Close of the Middle Ages.* Oxford: Clarendon Press, 1927.

Radzinowicz, Mary Ann. *Toward "Samson Agonistes": The Growth of Milton's Mind.* Princeton: Princeton University Press, 1978.

Rahner, H. *Greek Myths and Christian Mystery.* Trans. Brian Battershaw. London: Burns and Oates, 1963.

Reames, Sherry L. *The Legenda Aurea: A Reexamination of Its Paradoxical History.* Madison: University of Wisconsin Press, 1985.

——. "Saint Martin of Tours in the 'Legenda Aurea' and Before." *Viator* 12 (1981): 131–64.

Reardon, B. P., ed. *Collected Ancient Greek Novels.* Berkeley: University of California Press, 1989.

Richards, Jeffrey. *Consul of God: The Life and Times of Gregory the Great.* London and Boston: Routledge and Kegan Paul, 1980.

Robertson, D. W., Jr. *Abelard and Heloise.* New York: Dial Press, 1972.

——. "Chaucerian Tragedy." *ELH* 19 (1952): 1–37. In *Chaucer Criticism,* vol. 2, ed. Richard J. Schoeck and Jerome Taylor, 86–121. Notre Dame: University of Notre Dame Press, 1961.

Rosenmeyer, Thomas. *Senecan Drama and Stoic Cosmology.* Berkeley: University of California Press, 1989.

Rossi, Albert L. "*Miro gurge (Par.* XXX,68): Virgilian Language and Textual Pattern in the River of Light." *Dante Studies* 103 (1985): 79–101.

Rowe, Donald W. *O Love! O Charite! Contraries Harmonized in Chaucer's "Troilus."* Carbondale: Southern Illinois University Press, 1976.

Ryken, Leland. *The Apocalyptic Vision in "Paradise Lost."* Ithaca: Cornell University Press, 1970.

Sadler, Lynn Veach. *Consolation in "Samson Agonistes": Regeneration and Typology.* Elizabethan and Renaissance Studies. Salzburg: Institut für Anglistik und Amerikanistik, 1979.

Salmon, P. B. "The 'Three Voices' of Poetry in Medieval Literary Theory." *Medium Aevum* 30 (1961): 1–18.

Sarna, N. M. "Epic Substratum in the Prose of Job." *JBL* 76 (1957): 13–25.

Scheible, Helga. *Die Gedichte in der Consolatio Philosophiae des Boethius.* Heidelberg: Winter, 1972.

Schlauch, Margaret. *Chaucer's Constance and Accused Queens.* New York: New York University Press, 1927.

Segal, Charles P. "Dissonant Sympathy: Song, Orpheus, and the Golden Age in Seneca's Tragedies." In *Seneca Tragicvs: Ramus Essays on Senecan Drama*, ed. A. J. Boyle, 229–56. Berwick, Victoria: Aureal, 1983.

———. "'Like Winds and Winged Dream': A Note on Virgil's Development." *CJ* 69 (1973–74): 97–101.

———. "Orpheus and the Fourth *Georgic.*" *AJP* 87 (1966): 307–25.

Severs, J. Burke. "The Clerk's Tale." In *Sources and Analogues of Chaucer's Canterbury Tales*, ed. William Frank Bryan and Germaine Dempster, 296–331. 1941; repr. New York: Humanities Press, 1958.

———. "The Job Passage in the *Clerkes Tale.*" *MLN* 49 (1934): 461–62.

Shelton, Jo-Ann. "Revenge or Resignation: Seneca's *Agamemnon.*" In *Seneca Tragicvs: Ramus Essays on Senecan Drama*, ed. A. J. Boyle, 159–83. Berwick, Victoria: Aureal, 1983.

Singleton, Charles S. *An Essay on "The Vita Nuova."* Cambridge: Harvard University Press, 1949.

Smalley, Beryl. *The Study of the Bible in the Middle Ages.* Oxford: Blackwell, 1952; Notre Dame: University of Notre Dame, 1964.

Smith, Macklin. *Prudentius' Psychomachia: A Reexamination.* Princeton: Princeton University Press, 1976.

Sommerfeldt, John R. "The Social Theory of Bernard of Clairvaux." In *Studies in Medieval Cistercian History*, 35–48. Cistercian Studies, No. 13. Spencer, Mass.: Cistercian Publications, 1971.

Sørensen, Villy. *Seneca: The Humanist at the Court of Nero.* Trans. W. Glyn Jones. Edinburgh: Canongate; Chicago: University of Chicago Press, 1984.

Specht, Henrik. "'Ethopoeia' or Impersonation: A Neglected Species of Medieval Characterization." *Chaucer Review* 21.1 (1986): 1–15.

Stahl, William Harris, and Richard Johnson with E. L. Burge. *Martianus Capella and the Seven Liberal Arts.* 2 vols. Records of Civiliation Series 84. New York: Columbia University Press, 1971.

Stanford, William Bedell. *The Ulysses Theme: A Study in the Adaptability of a Traditional Hero.* 2d ed. Oxford: Blackwell, 1963.

Steadman, John H. *Milton's Epic Characters: Image and Idol.* Chapel Hill: University of North Carolina Press, 1959, repr. 1968.

Stein, Arnold. *Heroic Knowledge: An Interpretation of "Paradise Regained" and "Samson Agonistes."* Hamden: Archon Books, 1965.

Stock, Brian. *Myth and Science in the Twelfth Century: A Study of Bernard Silvester.* Princeton: Princeton University Press, 1972.

Straw, Carole. *Gregory the Great: Perfection in Imperfection.* Berkeley: University of California Press, 1988.

Stroud, Theodore A. "Boethius' Influence on Chaucer's *Troilus.*" *MP* 49 (1951–52): 1–9. In *Chaucer Criticism*, vol. 2, ed. Richard J. Schoeck and Jerome Taylor, 122–35.

Summers, Joseph. *The Muse's Method: An Introduction to "Paradise Lost."* Cambridge: Harvard University Press, 1962.

Tate, J. "On the History of Allegorism." *Classical Quarterly* 28 (1934): 105–14.

———. "Plato and Allegorical Interpretation." *Classical Quarterly* 23 (1929): 142–54 and 24 (1930): 1–10.

Tatlock, John. *The Development and Chronology of Chaucer's Works.* Gloucester: Peter Smith, 1963.

Tatum, James. *Apuleius and the Golden Ass.* Ithaca: Cornell University Press, 1979.

Taylor, Henry Osborn. *The Classical Heritage of the Middle Ages.* 4th ed. New York: Frederick Ungar, 1957.

Taylor, Karla. *Chaucer Reads "The Divine Comedy."* Stanford, Calif.: Stanford University Press, 1989.

Thompson, David. *Dante's Epic Journeys.* Baltimore: Johns Hopkins University Press, 1974.

Took, J. F. *Dante: Lyric Poet and Philosopher: An Introduction To the Minor Works.* Oxford: Clarendon Press, 1990.

Trinkhaus, Charles. *The Poet as Philosopher: Petrarch and the Formation of Renaissance Consciousness.* New Haven: Yale University Press, 1979.

Vance, Eugene. *Marvelous Signals: Poetics and Sign Theory in the Middle Ages.* Lincoln: University of Nebraska Press, 1986.

Van Dam, Raymond. "Images of St. Martin." *Viator* 19 (1988): 1–27.

Vinaver, Eugène. *The Rise of Romance.* New York and Oxford: Oxford University Press, 1971.

Von Moos, Peter. *Consolatio: Studien zur Mittellateinischen Trostliteratur über den Tod und zum Problem der Christlichen Trauer.* 4 vols. Munich: W. Fink, 1971–72.

———. "Le silence d'Héloïse et les idéologies modernes." In *Pierre Abélard, Pierre le vénérable,* 461–62.

Waddington, Raymond B. "The Death of Adam: Vision and Voice in Books XI and XII of *Paradise Lost.*" *MP* 70 (1972): 9–21.

———. "Melancholy against Melancholy: *Samson Agonistes* as Renaissance Tragedy." In *Calm of Mind: Tercentenary Essays on "Paradise Regained" and "Samson Agonistes,"* ed. Joseph Anthony Wittreich, Jr., 259–87. Cleveland: Case Western Reserve University Press, 1971.

Waszink, J. H. "Biene und Honig als Symbol des Dichters und der Dichtung in der griechischrömischen Antike." *Rheinisch-Westfälische Akademie der Wissenschaften* (1973), nr. G-196: 26–28.

Wetherbee, Winthrop. *Chaucer and the Poets: An Essay on "Troilus and Criseyde."* Ithaca: Cornell University Press, 1984.

———. *Platonism and Poetry in the Twelfth Century: The Literary Influence of the School of Chartres.* Princeton: Princeton University Press, 1972.

Whitbread, Leslie George, ed. and trans. *Fulgentius the Mythographer.* Columbus: Ohio State University Press, 1971.

White, Hayden. *Metahistory: The Historical Imagination in Nineteenth-Century Europe.* Baltimore: Johns Hopkins University Press, 1973.

Whitman, Jon. *Allegory: The Dynamics of an Ancient and Medieval Technique.* Oxford: Clarendon Press, 1987.

Winkler, Martin M. "The Function of Epic in Juvenal's Satires." *Studies in Latin Literature and Roman History* 5 (Brussels: Latomus Revue d'Études Latines, 1989): 414–43.

——. "Juvenal's Attitude toward Ciceronian Poetry and Rhetoric." *Rheinisches Museum für Philologie* 131.1 (Frankfurt am Main: J. D. Sauerlander, 1988): 84–97.

Wittreich, Joseph Anthony, Jr. *Interpreting "Samson Agonistes."* Princeton: Princeton University Press, 1986.

——. *Visionary Poetics: Milton's Tradition and His Legacy.* San Marino, Calif.: Huntington Library, 1979.

Wood, Chauncey. "Chaucer's Man of Law as Interpreter." *Traditio* 23 (1967): 149–90.

Zupinck, Irving L. "Saint Sebastian: The Vicissitudes of the Hero as Martyr." In *Concepts of the Hero in the Middle Ages and the Renaissance*, ed. Norman T. Burns and Christopher J. Reagan, 239–67. Albany: State University of New York Press, 1975.

INDEX